14th Edition

Leases & Rental Agreements

**Attorneys Janet Portman
& Ann O'Connell**

FOURTEENTH EDITION	AUGUST 2021
Book Design	SUSAN PUTNEY
Editor	ANN O'CONNELL
Proofreading	JOCELYN TRUITT
Index	ACCESS POINTS INDEXING
Printing	BANG PRINTING

ISSN: 1555-5291 (print)

ISSN: 2328-059X (online)

ISBN: 978-1-4133-2907-0 (pbk)

ISBN: 978-1-4133-2908-7 (ebook)

This book covers only United States law, unless it specifically states otherwise.

Please note

Accurate, plain-English legal information can help you solve many of your own legal problems. But this text is not a substitute for personalized advice from a knowledgeable lawyer. If you want the help of a trained professional— and we'll always point out situations in which we think that's a good idea— consult an attorney licensed to practice in your state.

About the Authors

Janet Portman, an attorney and Nolo's Executive Editor, received undergraduate and graduate degrees from Stanford and a law degree from Santa Clara University. She is an expert on landlord-tenant law and the coauthor of *Every Tenant's Legal Guide, Renters' Rights, The California Landlord's Law Book: Rights & Responsibilities, California Tenants' Rights, Every Landlord's Legal Guide, First-Time Landlord, Negotiate the Best Lease for Your Business*, and the author of *Every Landlord's Guide to Finding Great Tenants*.

Ann O'Connell is a legal editor at Nolo specializing in landlord-tenant and real estate law. She is a coauthor of *Nolo's Essential Guide to Buying Your First Home* and *Every Landlord's Legal Guide*. Before joining Nolo, Ann was a freelance writer for other publications and law firms. She is a member of the bar in California, Nevada, and Colorado, where she is both an active attorney and a real estate broker. Ann has practiced in California and Colorado, and had her own firm in Colorado, where she focused on real estate, landlord-tenant, and small business law. Ann earned her B.A. from Boston College and her J.D. from UC Berkeley Law.

Table of Contents

Appendixes

Your Lease and Rental Documents Companion

The month-to-month rental agreement or long-term lease that you and your tenant sign forms the contractual basis of your relationship. Taken together with federal, state, and local laws, it sets out almost all the legal and practical rules you and your tenant must follow, such as how many people may occupy the rental and for how long, the rent and deposit, and your (and your tenant's) repair and maintenance responsibilities.

We'll take you step by step through preparing a lease or rental agreement and the key forms that supplement them. These forms include a rental application to help you choose the best tenants (and weed out the bad ones), and a landlord-tenant checklist to document the condition of the rental unit at the beginning and end of the tenancy (and avoid disputes over security deposits).

Fortunately, you don't need a lawyer to draft these important rental documents—just this book. Here's how we can help you:

State-specific legal information. We'll show you how to use the detailed state law charts in Appendix A to write legally compliant clauses. For example, the "State Security Deposit Rules" chart has what you need, including the deposit limit, whether you need to keep the deposit in a separate account or pay interest on it, when you must return the deposit, and whether you're exempt from the rules based on the number of rental properties you own.

Where to find the forms. You'll find the lease and rental agreement, rental application, and other forms in this book on the Nolo website,

available for downloading at a special companion page for this book (described below). In addition, this book's print copy and e-book include blank versions of the forms (found in Appendix C). To help you understand and complete the forms, we provide filled-out samples in the text.

 CAUTION

Who shouldn't use our lease or rental agreement? Don't use the forms in this book if you're renting out property that is subsidized by the government, mobile homes, hotels, or commercial property. Landlords who accept Section 8 vouchers will need to use the HUD addendum, which will add to the terms and conditions of the lease you draft using this product (the HUD terms will prevail in case of any inconsistencies). If you are renting out your condominium or townhouse, use these forms in conjunction with your homeowners' association CC&Rs (covenants, conditions, and restrictions).

Get Updates, Forms, and More at This Book's Companion Page on Nolo.com

You can download the lease, rental agreement, and all of the other forms in this book at its "companion page":

www.nolo.com/back-of-book/LEAR.html

When important changes affect the information in this book, we'll post updates on this page. (See Appendix B, "How to Use the Downloadable Forms on the Nolo Website," for a complete list of forms available on Nolo.com.)

Other Helpful Nolo Titles and Online Information and Resources for Landlords

A lease or rental agreement is only one part of a landlord-tenant legal relationship. Nolo publishes several other books for landlords (most with legal forms and state-by-state information) that complement this book, including:

- *Every Landlord's Legal Guide.* A comprehensive explanation of landlord-tenant laws and the practical steps rental property owners can take to comply with them (while at the same time running an efficient and profitable business). It covers most key laws affecting landlords in all 50 states, including your repair and maintenance responsibilities and your liability for crime and environmental health hazards such as lead, mold, and bed bugs; rules and procedures for collecting and returning security deposits; anti-discrimination laws; privacy rules; employment laws affecting managers; tenants' rights to break a lease and leave early; how to resolve problems with tenants or begin the eviction process; issues such as meth labs; and more.
- *First-Time Landlord: Your Guide to Renting Out a Single-Family Home.* A starter guide for people who are renting out a house for the first time (or are considering doing so) and want a basic overview of the legal, practical, and financial issues involved, including estimating costs and profits, co-owning rental property with family, and managing rental income to maximize tax deductions.
- *Every Landlord's Guide to Finding Great Tenants.* A detailed guide to attracting, screening, and choosing the best tenants.

- *Every Landlord's Guide to Managing Property.* Provides practical and legal compliance advice for small-time landlords who manage property and tenants on the side. Includes do-it-yourself advice on handling day-to-day issues, such as nitty-gritty maintenance and conflicts with tenants regarding late rent, pets, and unauthorized occupants.
- *Every Landlord's Tax Deduction Guide.* A comprehensive explanation of deductions and other tax write-offs available to landlords, such as depreciation and insurance. Includes instructions for filling out Schedule E.
- For California landlords: *The California Landlord's Law Book: Rights & Responsibilities.* This book contains all the information California landlords need to run their business.

You can order these landlord titles from Nolo's website (Nolo.com) or by phone (800-728-3555). You can also find Nolo books at bookstores and libraries.

The Nolo website has many online state-specific leases and other landlord forms for sale, plus lots of free information of interest to landlords—including legal updates—and 50-state charts of state laws, such as tenants' rights to withhold rent, eviction rules, restrictions on smoking in residential units, and small claims court limits. (Check out the "Landlords and Tenants" section at Nolo.com.) The "Legal Research" section on the Nolo website will also help you find federal and state laws that affect your property (look for the "Legal Research" link at the bottom of Nolo.com).

11 Tips for Being a Successful Landlord

1. **Don't rent to anyone before checking credit history, references, and background.** Haphazard screening too often results in problem tenants who pay the rent late or not at all, trash your place, move in undesirable friends, or worse.

2. **Avoid illegal discrimination.** Comply with all federal, state, and local laws prohibiting discrimination on the basis of race or color, national origin, gender, age, familial status, disability, and other protected categories.

3. **Get all the important terms of the tenancy in writing.** Beginning with the rental application and lease or rental agreement, be sure to document your relationship with your tenants—including when and how you handle tenant complaints and repair problems, the amount of notice you must give to enter a tenant's apartment, and the like.

4. **Establish a clear, fair system of setting, collecting, holding, and returning security deposits.** Inspect and document the condition of the rental unit before the tenant moves in to avoid disputes over security deposits when the tenant moves out.

5. **Stay on top of repair and maintenance needs and make repairs when requested.** If the property is not kept in good repair, you'll alienate good tenants. And they might have the right to withhold rent, sue for any injuries caused by defective conditions, or move out without notice.

6. **Don't let your tenants and property be easy marks for a criminal.** You could be liable for the tenant's injuries and losses.

7. **Respect your tenants' privacy.** Notify tenants whenever you plan to enter their rental unit, and provide at least 24 hours' notice or the minimum amount required by state law.

8. **Disclose environmental hazards such as lead.** Landlords are increasingly being held liable for tenant health problems resulting from exposure to environmental poisons in the rental premises.

9. **Choose and supervise your manager carefully.** If a manager commits a crime or is incompetent, you could be held financially responsible. Do a thorough background check and clearly spell out the manager's duties to help prevent problems down the road.

10. **Purchase enough liability and other property insurance.** A well-designed insurance program can protect your rental property from losses caused by everything from fire and storms to burglary, vandalism, and personal injury and discrimination lawsuits.

11. **Try to resolve disputes with tenants without lawyers and lawsuits.** If you have a conflict with a tenant over rent, repairs, your access to the rental unit, noise, or some other issue that doesn't immediately warrant an eviction, meet with the tenant to see if the problem can be resolved informally. If that doesn't work, consider mediation by a neutral third party, often available at little or no cost from a publicly funded program. If your dispute involves money and all attempts to reach agreement fail, try small claims court, where you can represent yourself. Use it to collect unpaid rent or to seek money for property damage after a tenant moves out and the deposit is exhausted.

Get a Little Help From Your Friends

Many landlords have discovered the value of belonging to a local or state association of rental property owners. These organizations range from small, volunteer-run groups to substantial city, county, or statewide organizations. Many offer a wide variety of services to members, including:

- legal information and updates through newsletters and seminars
- tenant-screening and credit check services
- training and practical advice on compliance with legal responsibilities
- a place to meet other rental property owners and exchange information and ideas, and
- referrals to professionals, including attorneys, accountants, maintenance firms, and property management companies.

If you can't find an association of rental property owners online, ask other landlords for references. You can also contact the National Apartment Association (www.naahq.org), a national organization whose members include many individual associations.

Preparing a Lease or Rental Agreement

This chapter begins by explaining the differences between leases and rental agreements. You can use this information to decide which is right to use with your tenants. The chapter continues with step-by-step instructions on how to complete and customize your lease or rental agreement, taking into account important issues and legal considerations that we'll walk you through each step of the way.

SEE AN EXPERT

The lease and rental agreement forms are legally sound as designed. If you change important terms or make major changes, however, you might affect a form's legal validity. Rather than take a chance, you might wish to have your work reviewed by an experienced landlord-tenant lawyer.

Which Is Better, a Lease or a Rental Agreement?

One of the first decisions you need to make is whether to use a lease or a rental agreement. Often, your choice will depend on how long you want a tenant to stay. However, other factors come into play, so carefully read what follows before evaluating your own situation and making a decision.

Month-to-Month Rental Agreement

A written rental agreement establishes a tenancy for a short period of time. The law refers to these agreements as periodic or month-to-month tenancies, although it is often legally possible to base them on other time periods, as would be the case if the rent must be paid every two weeks. A month-to-month tenancy automatically renews each month—or other agreed-upon period— unless the landlord or tenant gives the other the proper amount of written notice (typically 30 days) that terminates the agreement.

Month-to-month rental agreements give landlords more flexibility than leases. You can increase the rent or change other terms of the tenancy on relatively short notice (subject to any restrictions of rent control ordinances— see "Rent Control," below). And with proper notice, you can also end the tenancy at any time (again, subject to any rent control restrictions, anti-retaliation laws, and fair housing dictates). (Chapter 4 discusses notice requirements to change or end a rental agreement.) Not surprisingly, many landlords prefer to rent month to month, particularly in urban areas with tight rental markets where new tenants are usually easily found and rents are trending upwards.

On the flip side, a month-to-month tenancy almost guarantees more tenant turnover. Tenants who can legally move out with only 30 days' notice will be more inclined to leave than tenants who make a longer commitment (leaving before a lease is up carries financial risks). Some landlords base their rental business strategy on painstakingly seeking high-quality, long-term renters. If you're one of those, or if you live in an area where it's difficult to fill vacancies, you will probably want tenants to commit for a longer period, such as a year. As discussed below, a fixed-term lease, especially when combined with tenant-friendly management policies, might encourage tenants to stay longer.

Fixed-Term Lease

A lease is a contract that obligates both you and the tenant for a set period of time—usually six months or a year, but sometimes longer. With a fixed-term lease, you can't raise the rent or change other terms of the tenancy until the lease runs out, unless the lease itself allows future changes or the tenant agrees in writing to the changes.

In addition, you usually can't prevail in an eviction lawsuit or even ask a tenant to move out before the lease term expires unless the tenant fails to pay the rent or violates another significant term of the lease or the law, such as repeatedly making too much noise or selling drugs on your property. This restriction can sometimes be problematic if you end up with a tenant you would like to be rid of but don't have sufficient cause to evict.

Say, for example, that you wish to sell the property halfway into the lease term. The new owner usually purchases all the obligations of the previous owner, including the obligation to honor existing leases. The existence of long-term tenants—especially if the buyers want to occupy the property as their home—could be an obstacle to a sale (as would the presence of long-term tenants with a below-market rent). Of course, the opposite can also be true: If you have good, long-term tenants paying a fair rent, the property might be very attractive to potential investment-property buyers.

At the end of the lease term, you have several options. You can:

- decline to renew the lease (except in areas where that's prohibited by local rent control)
- sign a new lease for a set period, or
- do nothing—which means, under the law of most states, that your lease will usually turn into a month-to-month tenancy if you continue to accept monthly rent from the tenant.

Although leases restrict your flexibility, there's often a big plus to having long-term tenants. Some tenants make a serious personal commitment when they enter into a long-term lease, in part because they think they'll be liable for several months' rent if they leave early. And people who plan to be with you over the long term are often more likely to respect your property and the rights of other tenants, making the management of your rental units easier and more pleasant than catering to an endless stream of short-termers.

You'll probably prefer to use leases in areas where there is a high vacancy rate or it is difficult to find tenants for one season of the year. For example, if you are renting near a college that is in session for only nine months a year, or in a vacation area that is deserted for months, you are far better off with a year's lease. This is especially true if you have the market clout to charge a large deposit, so that a tenant who wants to leave early has an incentive to find someone to take over the tenancy.

Getting All the Rent Under a Lease Isn't a Sure Thing

In theory, tenants who sign a year-long lease will pay the rent 12 times. Alas, that doesn't always happen. Leases can end early, and you'll be out the rent, in the following circumstances:

- **State law allows certain tenants to leave.** In some states, tenants can leave, for example, if they need to move to a nursing home.
- **Your shortcomings give tenants a legal reason to break the lease.** In most states, persistent and significant failures to keep the property habitable will justify an early move-out, as will repeated violations of tenant privacy.
- **Federal law gives servicemembers the right to leave.** Tenants in active military service are entitled to break a lease if required by their orders, as explained in "Special Rules for Active Military Tenants" in Chapter 4.
- **Landlords must make reasonable efforts to rerent.** Tenants who leave without a legal reason are on the hook for the rent, but landlords in most states must make reasonable efforts to rerent. Once the place is rerented, the original tenant's obligation ends. If your property is attractive and easily rented, the original tenant might owe you no more than a month or two of rent— probably equal to their security deposit.

Finally, even tenants who leave without legal justification can often escape without paying the balance of the rent. It's usually a losing proposition to try to collect from a tenant who is either judgment-proof or long gone.

 TIP
Always put your agreement in writing. Oral leases or rental agreements are perfectly legal for month-to-month tenancies and for leases of a year or less in most states. While oral agreements are easy and informal, it is never wise to use one. You can almost count on tenants claiming that you made, but didn't keep, certain oral promises—for example, to repaint the kitchen or to not increase the rent. Tenants might also forget what restrictions they agreed to, such as a no-subletting policy. And other issues—for example, how deposits can be used—probably weren't discussed at all. Especially dangerous is the fact that the parties might not accurately recall how long they intended the tenancy to last. If something goes wrong with an oral rental agreement or lease, you and your tenants are all too likely to end up in court, arguing over who said what to whom, when, and in what context.

Tips for Landlords Taking Over Rental Property

If you've recently bought (or inherited) rental property, you will likely be taking on tenants with existing rental agreements or leases. Be sure the last owner gives you copies of all tenant and property files, including leases and rental agreements, details on deposits (location and amounts, along with the deposits themselves), house rules, maintenance and repair records, and all other paperwork and records relevant to the property. If you want to change any of the terms of the lease or rental agreement, follow our advice in the first part of Chapter 4.

Instructions for Completing the Lease or Rental Agreement Form

This section explains each clause in the lease and rental agreement forms in this book, and how to fill in any blanks (in many cases, there will be nothing to fill in). When relevant, you will be asked to check the state law charts in Appendix A to see whether your state has a specific rule that you'll need to enter, such as the amount of notice you give tenants before entering the rental property. Except for Clause 4, Term of the Tenancy, the lease and rental agreement forms are identical, covering the basic terms of the tenancy, such as the amount of rent and due date.

Check Your Local Laws

In some cities or counties, local ordinances or laws (particularly rent control laws) might apply to your rental business. In addition, these laws might affect the lease itself by requiring certain language or information to be in the document. We cannot list the requirements for every locality in the United States, but we can suggest that, to be extra careful, you take a moment to find out whether local laws affect your residential lease.

Fortunately, many cities and counties have placed their laws online. To find out whether your local government has done so, go to www.statelocalgov.net and look for your state and city. A useful source of city codes is www.municode.com. Or, simply call your local government offices, ask whether residential rentals are covered by local ordinances and, if so, where you can obtain a copy.

If local law varies from your state law—by imposing an interest requirement for security deposits, for example—be sure to follow the local rule. You might need to modify this lease accordingly.

How to Edit (or Add) a Lease or Rental Agreement Clause

You might want to change our lease and rental agreement forms in some situations, and the instructions suggest possible modifications for doing so, including how to prepare an attachment (see "How to Prepare an Attachment Page," below, for advice).

It's easy to make changes to the lease or rental agreement form by using the electronic versions available for download on the Nolo website—for example, if you want to:

- edit or add something to a clause
- delete a clause (for example, Clause 20 on tenant rules and regulations, if you don't have a separate set of these), or
- add a new clause.

If your additions or modifications are very slight, and can be done in the margins of the lease or rental agreement, you could instead enter them on the hard copy. If you do this, be sure that you and all tenants initial and date the insertions.

Be sure to renumber the clauses if you add or delete a clause. And if you make extensive changes on your own, you might wish to have your work reviewed by an experienced landlords' lawyer.

TIP

Don't be tempted to cram too many details into your lease or rental agreement. Instead, send new tenants a move-in letter that dovetails with your lease or rental agreement and highlights important terms of the tenancy—for example, how and where to report maintenance problems, procedures for returning security deposits, or special rules for use of a pool or laundry room. (See Chapter 3 for advice on preparing a move-in letter.)

You might be tempted to simply use the form in the back of this book (if you're using a print copy), or download the lease or rental agreement from the Nolo website, and skip the detailed instructions. This would be a mistake. If there is one area of landlord-tenant law where details count, this is it. Make sure you really do have the information necessary to create a lease or a rental agreement that accurately reflects your business strategy and complies with all the laws of your state.

You might be tempted to simply use the form in the back of this book (if you're using a print copy), or download the lease or rental agreement from the Nolo website, and skip over detailed instructions. This would be a mistake. If there is one area of landlord-tenant law where details count, this is it. Make sure you really do have the information necessary to create a lease or a rental agreement that accurately reflects your business strategy and complies with all the laws of your state.

FORM

Rental agreement and lease forms. You'll find copies of the Month-to-Month Residential Rental Agreement and the Fixed-Term Residential Lease (in English and in Spanish) in Appendix C. You can also download these forms on the Nolo website; the link is included in Appendix B. A filled-in sample rental agreement is shown at the end of this chapter.

Clause 1. Identification of Landlord and Tenant

This Agreement is between _____
_____ ("Tenant")
and _____
("Landlord"). Each Tenant is jointly and severally liable for the payment of rent and performance of all other terms of this Agreement.

Every lease or rental agreement must identify the tenant and the landlord or property owner—usually called the "parties" to the agreement. The term "Agreement" (a synonym for "contract") refers to either the lease or the rental agreement.

Any competent adult—at least 18 years of age —may be a party to a lease or rental agreement. (Teenagers who are younger than age 18 and who have achieved legal adult status through court order, military service, or marriage may also be parties to a lease.)

Joint and several liability. The last sentence of Clause 1 states that if you have more than one tenant, they (the cotenants) are all "jointly and severally" liable (legally responsible) for paying rent and abiding by all the terms of the agreement. This essential bit of legalese simply means that each tenant is legally responsible for the whole rent and complying with the lease. This part of the clause gives you important rights; it means you can legally seek the entire rent from any one of the tenants should the others skip out or be unable to pay. A "jointly and severally liable" clause also gives you the right to evict all of the tenants even if just one has broken the terms of the lease—for example, by seriously damaging the property.

How to Fill in Clause 1

In the first blank, fill in the names of all tenants—all adults who will live in the rental, including both members of a married couple. This is a crucial step: By requiring everyone who lives in the unit to sign the lease or rental agreement, you emphasize your expectation that each individual is responsible for the rent, the use of the property, and all terms of the agreement. Also, make sure all tenants' names match their legal documents, such as a driver's license. You can set a reasonable limit on the number of people per rental unit. (See "How Many Tenants to Allow," below.)

In the second blank, list the names of all landlords or property owners who will be signing the lease or rental agreement. If you are using a business name, enter your name, followed by your business name.

> **EXAMPLE:** Joe Smith, doing business as Apple Lane Apartments.

If more than one landlord or owner is signing the lease (such as married property owners), you might want to put both names on the agreement if you both plan to actively participate in managing the property.

 RELATED TOPIC
More on choosing tenants. Chapter 2 provides detailed advice on choosing tenants.

Clause 2. Identification of Premises

> Subject to the terms and conditions set forth in this Agreement, Landlord rents to Tenant, for residential purposes only, the premises located at
> _____ ("the Premises").
> Rental of the Premises also includes _____
> _____ .
> Rental of the Premises excludes _____
> _____ .

Clause 2 identifies the street address of the property being rented (the premises) and provides details on extras such as furnishings and parking spaces. The words "for residential purposes only" are to prevent a tenant from using the property for conducting a business that might affect your insurance or violate zoning laws, or that might burden other tenants or neighbors. Don't go overboard enforcing this against people who work from home and whose activities don't negatively affect their neighbors or your property. The COVID pandemic has made such work commonplace, if not necessary.

Home Businesses on Rental Property

About half of all small businesses in the U.S. are home-based. If a tenant wants you to modify Clause 2 to allow the operation of a business, you have some checking to do—even if you are inclined to say yes. For starters, you'll need to check local zoning laws for restrictions on home-based businesses, including the type of businesses allowed (if any), the amount of car and truck traffic the business can generate, outside signs, on-street parking, the number of employees, and the percentage of floor space devoted to the business. And if your rental is in a planned unit or a condominium development, check the CC&Rs of the homeowners' association.

You'll also want to find out if your insurance company requires a special policy to cover the potential liability of tenants' employees or guests. In many situations, a home office for occasional use will not be a problem. But if the tenant wants to operate a business that involves people and deliveries coming and going, such as a therapy practice, jewelry importer, or small business consulting firm, you should seriously consider expanding or increasing your coverage. You might also want to require that the tenant maintain certain types of liability insurance, so that you won't wind up paying if the tenant's business somehow results in an injury occurring on the rental property—for example, a business customer who trips and falls on the front steps.

Finally, be aware that if you allow a residence to be used as a commercial site, your property might need to meet the accessibility requirements of the federal Americans with Disabilities Act (ADA). For more information on the ADA, see www.ADA.gov or contact the U.S. Department of Justice, Disability Rights Section, Civil Rights Division, in Washington, D.C., at 800-514-0301.

> **CAUTION**
>
> **You might not be able to restrict a child care home business.** A tenant who wants to operate a child care business in the rental might be entitled to do so, despite your general prohibition against businesses. In California and New York, for example, legislators and courts have declared a strong public policy in favor of home-based child care, in single-family homes or in multifamily settings, and have limited a landlord's ability to say no. (Cal. Health & Safety Code §§ 1597.40 and 1597.41; *Haberbaum v. Gotbaum*, 698 NYS 2d 406 (N.Y. City Civ. Ct. 1999).) If you're concerned about a tenant running a child care business in the apartment, check with your state's office of consumer protection (find yours at www.USA.gov) for information on laws that cover in-home child care in residential properties.

If you decide to allow a tenant to run a business from your rental property, you might want to provide details in Clause 24 (Additional Provisions) of your lease or rental agreement.

How to Fill in Clause 2

In the first blank, fill in the street address of the unit or house you are renting. Specify the apartment or building number, if any, as well as the city, state, and zip code.

In the second blank, add details on furnishings and appliances. If the rental unit has only a few basic furnishings, list them in the text of Clause 2.

EXAMPLE: Double bed, night table, blue sofa, and round kitchen table and two matching chairs.

If the rental is fully furnished, it makes sense to attach a separate room-by-room list to the lease or rental agreement. In this case, simply write in something like this: "The rental unit is fully furnished. See Attachment 1, Addition to Clause 2, Identification of Premises, for a complete list of furnishings." Or you can provide information on furnishings on the Landlord-Tenant Checklist included in Chapter 3.

Also use line two to elaborate on other items that the rental includes (do so in the third blank of Clause 2). For example, if the rental includes a parking space, storage in the garage or basement, or access to other parts of the property, such as a gardening shed in the backyard or an on-site gym, include it in your description of the premises.

EXAMPLES:

Parking space #5 in underground garage

Open parking in lot on west side of building

Storage unit #5 in basement

Storage space available on west side of garage

How to Prepare an Attachment

An attachment is simply a separate document with specific details relevant to a clause, such as a list of furnishings (Clause 2) or detailed rules and regulations (Clause 20). Every time you make an attachment, number and name it by referring to the relevant clause—for example, "Attachment 1, Addition to Clause 2, Identification of Premises," "Attachment 2, Addition to Clause 20, Tenant Rules and Regulations." Then, in the agreement itself, refer to the attachment by name, like this: "See 'Attachment 2, Addition to Clause 20, Tenant Rules and Regulations.'" Everyone signing the lease or rental agreement should sign and date each page of an attachment, and you should staple the attachment to all physical copies of the lease or rental agreement.

If your rules about parking or access to other areas of the property are quite detailed—for example, guest parking rules and gym use rules—you probably should include them in Clause 20 (Tenant Rules and Regulations) of your lease or rental agreement.

If the rented premises will not include a particular part of the rental property that a tenant might reasonably assume is included, such as a garage or storage shed you wish to use yourself or rent to someone else, explicitly exclude it from your description of the premises. You can do this by entering details about the items that are excluded on the third blank.

Clause 3. Limits on Use and Occupancy

> The Premises are to be used only as a private residence for Tenant(s) listed in Clause 1 of this Agreement, and their minor children: _____. Occupancy by guests for more than _____ is prohibited without Landlord's written consent and will be considered a breach of this Agreement.

Clause 3 specifies that the rental unit is the residence of the tenants and their minor children only. It lets the tenants know that they may not move anyone else in as a permanent resident without your consent. The value of this clause is that a tenant who tries to move in a relative or friend for a longer period has clearly violated a defined standard, which gives you grounds for eviction. (New York landlords, however, are subject to the "Roommate Law." See "How Many Tenants to Allow," below, for details.)

How Many Tenants to Allow

Two kinds of laws affect the number of people who may live in a rental unit.

State and local health and safety codes typically set *maximum* limits on the number of tenants, based on the size of the unit and the number of bedrooms and bathrooms.

Even more important, the federal government has taken the lead in establishing *minimum* limits on the number of tenants, through passage of the Fair Housing Act (42 U.S.C. §§ 3601–3619, 3631) and by means of regulations from the Department of Housing and Urban Development (HUD). HUD generally considers a limit of two persons per bedroom a reasonable occupancy standard. Because the number of bedrooms is not the only factor—the size of the bedrooms and configuration of the rental unit are also considered—the federal test has become known as the "two per bedroom plus" standard. States and localities can set their own occupancy standards as long as they are more generous than the federal government's—that is, by allowing more people per rental unit.

The Fair Housing Act is designed primarily to disallow illegal discrimination against families with children, but it also allows you to establish your own "reasonable" restrictions on the number of people per rental unit—as long as your policy is truly tied to health and safety needs. In addition, you can adopt standards that are driven by a legitimate business reason or necessity, such as the capacities of the plumbing or electrical systems. Your personal preferences (such as a desire to reduce wear and tear by limiting the number of occupants or to ensure a quiet, uncrowded environment for upscale tenants),

however, do not constitute a legitimate business reason. If your occupancy policy limits the number of tenants for any reason other than health, safety, and legitimate business needs, you risk charges that you are discriminating against families.

Figuring out whether your occupancy policy is legal is not always a simple matter. Furthermore, laws on occupancy limits often change. For more information, call HUD's Housing Discrimination Hotline at 800-669-9777, or check the HUD website at www.HUD.gov. Check your local and state housing authority for other occupancy standards that might affect your rental property. The HUD website includes contact information for these agencies.

> **TIP**
>
> **New York landlords should check out the state's "Roommate Law."** New York landlords must comply with the "Unlawful Restrictions on Occupancy" law, commonly known as the Roommate Law. (N.Y. RPL § 235-f.) The Roommate Law prohibits New York landlords from limiting occupancy of a rental unit to just the tenant named on the lease or rental agreement. It permits tenants to share their rental units with their immediate family members, and, in many cases, with unrelated, nontenant occupants, too, so long as a tenant (or tenant's spouse) occupies the unit as a primary residence. The number of total occupants is still restricted, however, by local laws governing overcrowding.

Clause 3 also allows you to set a time limit for guest stays. Even if you do not plan to strictly enforce restrictions on guests, this provision will be very handy if a tenant tries to move in a friend or relative for a month or two, calling that person a guest. It will give you the leverage you need to ask the guest to leave, request that the guest apply to become a tenant with an appropriate increase in rent, or, if necessary, evict the tenant for violating this lease provision.

How to Fill in Clause 3

In the first blank, have your tenant write the full name of all minors who will be living in the rental. In the second blank, fill in the number of days you allow guests to stay over a given time period without your consent.

We suggest you allow up to two consecutive weeks in any six-month period, but, of course, you might want to modify this based on your own preferences. For example, you could write in the blank, "two weeks in any six-month period."

 CAUTION

Don't discriminate against families with children. You can legally establish reasonable space-to-people ratios, but you cannot use overcrowding as an excuse for refusing to rent to tenants with children, especially if you would rent to the same number of adults. (See "How Many Tenants to Allow," above.) Discrimination against families with children is illegal, except in housing reserved for senior citizens only. Just as important as adopting a reasonable people-to-square-foot standard in the first place is the maintenance of a consistent occupancy policy. If you allow three adults to live in a two-bedroom apartment, you had better let a couple with a child live in the same type of unit, or you are leaving yourself open to charges that you are illegally discriminating.

Clause 4. Term of the Tenancy

This clause sets out the key difference between a lease and a rental agreement: how long a rent-paying tenant is entitled to stay. The early part of this chapter discusses the pros and cons of leases and rental agreements.

Lease Provision

The term of the rental will begin on _____ , and end on _____ .

This lease provision sets a definite date for the beginning and the expiration of the lease and obligates both the landlord and the tenant for a specific term.

Most leases run for one year. This makes sense, because it allows you to raise the rent at reasonably frequent intervals if market conditions allow. Leases can be shorter (six months) or longer (24 months). This, of course, is up to you and the tenants. A long period—two, three, or even five years—can be appropriate, for example, if you're renting out your own house because you're taking a two-year sabbatical or if you have agreed to allow tenants to make major repairs or remodel your property at their expense.

How to Fill in Clause 4 (Lease)

In the first blank, fill in the starting date of the lease. The starting date is the date the tenant has the right to move in, such as the first of the month. This date is usually not the date that you and the tenant sign the lease. The lease signing date is simply the date that you're both bound to the terms of the lease. If the tenant moves in before the regular rental period—such as the middle of the month and you want rent due on the first of every month—you will need to prorate the rent for the first partial month as explained in Clause 5 (Payment of Rent).

In the second blank, fill in the expiration date—in most leases, this will be a year from the starting date. Leases may be shorter (six months) or longer (two years), depending on your situation.

Rental Agreement Provision

The rental will begin on _____ , and continue on a month-to-month basis. Landlord may terminate the tenancy or modify the terms of this Agreement by giving the Tenant ____ days' written notice. Tenant may terminate the tenancy by giving the Landlord ____ days' written notice.

This rental agreement provides for a month-to-month tenancy and specifies how much written notice you must give a tenant to change or end a tenancy, and how much notice the tenant must provide you before moving out. (Chapter 4 discusses changing or ending a month-to-month rental agreement.)

How to Fill in Clause 4 (Rental Agreement)

In the first blank, fill in the date the tenancy will begin. The date the tenancy will begin is the date the tenant has the right to move in, such as the first of the month. This date is usually not the date that you and the tenant sign the rental agreement. The agreement signing date is simply the date that you're both bound to the terms of the rental agreement. If the tenant moves in before the regular rental period—such as the middle of the month, and you want rent due on the first of every month—you will need to prorate the rent for the first partial month as explained in Clause 5 (Payment of Rent).

In the next two blanks, fill in the amount of written notice you'll need to give tenants to end or change a tenancy and the amount of notice tenants must provide to end a tenancy. In most cases, to comply with the law of your state, this will be 30 days for both landlord and tenant in a month-to-month tenancy. (See the "State Rules on Notice Required to Change or Terminate a Month-to-Month Tenancy" chart in Appendix A for a list of each state's notice requirements.)

Possible Modifications to Clause 4 (Rental Agreement)

This rental agreement is month-to-month, although you can change it to a different interval as long as you don't go below the minimum notice period required by your state's law. If you do, be aware that notice requirements to change or end a tenancy might also need to differ from those required for standard month-to-month rental agreements, because state law often requires that all key notice periods be the same.

RENT CONTROL

Rent control might limit your right to terminate or change the terms of a tenancy. Even a month-to-month tenancy can be limited by a rent control law. Check state or local rent control laws for details.

Clause 5. Payment of Rent

Regular monthly rent.

Tenant will pay to Landlord a monthly rent of $_____ , payable in advance on the first day of each month, except when that day falls on a weekend or legal holiday, in which case rent is due on the next business day. Rent will be paid as follows, or in another manner as Landlord designates from time to time:

Delivery of payment.

Rent will be paid:
- ☐ by mail, to _____
- ☐ in person, at _____
- ☐ electronically, to _____

Form of payment.

Landlord will accept payment the form of:
- ☐ cash
- ☐ personal check made payable to _____
- ☐ certified funds or money order made payable to _____
- ☐ credit or debit card
- ☐ other electronic funds transfer

Prorated first month's rent.

- ☐ On signing this Agreement, Tenant will pay to Landlord for the period of _____ through _____ the sum of $_____ as rent, payable in advance of the start of the tenancy.
- ☐ Upon move-in, Tenant will owe as rent the prorated rent specified above, plus one full month's rent in the amount designated above, for a total of $_____.

This clause provides details on the amount of rent and when, where, and how it's paid. It requires the tenant to pay rent monthly on the first day of the month, unless the first day falls on a weekend or a legal holiday, in which case rent is due on the next business day. (Extending the rent due date for holidays is legally required in some states and is a general rule in most.) Clause 5 also covers prorating rent if a tenant moves in before the regular rental period.

How to Fill in Clause 5

Regular monthly rent. In the first blank, state the amount of monthly rent. Unless your premises are subject to a local rent control ordinance, you can legally charge as much rent as you want (or, more practically speaking, as much as the market will bear).

Delivery of payment. Next, specify to whom and where the rent is to be paid. If you accept payment by mail (most common), list the specific person (such as yourself) to whom rent checks will be mailed. Be sure the tenant knows the exact address, including the building or office name and suite number for mailing rent checks. If the tenant will pay rent in person, specify the address, such as your office or the manager's unit at the rental property. Be sure to specify the hours when rent can be paid in person, such as 9 a.m. to 5 p.m. weekdays and 9 a.m. to noon on Saturdays.

CAUTION

California landlords should take special care to inform tenants of where and how rent is paid. State law (Cal. Civ. Code §§ 1962 and 1962.5) requires landlords to notify tenants (either in a separate writing or in a written rental agreement or lease) of the name and street address of the owner or manager responsible for collection of rent, how rent is to be paid, and who is available for services of notices. A landlord in California may not evict for nonpayment of any rent that came due during any period that the landlord was not in compliance with this requirement.

Form of payment. Note all the forms of payment you'll accept, such as personal check and electronic funds transfer, and to whom payment must be made. You can require that tenants pay rent only by check, or give them several options, such as personal check, money order, cashier's check, credit card, automatic credit card debit, or other electronic funds transfer, such as PayPal.

TIP

Looking for ways to ensure that rent payments are timely and reliable? Credit card and automatic debit are two common methods, especially for landlords with large numbers of rental units. If you accept credit cards, you must pay a fee—a percentage of the amount charged—for the privilege, but the cost could be worth it if accepting credit cards results in more on-time rent payments and less hassle for you and your tenants. In terms of automatic debit, you can get tenants' permission to have rent payments debited automatically each month from the tenants' bank accounts and transferred into your account. Some tenants will resist this idea, however, and it's not worth insisting on.

CAUTION

Don't accept cash unless you have no choice. You face an increased risk of robbery if word gets out that you are taking in large amounts of cash once or twice a month. We recommend that you insist that rent be paid by check, money order, or credit card. If you do accept cash, be sure to provide a written, dated receipt stating the tenant's name and the amount of rent paid. Such a receipt is required by law in a few states, and it's a good idea everywhere. Also, check your state law for any other restrictions regarding cash payments. For example, California landlords cannot demand that rent be paid only in cash, unless a tenant has previously bounced a check and the landlord has given the tenant notice to that effect; and in that event, the landlord's demand for cash only may last no longer than three months. (Cal. Civ. Code § 1947.3.)

Prorated first month's rent. If the tenant moves in before the regular rental period—say in the middle of the month, and you want rent due on the first of every month—you can specify the prorated amount due for the first partial month. To figure out prorated rent, divide the monthly rent by 30 days and multiply by the number of days in the first (partial) rental period. That will avoid confusion about what you expect to be paid. Enter the move-in date, such as "June 21, 20xx," and the amount of prorated monthly rent.

> **EXAMPLE:** Meg rents an apartment for $2,100 per month, with rent due on the first of the month. She moves in on June 21, so she should pay ten days' prorated rent of $700 when she moves in. ($2,100 ÷ 30 = $70 x 10 days = $700.) Beginning with July 1, Meg's full $2,100 rent check is due on the first of the month.

You'll see two options for when the tenant will pay the prorated rent. The first option is for the tenant to pay the prorated amount at the time of signing the lease or rental agreement. The second option is for the tenant to pay the prorated rent plus the full amount of the first month's rent at move-in. Check the box next to the option that best applies to your situation.

If the tenant is moving in on the first of the month, you can ignore or delete this section of the clause.

Possible Modifications to Clause 5

Here are a few common ways to modify Clause 5.

Rent due date. You can establish a rent due date different from the first of the month, such as the day of the month on which the tenant moves in. For example, if the tenant moved in on July 10, rent would be due on that date, a system which of course saves the trouble of prorating the first month's rent.

Frequency of rent payments. You are not legally required to have your tenant pay rent on a monthly basis. You can modify the clause and require that the rent be paid twice a month, each week, or by whatever schedule suits you.

Rent Control

"Rent control" is the common term for laws that regulate rent increases and usually also limit the situations in which landlords can terminate tenancies. Rent control also goes by the names "rent stabilization" and "rent regulation." Maryland, New Jersey, and New York allow cities and counties to enact local rent control ordinances. Two states—California and Oregon—have statewide rent control, and Washington, D.C. has district-wide rent control. Although rent control ordinances used to be found mostly in larger cities only (such as San Francisco, Los Angeles, New York City, and Newark), many smaller communities have now adopted some form of rent regulation. Rent control laws usually regulate much more than rent. As mentioned above, many laws restrict the ability of owners to terminate tenancies (known as "just cause" eviction protections), and impose additional procedural steps when landlords terminate tenancies. Many laws also require landlords to disclose certain information in a lease or rental agreement—for example, the address of the local rent control board.

If you own rental property in an area subject to rent control, you should always have a current copy of the ordinance and any regulations interpreting it.

Check with your local rent control board or city manager's or mayor's office for more information on rent control, and modify our forms accordingly. If you're an Oregon landlord, consider contacting or joining a rental-related association, such as the Oregon Rental Housing Alliance or the Oregon Rental Housing Association, Inc., to stay on top of Oregon rent control developments.

Prorated first month's rent. You could make any other arrangement for collecting the prorated first month's rent. For example, you could have the tenant pay the prorated amount at move-in without requiring the payment of the first full month's rent at the same time. This might be a good option if the tenant is moving in early in the month and has a few weeks before the first of the next month.

RELATED TOPIC

See the following chapters for rent-related discussions:

- collecting deposits and potential problems with calling a deposit the "last month's rent": Clause 8, this chapter
- the value of highlighting your rent rules in a move-in letter to new tenants, and collecting the first month's rent: Chapter 3
- tenant's obligations to pay rent when breaking a lease: Chapter 4, and
- legal citations for state rent rules: Appendix A.

Clause 6. Late Charges

Because Landlord and Tenant agree that actual damages for late rent payments are very difficult or impossible to determine, Landlord and Tenant agree to the following:

- Tenant will pay Landlord a late charge if Tenant fails to pay the rent in full within _____ days after the date it is due.
- The late charge will be $_____, plus $_____ for each individual day that the rent continues to be unpaid. The total late charge for any one month will not exceed $_____.

Landlord does not waive the right to insist on payment of the rent in full on the date it is due.

It is your legal right in most states to charge a late fee if rent is not paid on time. This clause spells out the details of your policy on late fees. Charging a late fee does not mean that you give up your right to insist that rent be paid on the due date. To bring this point home, Clause 6 states that

you do not waive the right to insist on full payment of the rent on the date it is due. A late fee is simply one way to motivate tenants to pay rent on time.

A few states have statutes that put precise limits on the amount of late fees or when they can be collected. (See the Late Fees column in the "State Rent Rules" chart in Appendix A before completing this clause.)

RENT CONTROL

Some rent control laws also regulate late fees. If you own rental units in a state or city with rent control, check the laws carefully.

But even if your state doesn't have specific rules restricting late fees, you are still bound by general legal principles (often expressed in court decisions) that prohibit unreasonably high fees. Unless your state imposes more specific statutory rules on late fees, you should be on safe ground if you adhere to these principles:

- The total late charge should not exceed 4%–5% of the rent. That's $40 to $50 on a $1,000-per-month rental.
- If the late fee increases each day the rent is late, it should be moderate and have an upper limit. A late charge that increases without a maximum could be considered interest charged at an illegal ("usurious") rate. Although state usury laws don't directly apply to late charges, judges often use these laws as one guideline in judging whether a particular provision is reasonable. Most states set the maximum interest rate that may be charged for a debt at about 10% to 12%. A late charge that would generally be acceptable for a monthly rent of $1,000 would be a charge of $10 if rent is not paid by the end of the second business day after it is due, plus $5 for each additional day, up to a maximum of 5% of the monthly rental amount.

CAUTION

Don't try to disguise excessive late charges by giving a "discount" for early payment. One landlord we know concluded that he couldn't get away with charging a $100 late charge on an $850 rent payment, so, instead, he designed a rental agreement calling for a rent of $950 with a $100 discount if the rent was not more than three days late. Ingenious as this ploy sounds, it is unlikely to stand up in court in many states, unless the discount for timely payment is modest. Giving a relatively large discount is, in effect, the same as charging an excessive late fee, and a judge is likely to see it as such.

How to Fill in Clause 6

In the first blank, specify how many days (if any) you will allow as a grace period before you charge a late fee. You don't have to give a grace period, but many landlords don't charge a late fee until the rent is two or three days late. If you don't allow any grace period, simply cross out "within ____ days after," so that the first bullet point reads "Tenant will pay Landlord a late charge if Tenant fails to pay the rent in full the date it is due."

In the second bullet point, the first blank is for entering the amount of your late charge when the grace period (if any) has expired. The second blank is for the amount that you will charge for each additional day that the rent is late. The third blank is for the maximum total in late fees you will charge.

Possible Modifications to Clause 6

If you decide not to charge a late fee (something we consider highly unwise), you can simply delete this clause, or write the words "N/A" or "Not Applicable" on it.

Clause 7. Returned Check and Other Bank Charges

> If any check offered by Tenant to Landlord in payment of rent or any other amount due under this Agreement is returned for lack of sufficient funds, a "stop payment," or any other reason, Landlord will make a demand for payment and otherwise pursue remedies as allowed by law.

As with late charges, any bounced-check charges you demand must be reasonable. Some states regulate the amount you can charge; in the absence of such regulation, you should seek no more than the amount your bank charges you for a returned check, probably $25 to $35 per returned item, plus a few dollars for your trouble. Some states regulate the maximum amount you can charge. Check with your state consumer protection agency for any restrictions on bounced-check charges. A list of state consumer protection agencies is available at www.USA.gov.

 TIP

Don't tolerate repeated bad checks. If a tenant habitually pays rent late or gives you bad checks, give written notice demanding that the tenant pay the rent or move within a few days. How long the tenant is allowed to stay depends on state law; in most places, it's about three to 15 days. In most instances, tenants who receive this kind of "pay rent or quit" notice pay up and reform their ways, and that's the end of it. But, if the tenant doesn't pay the rent (or move), you can file an eviction lawsuit. An alternative is to serve the tenant with a 30-day notice to change Clause 5 of the lease or rental agreement to require payment with a money order or a verified credit card transaction.

How to Fill in Clause 7

You do not need to add anything to this clause.

Clause 8. Security Deposit

> On signing this Agreement, Tenant will pay to Landlord the sum of $ _____ as a security deposit. Tenant may not, without Landlord's prior written consent, apply this security deposit to the last month's rent or to any other sum due under this Agreement. Within _____ after Tenant has vacated the Premises, returned the keys, and provided Landlord with a forwarding address, Landlord will return the deposit in full or give Tenant an itemized written statement of the reasons for, and the dollar amount of, any of the security deposit retained by Landlord, along with a check for any deposit balance.

Most landlords quite sensibly ask for a security deposit before entrusting hundreds of thousands of dollars' worth of real estate to a tenant. But it's easy to get into legal trouble over deposits, because they are strictly regulated by state law and, sometimes, also by city ordinance. The law of most states dictates how large a deposit you can require, how you can use it, when you must return it, and more. Several states and cities require you to put deposits in a separate account and pay interest on them.

The use and return of security deposits is a frequent source of disputes between landlords and tenants. To avoid confusion and legal hassles, this clause is clear on the subject, including:

- the dollar amount of the deposit
- the fact that the deposit may not be used for the last month's rent without your prior approval, and
- when the deposit will be returned, along with an itemized statement of deductions.

This section discusses the basic information you need to complete Clause 8. Check the "State Security Deposit Rules" chart in Appendix A for specific details that apply to your situation.

If, after reviewing these tables, you have any questions of what's allowed in your state,

get a current copy of your state's security deposit statute or a summary from a landlords' association. In addition, be sure to check local ordinances in all areas where you own property. Cities, particularly those with rent control, might have additional rules on security deposits, such as a requirement that you pay interest on deposits.

Basic State Rules on Security Deposits

The general purpose of a security deposit is to give the landlord a source of funds if a tenant fails to pay the rent when it is due or doesn't pay for damage to the rental unit. Rent you collect in advance for the first month is not considered part of the security deposit. Specifically:

- Many states limit the amount you can collect to a maximum of one or two months' rent. The limit might be higher for furnished units.
- Several states and cities (particularly those with rent control) require landlords to pay interest, and specify the interest rate that must be paid and when payments must be made. Some states require you to put deposits in a separate account, sometimes called a "trust" account, rather than mixing the funds with your personal or business accounts. In most states, however, you don't have to pay tenants interest on deposits or put them in a separate bank account. In other words, you can put the money in your bank account and use it, as long as you have it available when the tenant moves out.
- When a tenant moves out, you will have a set amount of time (usually from 14 to 30 days, depending on the state) to either return the tenant's entire deposit or provide an itemized statement of deductions and refund any deposit balance, including any interest that is required.
- You can withhold all or part of the deposit to pay for:
  - unpaid rent

Don't Charge Nonrefundable Fees

State laws are often muddled on the subject of whether charging nonrefundable deposits and fees is legal. Some specifically allow landlords to collect a fee that is not refundable—such as for pets, cleaning, or redecorating—as long as this is clearly stated in the lease or rental agreement. In addition, most states allow landlords to charge prospective tenants a nonrefundable fee for the cost of a credit report and related screening fees (discussed in Chapter 3).

But many states—and this is clearly the trend—specifically prohibit nonrefundable fees such as a fixed fee for cleaning drapes or carpets or for painting. All such fees are legally considered security deposits, no matter what their label, and must be refundable. It is also illegal in many states to make the return of deposits contingent upon a tenant staying for a minimum period of time.

Generally, it's best to avoid the legal uncertainties and not try to collect any nonrefundable fees from tenants. In addition, most landlords have found that making all deposits refundable avoids many time-consuming arguments and even lawsuits with tenants. We believe it's much simpler just to consider the expenses these fees cover as part of your overhead and figure them into the rent, raising it, if necessary.

If you have a specific concern about a particular tenant—for example, you're afraid a tenant's pet will damage the carpets or furniture—just ask for a higher security deposit (but do check your state's maximum). That way, you're covered if the pet causes damage, and if it doesn't, the tenant won't have to shell out unnecessarily.

If, despite our advice, you want to charge a nonrefundable fee, check your state's law to find what (if any) kinds of nonrefundable fees are allowed. Then, make sure your lease or rental agreement is clear on the subject.

- repairing damage to the premises (except for "ordinary wear and tear") caused by the tenant, a family member, or a guest
- cleaning necessary to restore the rental unit to its condition at the beginning of the tenancy (over and above "ordinary wear and tear"), and
- restoring or replacing rental unit property taken or damaged or destroyed by the tenant. States typically also allow you to use a deposit to cover the tenant's other obligations under the lease or rental agreement, which might include payment of utility charges.

The laws of many states set heavy penalties for violations of security deposit statutes. See Chapter 4 for a discussion of inspecting the rental unit and returning deposits when a tenant leaves.

How Much Deposit Should You Charge?

Normally, the best advice is to charge as much as the market will bear, within legal limits. The more the tenant has at stake, the better the chance your property will be respected. And, the larger the deposit, the more financial protection you will have if a tenant leaves owing you rent or needing to do expensive repairs.

Market forces, however, often require that you settle for a deposit that is lower than the maximum allowed by law. Your common sense and your business sense need to work together in setting security deposits. Here are a number of considerations to keep in mind:

Charge the full limit in high-risk situations: For example, where there's a lot of tenant turnover, or the tenant has a pet and you're concerned about damage, or the tenant's credit is shaky and you're worried about unpaid rent, you'll want as large a cushion as possible.

- **Consider the psychological advantage of a higher rent rather than a high deposit.** Many tenants would rather pay a slightly higher rent than an enormous deposit. Also, many acceptable, solvent tenants have a hard time coming up with several months' rent, especially when they are still in a rental unit and are awaiting the return of a previous security deposit.

- **Charge a bigger deposit for single-family homes.** Unlike multiunit residences, where close-by neighbors or a manager can spot, report, and quickly stop any destruction of the premises, the single-family home is somewhat of an island. The condition of the interior and even the exterior might be hard to assess, unless you live close by or can frequently check the condition of a single-family rental. And, of course, the cost of repairing damage to a house is likely to be higher than for an apartment.

- **Gain a marketing advantage by allowing a deposit to be paid in installments.** If rentals are plentiful in your area, with comparable units renting at about the same price, you might gain a competitive edge by allowing tenants to pay the deposit in several installments, rather than one lump sum.

TIP

Require renters' insurance as an alternative to a high security deposit. If you're worried about damage but don't think you can raise the deposit any higher, require renters' insurance. You can give your property an extra measure of protection by insisting that the tenant purchase renters' insurance, which might cover damage done by the tenant or guests. (See the discussion of renters' insurance under Clause 15.)

Last Month's Rent

It's a common—but often unwise—practice to collect a sum of money called "last month's rent" from a tenant who's moving in. Landlords tend to treat this money as just another security deposit, and use it to cover not only the last month's rent, but also other expenses such as repairs or cleaning.

Problems can arise because some states restrict the use of money labeled as the "last month's rent" to its stated purpose: the rent for the tenant's last month of occupancy. If you use any of it to repair damage by the former tenant, you're violating the law. Also, using the "last month's rent" for cleaning and repairs could lead to a dispute with a tenant who feels that the last month's rent is taken care of and resents having to pay all or part of it. You would be better off if the tenant paid the last month's rent when it came due, leaving the entire security deposit available to cover any necessary cleaning and repairs.

Avoiding the term "last month's rent" also keeps things simpler if you raise the rent, but not the deposit, before the tenant's last month of occupancy. The problem arises when rent for the tenant's last month becomes due. Has the tenant already paid in full, or does the tenant owe more because the monthly rent is now higher? Legally, there is often no clear answer. In practice, it's a hassle you can easily avoid by not labeling any part of the security deposit "last month's rent."

Clause 8 of the form agreements makes it clear that the tenant may not apply the security deposit to the last month's rent without your prior written consent.

How to Fill in Clause 8

Once you know how much security deposit you can charge (see "State Security Deposit Rules" in Appendix A), fill in the amount in the first blank.

Unless there's a lower limit, we suggest about two months as your rent deposit. (See "How Much Deposit Should You Charge?" above.) In no case is it wise to charge less than one month's rent.

Next, fill in the time period when you will return the deposit, also using the chart "State Security Deposit Rules" in Appendix A. If your state has no statutory deadline for returning the deposit, we recommend 14 to 21 days as a reasonable time to return a tenant's deposit. (See the discussion of returning security deposits in Chapter 4.)

Possible Modifications to Clause 8

The laws of several states require you to give tenants written information on various aspects of the security deposit, including where you are holding the security deposit, interest payments, and the terms of and conditions under which the security deposit may be withheld. The "State Security Deposit Rules" chart in Appendix A gives you information on disclosures you might need to add to Clause 8.

Even if it's not required, you might want to provide additional details on security deposits in your lease or rental agreement. Here are optional clauses you can add to the end of Clause 8.

OPTIONAL CLAUSES

> The security deposit will be held at: _____
> *(name and address of financial institution)* .
> Landlord will pay Tenant interest on all security deposits at the prevailing bank rate.

> Landlord may withhold only that portion of Tenant's security deposit necessary to: (1) remedy any default by Tenant in the payment of rent; (2) repair damage to the Premises, except for ordinary wear and tear caused by Tenant or Tenant's guests; (3) clean the Premises, if necessary; and (4) compensate Landlord for any other losses as allowed by state law.

Disclose Shared Utility Arrangements

When you do not have separate gas and electric meters for each unit, or a tenant's meter serves any areas outside the tenant's unit (such as a water heater used in common with other tenants or even a lightbulb not under the tenant's control in a common area), you should disclose this in your lease or rental agreement. Simply add details to Clause 9. This type of disclosure is required by law in some states, and is fair in any case. The best solution is to put in a separate meter for the areas served outside the tenant's unit. If you don't do that, you should:

- pay for the utilities measured by the tenant's meter yourself by placing that utility in your name (and possibly upping the rent a little bit; do this before advertising the rental).
- reduce the tenant's rent to compensate for payment of utility usage outside of the tenant's unit (this will probably cost you more in the long run than if you either added a new meter or simply paid for the utilities yourself), or
- sign a separate written agreement with the tenant, under which the tenant explicitly agrees to pay for others' utilities, too.

Clause 9. Utilities

> Tenant will pay all utility charges, except for the following, which will be paid by Landlord:
> _____
> _____ .

This clause helps prevent misunderstandings as to who's responsible for paying utilities. Normally, landlords pay for garbage (and sometimes water, if there is a yard) to help make sure that the premises are well maintained. Tenants usually pay for other services, such as gas, electricity, cable TV, and Internet access.

How to Fill in Clause 9

In the blank, fill in the utilities you—not the tenants—will be responsible for paying. If you will not be paying for any utilities, simply delete the last part of the clause so that the clause reads, "Tenant will pay all utility charges."

Clause 10. Prohibition of Assignment and Subletting

Tenant will not sublet any part of the Premises or assign this Agreement without the prior written consent of Landlord. Violating this clause is grounds for terminating the tenancy.

☐ a. Tenant will not sublet or rent any part of the Premises for short-term stays of any duration, including but not limited to vacation rentals.

☐ b. Short-stay rentals are prohibited except as authorized by law. Any short-stay rental is expressly conditioned upon the Tenant's following all regulations, laws, and other requirements as a condition to offering a short-stay rental. Failure to follow all laws, ordinances, regulations, and other requirements, including any registration requirement, will be deemed a material, noncurable breach of this Agreement and will furnish cause for termination.

Clause 10 is an antisubletting clause, the breach of which is grounds for eviction. It prevents a tenant from subleasing during a vacation or renting out a room to someone unless you specifically agree.

Clause 10 is also designed to prevent assignments, a legal term that means your tenant transfers the tenancy to someone else. Practically, you need this clause to prevent your tenant from leaving in the middle of the month or lease term and moving in a replacement—maybe someone you wouldn't choose to rent to—without your consent.

Should You Allow a Sublet or Assignment?

As a general rule, your best bet when a tenant asks to sublease or assign is to insist that the tenancy terminate and a new one begin—with the proposed "subtenant" or "assignee" as the new tenant who (assuming you approve of the subtenant) signs a new lease or rental agreement. This gives you the most direct legal relationship with the substitute. In a few situations, however, you might want to agree to a subtenancy or assignment.

You might, for example, want to accommodate—and keep—an exceptional, long-term tenant who has every intention of returning and whose judgment and integrity you have always trusted. If the proposed stand-in meets your normal tenant criteria, you might decide that it is worth the risk of a subtenancy or assignment in order to keep the original tenant.

Another good reason is a desire to have a sure source of funds in the background. This might come up if your original tenant is financially sound and trustworthy, but a proposed stand-in is less secure but acceptable in every other respect. By agreeing to a sublet or assignment, you have someone in the background (the original tenant) still responsible for the rent. The risk you incur by agreeing to set up a subtenancy or assignment and the hassle that comes with dealing with more than one person might be worth what you gain in keeping a sure and reliable source of funds on the hook.

By including Clause 10 in your lease or rental agreement, you have the option to decline the person your tenant proposes to take over the lease. Under the law of most states, however, you should realize that if a tenant who wishes to leave early provides you with another suitable tenant, you can't both unreasonably refuse to rent to this person and hold the tenant financially liable for breaking the lease. Typically, state law requires that you must try to rerent the property reasonably quickly and subtract any rent you receive from the amount the original tenant owed you for the remainder of the agreed-upon rental period. Lawyers call this the mitigation-of-damages rule, a bit of legalese that's valuable to know.

Subletting and Short-Term Stays (Airbnb)

Online businesses such as Airbnb act as clearing-houses for short-term, or short-stay rentals (less than 30 days), for use by vacationers or visiting businesspersons. Tenants using these platforms sublet their rentals and pocket the rent, turning your property into a hotel. Landlords are universally opposed to this practice, though even they have joined the bandwagon, taking regular rental property out of circulation in order to operate it solely as a short-term rental.

If you want to restrict tenants from running a short-term rental business, be sure your lease is clear on this. First, however, check local law: Bowing to political pressure, many municipalities are changing their laws concerning short-stay tenancies, by requiring registration and limiting the number of short-stay days per year. It is possible that your locality has granted tenants the right to rent on Airbnb or other services under specific conditions and requirements.

How to Fill in Clause 10

After you have determined whether any local ordinances regulate short-term rentals, choose the appropriate alternative language for Clause 10. Alternate (a) flatly prohibits such rentals, while alternate (b) advises tenants that they must follow the short-term-stay law or risk termination of their tenancy.

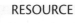 **RESOURCE**
For a related discussion of subleases, assignments, and the landlord's duty to mitigate damages, see Chapter 4.

Clause 11. Tenant's Maintenance Responsibilities

Tenant agrees to: (1) keep the Premises clean, sanitary, and in good condition and, upon termination of the tenancy, return the Premises to Landlord in a condition identical to that which existed when Tenant took occupancy, except for ordinary wear and tear; (2) immediately notify Landlord of any defects or dangerous conditions in and about the Premises of which Tenant becomes aware; and (3) reimburse Landlord, on demand by Landlord, for the cost of any repairs to the Premises, including Landlord's personal property therein, damaged by Tenant or Tenant's guests or business invitees through misuse or neglect.

Tenant has examined the Premises, including appliances, fixtures, carpets, drapes, and paint, and has found them to be in good, safe, and clean condition and repair, except as noted in the Landlord-Tenant Checklist.

Clause 11 makes the tenant responsible for keeping the rental premises clean and sanitary, and makes it clear that if the tenant damages the premises (for example, by breaking a window or scratching hardwood floors) or the landlord's personal property (for example, any furnishings included with the rental), it's the tenant's responsibility to pay for the damage.

It is the law in some states (and a wise practice in all) to notify tenants in writing of procedures for making complaint and repair requests. Clause 11 requires the tenant to alert you to defective or dangerous conditions.

Clause 11 also states that the tenant has examined the rental premises, including appliances, carpets, and paint, and found them to be safe and clean, except as noted in a separate form (the Landlord-Tenant Checklist, described in Chapter 4). Before the tenant moves in, you and the tenant should inspect the rental unit and fill

Ten Elements of a Good Maintenance and Repair System

As a general rule, landlords are legally required to offer livable premises when a tenant originally rents an apartment or rental unit and to maintain the premises throughout the rental term. If rental property is not kept in good repair, the tenant might have the right to repair the problem and deduct the cost from the rent, withhold rent, sue for any injuries caused by defective conditions, or move out without notice. Your best defense against rent withholding hassles and other disputes with tenants is to establish and communicate a clear, easy-to-follow procedure for tenants to ask for repairs, and for you to document all complaints, respond quickly when complaints are made, and schedule annual safety inspections. And, if you employ a manager or management company, make sure they fully accept and implement your guidelines.

Follow these steps to avoid maintenance and repair problems with tenants:

1. **Regularly look for dangerous conditions on the property and fix them promptly.** Reduce risk exposure as much as possible—for example, by providing sufficient lighting in hallways, parking garages, and other common areas, strong locks on doors and windows, and safe stairs and handrails.

2. **Scrupulously comply with all public health and safety codes.** Your local building or housing authority and health or fire department can provide any information you need. Also, check state housing laws governing landlords' repair and maintenance responsibilities. (Appendix A includes citations for the major state laws affecting landlords. Check your statutes for headings such as "Landlord Obligations to Maintain Premises.")

3. **Clearly set out the tenant's responsibilities for repair and maintenance in your lease or rental agreement.** (See Clauses 11, 12, and 13 of the agreements in this chapter.)

4. **Use the written Landlord-Tenant Checklist form in Chapter 3 to check over the premises and fix any problems before new tenants move in.**

5. **Encourage tenants to immediately report plumbing, heating, weatherproofing, or other defects and safety or security problems.** They should report problems in the tenant's unit as well as in common areas like hallways and parking garages.

6. **Handle repairs (especially urgent ones, such as a broken door lock or lack of heat in winter) as soon as possible.** Notify the tenant by phone, text, or email and follow up in writing if repairs will take more than 48 hours, excluding weekends. Keep the tenant informed—for example, if you have problems scheduling a plumber, let your tenant know. For nonurgent repairs, be sure to give the tenant proper notice as required by state law. (See Clause 17 for details on notice required to enter rental premises.)

7. **Keep a written log of all tenant complaints, including those made orally.** Record your immediate and any follow-up responses (and subsequent tenant communications), with details as to how and when the problem was fixed, including reasons for any delay.

8. **Twice a year, give your tenants a checklist on which to report any potential safety hazards or problems that might have been overlooked.** For example, low water pressure in the shower, peeling paint, or noisy neighbors. This is also a good time to remind tenants of their repair and maintenance responsibilities. Respond promptly and in writing to all repair requests, keeping copies in your file.

9. **Once a year, inspect all rental units for safety and maintenance problems, using the Landlord-Tenant Checklist as a guide.** Make sure smoke detectors, heating and plumbing systems, and major appliances are safe and in good working order. (Keep copies of the filled-in checklist in your file.)

10. **Get a good liability insurance policy to cover injuries or losses suffered by others as the result of defective conditions on the property, and lawyers' bills for defending personal injury suits.**

out the Landlord-Tenant Checklist, describing what is in the unit and noting any problems. Doing so will help you avoid security deposit disputes when the tenant moves out.

Common Terms

Tenant. Someone who has signed a lease or a rental agreement, or who has gained the status of a tenant because the landlord has accepted that person's presence on the property or has accepted rent from the person.

Cotenants. Two or more tenants who rent the same property under the same lease or rental agreement, each 100% responsible for carrying out the agreement, including paying all the rent.

Subtenant. Someone who subleases (rents) all or part of the premises from a tenant and does not sign a lease or rental agreement with the landlord. A subtenant may either rent (sublet) an entire dwelling from a tenant who moves out temporarily—for example, for the summer—or rent one or more rooms from the tenant, who continues to live in the unit. The key to subtenant relationships is that the original tenant retains the primary relationship with the landlord and continues to exercise some control over the rental property, either by occupying part of the unit or by reserving the right to retake possession at a later date.

Assignment. The transfer by a tenant of all rights of tenancy to another tenant (the "assignee"). Unlike a subtenant, an assignee rents directly from the landlord.

Roommates. Two or more people, usually unrelated, living under the same roof and sharing rent and expenses. A roommate is usually a cotenant, but in some situations might be a subtenant.

How to Fill in Clause 11

You do not need to add anything to this clause.

 RESOURCE

Comprehensive landlord law resource. Several times in this book, we recommend *Every Landlord's Legal Guide*, by Marcia Stewart, Janet Portman, and Ann O'Connell (Nolo). It is especially useful for its detailed discussion of landlords' and tenants' rights and responsibilities for repair and maintenance under state and local laws and judicial decisions. It provides practical advice on how to stay on top of repair and maintenance needs and minimize financial losses and legal problems with tenants. It discusses tenants' rights if you do not meet your legal responsibilities and the pros and cons of delegating repairs and maintenance to the tenant. *Every Landlord's Legal Guide* also includes chapters on landlords' liability for tenant injuries from defective housing conditions, such as a broken step or defective wiring; liability for environmental hazards such as asbestos and lead; and responsibility to provide secure premises and protect tenants from assault or criminal activities, such as drug dealing.

Clause 12. Repairs and Alterations by Tenant

> a. Except as provided by law or as authorized by the prior written consent of Landlord, Tenant will not make any repairs or alterations to the Premises, including nailing holes in the walls or painting the rental unit.
>
> b. Tenant will not, without Landlord's prior written consent, alter, rekey, or install any locks to the Premises or install or alter any security alarm system. Tenant will provide Landlord with a key or keys capable of unlocking all such rekeyed or new locks as well as instructions on how to disarm any altered or new security alarm system.

Clause 12 makes it clear that the tenant may not make alterations and repairs without your consent, including painting the unit or putting nails in the walls.

And, to make sure you can take advantage of your legal right of entry in an emergency situation, Clause 12 specifically forbids the tenant from rekeying the locks or installing a security alarm system without your consent. If you do grant permission, make sure your tenant gives you duplicate keys or the name and phone number of the alarm company or instructions on how to disarm the alarm system so that you can enter in case of emergency.

The "except as provided by law" language in Clause 12 is a reference to the fact that, in certain situations and in certain states, tenants have a narrowly defined right to alter or repair the premises, regardless of what you've said in the lease or rental agreement. Examples include:

- **Alterations by a person with a disability, such as lowering countertops for a tenant who uses a wheelchair.** Under the federal Fair Housing Act, persons with disabilities may modify a living space to the extent necessary to make the space safe and comfortable, as long as the modifications will not make the unit unacceptable to the next tenant, or if the tenant with a disability agrees to undo the modification when the tenant leaves. Even so, the tenant must first approach you with the request. (42 U.S.C. § 3604(f)(3)(A).)
- **Use of the "repair and deduct" procedure.** In most states, tenants have the right to repair defects or damage that makes the premises uninhabitable or substantially interferes with the tenant's safe use or enjoyment of the premises. The tenant must first notify you of the problem and give you a reasonable amount of time to fix it.
- **Installation of satellite dishes and antennas.** Federal law gives tenants limited rights to install wireless antennas and small satellite dishes. (47 C.F.R. § 1.4000.)
- **Specific alterations allowed by state statutes.** Some states allow tenants to install energy conservation measures (like removable interior storm windows) or burglary prevention devices without the landlord's prior consent. Check your state statutes or call your local rental property association for more information on these types of laws.

How to Fill in Clause 12

If you do not want the tenant to make any repairs without your permission, you do not need to add anything to this clause.

You might, however, want to go further and specifically prohibit certain repairs or alterations by adding details in Clause 24 (Additional Provisions). For example, you could make it clear that any "fixtures"—a legal term that describes any addition that is attached to the structure, such as bolted-in bookcases or built-in dishwashers—are your property and may not be removed by the tenant without your permission.

If you do authorize the tenant to make any repairs, provide enough detail so that the tenant knows exactly what is expected, how much repairs can cost, and who will pay. For example, if you decide to allow the tenant to take over the repair of any broken windows, routine plumbing jobs, or landscaping, give specific descriptions and limits to the tasks.

 CAUTION

Do not delegate to a tenant your responsibility for major maintenance of essential services. The duty to repair and maintain heating, plumbing, and electrical and structural systems (the roof, for example) is yours. Absent unusual circumstances, and even then only after carefully checking state law, it's a mistake to try to delegate this responsibility to the tenant. Many courts have held that landlords cannot delegate to a tenant the responsibility for keeping the premises fit for habitation, fearing that the tenant will rarely be in the position, either practically or financially, to do the kinds of repairs that are often needed to bring a structure up to par.

Clause 13. Violating Laws and Causing Disturbances

> Tenant is entitled to quiet enjoyment of the Premises. Tenant and guests or invitees will not use the Premises or adjacent areas in such a way as to: (1) violate any law or ordinance, including laws prohibiting the use, possession, or sale of illegal drugs; (2) commit waste (severe property damage) or cause or tolerate a nuisance; or (3) annoy, disturb, inconvenience, or interfere with the quiet enjoyment and peace and quiet of any other tenant or nearby resident.

This type of clause is found in most leases and rental agreements. Although it contains some legal jargon, it's probably best to leave it as is, because courts have a lot of experience with these terms. As courts define it, the "covenant of quiet enjoyment" amounts to an implied promise that you will not act (or fail to act) in a way that interferes with or destroys the ability of the tenant to use the rented premises.

Examples of landlord violations of the covenant of quiet enjoyment include:

- allowing garbage to pile up

Waste and Nuisance: What Are They?

In legalese, committing **waste** means causing severe damage—way beyond ordinary wear and tear—to real estate, including a house or an apartment unit. Punching holes in walls, pulling out sinks and fixtures, and knocking down doors are examples of waste.

Nuisance means behavior that prevents neighbors from fully enjoying the use of their homes. Continuous loud noise and foul odors are examples of legal nuisances that could disturb nearby neighbors and affect their "quiet enjoyment" of the premises. So, too, is selling drugs or engaging in other illegal activities that greatly disturb neighbors.

- tolerating a major rodent infestation, or
- failing to control a tenant whose constant loud music makes it impossible for other tenants to sleep.

If you want more specific rules—for example, no loud music played after midnight—add them to Clause 20: Tenant Rules and Regulations, or to Clause 24: Additional Provisions.

How to Fill in Clause 13

You do not need to add anything to this clause.

How to Prevent Illegal Tenant Activity

You can take several practical steps to avoid trouble among your tenants and, in the event that hostilities do erupt, to limit your exposure to lawsuits:

- Screen tenants carefully and choose tenants who are likely to be law-abiding and peaceful. (Chapter 2 recommends a comprehensive system for screening prospective tenants, including checking out references from past landlords and employers.)
- Establish a system to respond to tenants' complaints and concerns about other tenants, especially those involving drug dealing.
- Make it clear that you will not tolerate tenants' disruptive behavior. An explicit lease or rental agreement provision such as Clause 13, prohibiting drug dealing and illegal activity, is the most effective way to make this point. If a tenant does cause trouble, act swiftly. Some situations, such as drug dealing, call for prompt efforts to evict the troublemaker. Your failure to evict drug-dealing tenants can result in lawsuits from tenants injured or annoyed by drug dealers, and local, state, or federal authorities might levy stiff fines for allowing the illegal activity to continue. In extreme cases, you could actually lose your property to the government under public nuisance abatement laws and forfeiture laws.

Clause 14. Damage to the Premises

In the event the Premises are partially or totally damaged or destroyed by fire or other cause, the following will apply:

a. Premises totally damaged and destroyed. Landlord will have the option to: (1) repair such damage and restore the Premises, with this Agreement continuing in full force and effect, except that Tenant's rent will be abated while repairs are being made; or (2) give written notice to Tenant terminating this Agreement at any time within thirty (30) days after such damage, and specifying the termination date; in the event that Landlord gives such notice, this Agreement will expire and all of Tenant's rights pursuant to this Agreement will cease.

b. Premises partially damaged by fire or other cause. Landlord will attempt to repair such damage and restore the Premises within thirty (30) days after such damage. If only part of the Premises cannot be used, Tenant must pay rent only for the usable part, to be determined by Landlord. If Landlord is unable to complete repairs within thirty (30) days, this Agreement will expire and all of Tenant's rights pursuant to this Agreement will terminate at the option of either party. Whether the Premises are totally or partially destroyed will be decided by Landlord, in the exercise of its sole discretion.

c. In the event that Tenant, or Tenant's guests or invitees, in any way caused or contributed to the damage of the Premises, Landlord will have the right to terminate this Agreement at any time, and Tenant will be responsible for all losses, including, but not limited to, damage and repair costs as well as loss of rental income.

d. Landlord will not be required to repair or replace any property brought onto the Premises by Tenant.

This clause outlines what will happen if all or part of the premises is destroyed or damaged. Because there's no way of knowing the exact situation under which you might need to use this clause, it gives you a lot of flexibility: As the landlord, you'll have the option to try to repair or rebuild, or terminate the lease. If the tenant or tenant's guests damage or destroy your property, you'll be able to hold the tenant responsible.

How to Fill in Clause 14

You do not need to add anything to this clause.

Clause 15. Renters' Insurance

Tenant acknowledges that Landlord's property insurance policy will not cover damage to or loss of Tenant's personal property. Tenant will obtain a renters' insurance policy that will:

- reimburse Landlord for cost of fire or water damage caused by Tenant or Tenant's guests, and vandalism to the Premises
- indemnify Landlord against liability to third parties for any negligence on the part of Tenant, Tenant's guests, or invitees; and
- cover damage to Tenant's personal possessions to a minimum of $100,000.

Tenant will provide Landlord with proof of such policy by giving Landlord a certificate of insurance issued by the insurance company within fifteen (15) days of _____. The policy will name Landlord as an "additional insured." Tenant will provide Landlord with a certificate of insurance upon every renewal. Tenant will not allow such policy to expire during the rental term. Failure to obtain and maintain a renters' insurance policy will be treated as a material breach of this Agreement.

This clause requires the tenant to obtain a renters' insurance policy. The policy will insure the tenant's personal property, and the liability portion will cover loss or damage to your rental property caused by the tenant's carelessness.

Tenants must give you proof that they have purchased a policy within 15 days after the tenancy begins. Be sure to ask for it, and stay on top of any renewals.

This clause warns tenants that if they fail to buy and maintain a renters' policy, they will have materially breached the agreement. This will entitle you to terminate the tenancy if you wish.

Renters' Insurance

Renters' insurance covers losses to the tenant's belongings as a result of fire or theft, as well as injury to other people or property damage caused by the tenant's negligence. Besides protecting the tenant from personal liability, renters' insurance benefits you, too: If damage caused by the tenant could be covered by either the tenant's insurance policy or yours, a claim made on the tenant's policy will affect the tenant's premiums, not yours. Renters' insurance will not cover intentional damage by the tenant.

Be advised that it might not be legal for you to require your tenants to carry renters' insurance (in particular, liability insurance). Judges in some states (including Oklahoma) have held that tenants are by implication coinsureds under the landlord's property policy, because their rent helps pay the landlord's premiums. The theory is that making tenants buy additional insurance that will cover any destruction they might cause to your property duplicates the insurance that you (and they, indirectly) already carry, and shouldn't be allowed.

Unfortunately, it's very hard to get a good handle on which states adopt this approach. Only Virginia has clear, statutory law on the subject: Virginia allows a landlord to require a tenant to pay for renters' insurance that's obtained by the landlord. However, if the landlord also requires a security deposit, the combined cost of the insurance premiums and the security deposit cannot exceed two months' rent. (Va. Code Ann.

§§ 55.1-1206, 1208.) Oregon also regulates landlords' requirements for renters' insurance (Or. Rev. Stat. Ann. § 90.222.)

Landlords subject to rent control might not be able to require renters' insurance, because a court might consider the premiums as a rent overcharge. Before requiring tenants to carry renters' insurance, you'll need to check with your agent or lawyer on the legality of such a requirement in your state or locality.

The average cost of renters' insurance is typically less than $20 or $30 per month, depending on the location and size of the rental unit and the value of the policyholder's possessions. Some carriers offer discounts for new policies to customers with existing policies, and additional discounts for tenants who don't smoke (smoking is a major cause of house fires) and who can demonstrate they have risk-reduction measures such as smoke alarms, safes, alarm systems, or double-bolt locks.

How to Fill in Clause 15

In the blank, type in the date that the tenancy will begin—refer back to the date you wrote into Clause 4. Keep in mind that this date might be different from the date you signed the agreement, and it might also be different from the date the tenant actually moves in.

If you decide to not require the tenant to obtain renters' insurance, delete this clause, and renumber the following clauses.

Clause 16. Pets

No animal may be kept on the Premises without Landlord's prior written consent, except animals needed by tenants who have a disability, as that term is understood by law, and under the following conditions: _____

_____

_____ .

This clause prevents tenants from keeping pets without your written permission. If you want, you can have a flat "no pets" rule, though many landlords, in fact, report that pet-owning tenants tend to be more appreciative, stable, and responsible than the norm. At the least, the clause provides you with a legal mechanism that will keep your premises from being waist-deep in Irish wolfhounds. Without this sort of provision, particularly if you use a longer-term lease that can't be terminated early save for a clear violation of one of its provisions, there's little to prevent your tenant from keeping multiple, dangerous, or nonhousebroken pets, except for city ordinances prohibiting exotic animals, and animal cruelty laws.

You have the right to prohibit all pets (including pets of guests), or to restrict the types of pets or dog breeds you allow, with the exception of trained dogs and some other animals used by people who have a mental or physical disability.

How to Fill in Clause 16

If you do not allow pets, simply delete the words "and: _____ under the following conditions: _____ _____."

If you allow pets, be sure to identify the type and number of pets in the first blank—for example, "one cat" or "one dog weighing less than 20 pounds." It's also wise to spell out your pet rules in the second blank.

> **EXAMPLE:**
>
> Tenant must keep the grounds and street free of all animal waste. Tenant's pet must be well behaved and under Tenant's control at all times and will not pose a threat or apparent threat to the safety of other tenants, their guests, or other people on or near the Premises.

Your tenant rules and regulations is another possible place to spell out your pet rules—in which case, add this language in the second blank: Tenant must comply with pet rules included in the Tenant Rules and Regulations (Clause 18) attached to this agreement.

Should You Require a Separate Security Deposit for Pets?

Some landlords allow pets but require the tenant to pay a separate deposit to cover any damage caused by the pet. The laws of a few states specifically allow separate, nonrefundable pet deposits. In others, charging a designated pet deposit is legal only if the total amount you charge for deposits does not exceed the state maximum for all deposits. (See Clause 8 for details on security deposits.)

Even where allowed, separate pet deposits can often be a bad idea, because they limit how you can use that part of the security deposit. For example, if the pet is well-behaved but the tenant trashes your unit, you can't use the pet portion of the deposit to clean up after the human. If you want to protect your property from damage done by a pet, you are probably better off charging a slightly higher rent or security deposit to start with (assuming you are not restricted by rent control or the upper security deposit limits).

If your tenant is a person with a disability and has a trained service animal, you cannot charge a separate pet deposit—service animals are not considered pets. But what about tenants with assistance animals—animals that provide emotional support and comfort or companionship? If your tenant is a person with a disability (as defined by law), you cannot charge a separate pet deposit if the tenant can demonstrate that the assistance animal provides some form of benefit that enables the tenant to live safely and equally on the premises.

Clause 17. Landlord's Right to Access

Landlord or Landlord's agents may enter the Premises in the event of an emergency, to make repairs or improvements, or to show the Premises to prospective buyers or tenants. Landlord may also enter the Premises to conduct an annual inspection to check for safety or maintenance problems. Except in cases of emergency, Tenant's abandonment of the Premises, court order, or where it is impractical to do so, Landlord will give Tenant _____ notice before entering.

Because you have a legal duty to keep the premises safe and habitable, as a practical matter you must keep monitoring the condition of the property. For this reason, and because it makes good sense to allow landlords reasonable access to their property, nearly every state clearly recognizes the right of a landlord to legally enter rented premises while a tenant is still in residence under certain broad circumstances, such as to deal with an emergency and when the tenant gives permission.

Many states have access laws specifying the circumstances under which landlords may legally enter rented premises. Most access laws allow landlords to enter rental units to make repairs and inspect the property and to show property to prospective tenants and purchasers. (See "General Rules of Entry," below.) State access laws typically specify the amount of notice required for such entry—usually 24 hours (unless it is impractical to do so—for example, in cases of emergency). A few states simply require the landlord to provide "reasonable" notice, often presumed to be 24 hours.

Clause 17 makes it clear to the tenant that you have a legal right of access to the property to make repairs or to show the premises for sale or rental, provided you give the tenant reasonable notice. (The chart "State Laws on Landlord's Access to Rental Property" in Appendix A provides details on a landlord's right to entry and notice requirements.)

How to Fill in Clause 17

In the blank, indicate the amount of notice you will provide the tenant before entering—at least the minimum required in your state. If your state law simply requires "reasonable" notice or has no notice requirement, we suggest you provide at least 24 hours' notice.

General Rules of Entry

Except in cases of emergency, or where it is impractical to do so, you generally must enter only at reasonable times, and you must give at least the amount and type of notice required in your state.

Emergency. In all states, you can enter rental property to respond to a true emergency—such as a gas leak.

To make repairs or inspect the property. By law, many states allow you and your repairperson to enter the tenant's home to make necessary or agreed-upon repairs, decorations, alterations, or improvements, and to supply necessary or agreed-upon services—for example, when you need to fix a broken oven.

To show property. Most states with access laws allow a landlord to enter rented property to show it to prospective tenants or to prospective purchasers. (See Chapter 2 for advice on renting property that's still occupied.)

With the permission of the tenant. You can always enter rental property, even without notice, if the tenant agrees.

Entry after the tenant has moved out. To state the obvious, you may enter the premises after the tenant has completely moved out—regardless of whether the tenant left voluntarily after giving back the key or involuntarily as a result of an eviction lawsuit. In addition, if you reasonably believe the tenant has abandoned the property—that is, skipped out without giving any notice or returning the key—you may legally enter.

Clause 18. Extended Absences by Tenant

> Tenant will notify Landlord in advance if Tenant will be away from the Premises for _____ or more consecutive days. During such absence, Landlord may enter the Premises at times reasonably necessary to maintain the property and inspect for damage and needed repairs.

Several states give landlords the specific right to enter the rental during a tenant's extended absence, to maintain the property as necessary and to inspect for damage and needed repairs. Extended absence is often defined as seven days or more. For example, if you live in a cold-weather place and temperatures take a dive, it makes sense to check the pipes in rental units when the tenant is away in the winter.

While many states do not address this issue, either by statute or court decision, you should be on safe legal ground to enter rental property during a tenant's extended absence, as long as you have a genuine reason to enter to protect the property from damage. You should enter only if something really needs to be done—that is, something tenants would do if they were home as part of their obligation to keep the property clean, safe, and in good repair.

To protect yourself, include Clause 18, which requires that the tenant notify you when they will be gone for an extended time and alerts the tenant of your intent to enter the premises during these times, if necessary.

How to Fill in Clause 18

In the blank, fill in the length of the tenant's expected absence that will trigger your tenant's duty to notify you. Ten or 14 days is common.

Clause 19. Possession of the Premises

> a. *Tenant's failure to take possession.* If, after signing this Agreement, Tenant fails to take possession of the Premises, Tenant will still be responsible for paying rent and complying with all other terms of this Agreement.
>
> b. *Landlord's failure to deliver possession.* If Landlord is unable to deliver possession of the Premises to Tenant for any reason not within Landlord's control, including, but not limited to, failure of prior occupants to vacate or partial or complete destruction of the Premises, Tenant will have the right to terminate this Agreement upon proper notice as required by law. In such event, Landlord's liability to Tenant will be limited to the return of all sums previously paid by Tenant to Landlord.

The first part of this clause (Part a) explains that a tenant who chooses not to move in (take possession) after signing the lease or rental agreement will still be required to pay rent and satisfy other conditions of the agreement. This does not mean, however, that you can sit back and expect to collect rent for the entire lease or rental agreement term. (As we explain in Chapter 4, in most states you must take reasonably prompt steps to rerent the premises, and you must credit the rent you collect against the first tenant's rent obligation.)

The second part of the clause (Part b) protects you if you're unable, for reasons beyond your control, to turn over possession after having signed the agreement or lease—for example, if a fire spreads from next door and destroys the premises. It limits your financial liability to the new tenant to the return of any prepaid rent and security deposits (the "sums previously paid," in the language of the clause).

$\left(\begin{array}{c}!\\○\end{array}\right)$ CAUTION
Clause 19 might not limit your liability if you cannot deliver possession because the old tenants are still on the premises—even when they are the subject of an eviction that you ultimately win. When a holdover tenant prevents the new tenant from moving in, landlords can be sued by the new tenant for not only the return of any prepaid rent and security deposits, but also the costs of temporary housing, storage costs, and other losses. In some states, an attempt in the lease to limit the new tenant's recovery to the return of prepaid sums alone would not hold up in court. To protect yourself, you will want to shift some of the financial liability to the holdover tenants. You'll have a stronger chance of doing this when the old tenants have given written notice of their intent to move out. (See Clause 4, above, which requires written notice.)

How to Fill in Clause 19

You do not need to add anything to this clause.

Clause 20. Tenant Rules and Regulations

☐ Tenant acknowledges receipt of, and has read a copy of, Tenant Rules and Regulations, which are labeled Attachment_____ and attached to and incorporated into this Agreement by this reference. Tenant understands that serious or repeated violations of the rules may be grounds for termination.

What's Covered in Tenant Rules and Regulations

Tenant rules and regulations typically cover issues like:
- elevator safety and use
- pool rules
- garbage disposal and recycling
- vehicles and parking regulations—for example, restrictions of repairs on the premises or types of vehicles (such as no RVs)
- lockout and lost key charges
- if you allow pets, rules about where pets are allowed
- security system
- use details on what's considered excessive noise
- storage of bikes, baby strollers, and other equipment in halls, stairways, and other common areas
- directions for using items in rental, such as how to use the fireplace
- use of the grounds and recreation areas
- maintenance of balconies and decks (for instance, no drying clothes on balconies)
- display of signs in windows, and
- laundry room rules.

Many landlords don't worry about detailed rules and regulations, especially when they rent single-family homes or duplexes. However, in larger buildings with many tenants, rules are usually important to control the use of common areas and equipment—both for the convenience, safety, and welfare of the tenants and as a way to protect your property from damage. Rules and regulations also help avoid confusion and misunderstandings about day-to-day issues such as garbage disposal, lost key charges, and parking rules.

When tenants break a rule or regulation, consider giving them a written warning to not engage in the behavior again, and keep a record of the tenant's violations. Depending on the circumstances, you might be able to terminate the tenancy of or evict a tenant who repeatedly or seriously violates your rules and regulations. Also, to avoid charges of illegal discrimination, make sure to apply the same rules, regulations, and consequences to all tenants.

Some rules do not belong in your rules and regulations: Very important rules—such as a no-smoking policy or a prohibition on waterbeds—go directly into your lease or rental agreement. A rule is important enough to put in the lease or rental agreement if repeated (or even single) violations would justify a lease termination. (Most of the time, the consequence of rule-breaking isn't so dire.) Putting very important rules in your lease or rental agreement gives you the option to terminate the tenancy of or evict a tenant who breaks the rule even just one time.

Because tenant rules and regulations are often lengthy and might be revised occasionally, we suggest you prepare a separate attachment. (See "How to Prepare an Attachment Page," above.) Be sure the rules and regulations (including any revisions) are dated on each page and signed or initialed by both you and the tenant.

How to Fill in Clause 20

If you have a set of tenant rules and regulations document, check the box and be sure to attach it. Fill in the blank with the label you assign to the attachment. For example, if this is the first attachment referenced in the lease, you could call it Attachment A. If it's the second or third, label it "B," "C," and so on. Do the same if your rental is in a community with homeowners' association or condo rules. If you do not have a separate set of tenant rules and regulations, simply delete this clause (in which case you will need to renumber the remaining clauses).

Clause 21. Payment of Court Costs and Attorneys' Fees in a Lawsuit

In any action or legal proceeding to enforce any part of this Agreement, the prevailing party ☐ will not / ☐ will recover reasonable attorneys' fees and court costs.

Many landlords assume that if they sue a tenant and win, the court will order the losing tenant to pay the landlord's court costs (filing fees, service of process charges, deposition costs, and so on) and attorneys' fees. This is not generally true. In most states, a court will order the losing tenant to pay your attorneys' fees only if a written agreement specifically provides for it.

If, however, you have an "attorneys' fees" clause in your lease, all this changes. If you hire a lawyer to bring a lawsuit and win, the judge will order your tenant to pay your costs and attorneys' fees. (In rare instances, a court will order the loser to pay costs and fees on its own, in the absence of a clause in the lease, if it finds that the behavior of the losing party was particularly egregious.)

But there's another important issue you need to know about: By law in many states, an attorneys' fees clause in a lease or a rental agreement works both ways, even if you haven't written it that way. That is, even if the lease states that only *you* are entitled to attorneys' fees if you win a lawsuit, your tenants will be entitled to collect their attorneys' fees from you if they prevail. The amount you would be ordered to pay would be whatever the judge decides is reasonable.

So, give some thought to whether you want to bind both of you to paying for the winner's costs and fees, especially if you live in a state that will read a "one-way" attorneys' fees clause as a two-way street. Remember, if you can't actually collect a judgment containing attorneys' fees from an evicted tenant (which often happens), the clause will not help you. But if the tenant prevails, you will be stuck paying the tenant's costs and fees. In addition, the presence of a two-way clause will make it far easier for a tenant to secure a willing lawyer for even a doubtful claim, because the source of the lawyer's fee (you, if you lose) will probably appear more financially solid than if the client were paying the bill himself or herself.

Especially if you intend to do all or most of your own legal work in any potential eviction or other lawsuit, you will almost surely be better off not to allow for attorneys' fees. Why? Because if the tenant wins, you will have to pay the tenant's fees; though it is true that if you win, the tenant will owe you nothing, because you didn't hire an attorney. You can't even recover for the long hours you spent preparing for and handling the case. (In addition, it won't always be clear who "won" a lawsuit that gets settled before trial, as the great majority do. You'll need a settlement agreement that names you as the prevailing party, which can be hard to negotiate.)

Finally, be aware that attorneys' fees clauses only cover lawsuits concerning the meaning or implementation of the lease—such as a dispute about rent, security deposits, or your right to access. An attorneys' fees clause would not apply in a personal injury or discrimination lawsuit.

CAUTION
If your rental property is in Ohio, do not include the attorneys' fees clause—it's prohibited by law in Ohio. (Ohio Rev. Code Ann. § 5321.13(c).)

How to Fill in Clause 21

If you don't want to allow for attorneys' fees, check the box before the words "will not" and delete or cross out the word "will."

Disclosures of Hidden Defects

Landlords have a duty to warn tenants and others about naturally occurring dangers (such as loose soil) and human-made dangers (like low doorways or steep stairs) that are hidden but that you know (or should know) about. Disclose hidden defects in Clause 22 of your lease or rental agreement, so that it can never be claimed that a tenant was not warned of a potentially dangerous condition. For example, if the building contains asbestos insulation that could be dangerous if anyone made a hole in the wall, disclose this to your tenants. If appropriate, also post warning signs near hazards, such as a ramp that's slippery when wet or a tree that drops entire strips of bark during windy weather.

While disclosure doesn't guarantee that you won't be legally liable, it will likely help (be sure your insurance protects you). Putting the tenant on notice that a problem exists will help prevent injuries and limit your liability should an injury occur from a defective condition in the rental unit or on the premises.

CAUTION
Some problems need to be fixed, not merely disclosed. Warning your tenants about a hidden defect does not absolve you of legal responsibility if the condition makes the dwelling uninhabitable or unreasonably dangerous. For example, you are courting liability if you rent an apartment with a gas heater that you know might blow up, even if you warn the tenant that the heater is faulty. Nor can you simply warn your tenants about prior crime on the premises and then fail to do anything (like installing dead bolts or an alarm system) to promote safety.

If you want to be entitled to attorneys' fees and costs if you win—and you're willing to risk paying them if you lose—check the box before the word "will" and delete or cross out the words "will not."

Clause 22. Disclosures

Tenant acknowledges that Landlord has made the following disclosures regarding the premises:

☐ *Disclosure of Information on Lead-Based Paint and/or Lead-Based Paint Hazards,* and the booklet *Protect Your Family From Lead in Your Home.*

☐ Other disclosures: _____

_____ .

Federal, state, or local laws might require you to make certain disclosures before a new tenant signs a lease or rental agreement or moves in.

Lead Disclosures

If your rental unit was built prior to 1978, before signing a lease or rental agreement you must tell new tenants about any known lead-based paint or lead-based paint hazards in the rental premises. This includes known hazards in both individual units and common areas, such as hallways, parking garages, or play areas. You must also give them an EPA pamphlet, *Protect Your Family From Lead in Your Home.* This is a requirement of the Residential Lead-Based Paint Hazard Reduction Act, commonly known as Title X (42 U.S.C. § 4852d), which is administered by the U.S. Environmental Protection Agency (EPA).

In addition, both you and the tenant must sign an EPA-approved form—*Disclosure of Information on Lead-Based Paint and/or Lead-Based Paint Hazards*—that will prove that you told your tenants what you know about these hazards on your premises. You must keep the disclosure form as part of your records for three years from the date of the start of the tenancy.

As discussed below, state laws on lead disclosure might also come into play.

FORM

Lead forms. You'll find copies of the *Disclosure of Information on Lead-Based Paint and/or Lead-Based Paint Hazards* form, and the EPA pamphlet *Protect Your Family From Lead in Your Home* (both in English and in Spanish) in Appendix C of this book. You can also download this form and pamphlet on the Nolo website; the link is included in Appendix B of this book.

CAUTION

Penalties are severe. Property owners who fail to comply with EPA regulations for disclosing lead-based paint hazards face penalties of up to $16,773 for each violation (24 C.F.R. 30.65) and treble (triple) damages if a tenant is injured by your willful noncompliance.

Rental Properties Exempt From Title X Regulations

Landlords who rent the following types of property are not required to comply with federal lead disclosure requirements:

- housing built after January 1978
- housing certified lead-free by an accredited lead inspector
- lofts, efficiencies, and studios
- short-term vacation rentals of 100 days or less
- a single room rented in a residential dwelling
- housing designed for persons with disabilities, unless children younger than age six are present, and
- retirement communities (housing designed for seniors, where one or more tenant is at least 62 years old), unless children younger than age six are present.

RESOURCE

Lead disclosure forms, copies of Title X regulations, and background information on the evaluation and control of lead can be obtained by calling the National Lead Information Center at 800-424-LEAD, or checking www.epa.gov/lead.

Many states have also addressed the lead issue by prohibiting the use of lead-based paint in residences and requiring the careful maintenance of existing lead-based building materials. Some states require property owners to disclose lead hazards to prospective tenants. If you are subject to a state statute, you must comply with it as well as federal law. Check with your state housing department or local office of the U.S. Department of Housing and Urban Development (www.HUD.gov) to find out if this applies to you.

Other Disclosures

State laws might impose disclosure requirements, too, such as for known radon hazard risks, shared utility arrangements, or a history of bed bug problems. Local rent control ordinances often require disclosures, such as the name and address of the government agency or elected board that administers the ordinance. Some states require landlords to inform tenants of the name and address of the bank where their security deposit is being held. (Clause 8 covers security deposits; see "Required Landlord Disclosures" and "State Security Deposit Rules," in Appendix A.)

How to Fill in Clause 22

If your rental property was built before 1978, you must meet federal lead disclosure requirements, so check the first box and follow the advice above.

If you are legally required to make other disclosures as described above, check the second box and provide details in the blank space, adding pages as necessary.

Also, if there is a hidden (not obvious) problem with the property that could cause injury or substantially interfere with your tenant's safe enjoyment and use of the dwelling, and it is impossible or highly impractical to fix it, you are better off legally if you disclose the defective or dangerous condition before the tenant signs the lease. Examples include naturally occurring dangers, such as loose soil, and man-made dangers, such as steep stairs. (See "Disclosures of Hidden Defects," above, for more on the subject.)

Clause 23. Authority to Receive Legal Papers

The Landlord, any person managing the Premises, and anyone designated by the Landlord are authorized to accept service of process and receive other notices and demands, which may be delivered to:

☐ The Landlord, at the following address:

_____

_____

☐ The manager, at the following address:

_____

_____

☐ The following person, at the following address:

_____

_____

It's the law in many states, and a good idea in all, to give your tenants information about everyone whom you have authorized to receive notices and legal papers, such as a tenant's notice ending a tenancy or a tenant's court documents as part of an eviction defense. You might want to handle all of this yourself or delegate it to a manager or management company. Make sure the person you designate to receive legal papers is almost always available to receive tenant notices and legal papers. Also, be sure to keep your tenants up to date on any changes in this information.

How to Fill in Clause 23

Provide your name and street address or the name and address of someone you authorize to receive notices and legal papers on your behalf, such as a property manager.

Clause 24. Additional Provisions

> Additional provisions are as follows: _____
> _____ .

In this clause, you can list additional provisions or agreements that are unique to this tenancy, such as a provision that allows limited business use of the premises—for example, allowing piano lessons on weekdays only.

If you don't have separate tenant rules and regulations (see Clause 20, above), you can spell out a few rules under this clause—for example, regarding lost key charges, use of a pool, or no-smoking rules.

How to Fill in Clause 24

List additional provisions or rules here or in an attachment. If you have no additional provisions, delete this clause or write "N/A" or "Not Applicable."

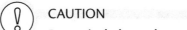
TIP

You needn't put every small detail you want to communicate to the tenant into your lease or rental agreement. Instead, prepare a welcoming, but no-nonsense, "move-in letter" that dovetails with the lease or rental agreement and highlights important terms of the tenancy—for example, how and where to report maintenance problems. You can also use a move-in letter to cover issues not included in the lease or rental agreement —for example, rules for use of a laundry room. (Chapter 3 covers move-in letters.)

CAUTION

Do not include exculpatory ("If there's a problem, I'm not responsible") clauses or hold harmless ("If there's a problem, you are responsible") clauses. Many form leases include provisions that attempt to absolve you in advance from responsibility for your legal misdeeds. For example, one lease form generated by a popular software package contains a broad provision stating that the landlord is not responsible for injuries to tenants and guests, even those caused intentionally. Many exculpatory clauses are blatantly illegal: If a tenant is injured because of a dangerous condition you failed to fix for several months, no boilerplate lease provision will protect you from civil—and possibly criminal—charges.

Clause 25. Validity of Each Part

> If a court holds any portion of this Agreement to be invalid, its invalidity will not affect the validity or enforceability of any other provision of this Agreement.

This clause is known as a "savings" clause, and it is commonly used in contracts. It means that, in the unlikely event that one of the other clauses in the Agreement is found to be invalid by a court, the remainder of the Agreement will remain in force.

How to Fill in Clause 25

You do not need to add anything to this clause.

Clause 26. Grounds for Termination of Tenancy

> The failure of Tenant or Tenant's guests or invitees to comply with any term of this Agreement, or the misrepresentation of any material fact on Tenant's rental application, is grounds for termination of the tenancy, with appropriate notice to the Tenant and procedures as required by law.

This clause states that any violation of the Agreement by the tenant, or by the tenant's business or social guests, is grounds for terminating the tenancy, according to the procedures established by your state or local laws. Making the tenant responsible for the actions of guests can be extremely important—for example, if you discover that the tenant's family or friends are dealing illegal drugs on the premises or have damaged the property. Clause 26 also tells tenants that if they have made false statements on a rental application concerning an important fact— such as their prior criminal history—you may terminate the tenancy and evict if necessary.

How to Fill in Clause 26

You do not need to add anything to this clause.

Clause 27. Entire Agreement

> This document constitutes the entire Agreement between the parties, and no promises or representations, other than those contained here and those implied by law, have been made by Landlord or Tenant. Any modifications to this Agreement must be in writing, signed by Landlord and Tenant.

This clause establishes that the lease or rental agreement and any attachments (such as tenant rules and regulations) constitute the entire agreement between you and your tenant. It means that oral promises (by you or the tenant) to do something else with respect to any aspect of the rental are not binding. Any changes or additions must be in writing. For example, if your lease prohibits pets, and your tenant wants to get a dog and you agree, you should amend the Pets clause of the lease accordingly. This will help ensure that a casual conversation about pets, which the tenant misconstrues, doesn't lead the tenant to bringing in a dog without your permission. (Chapter 4

discusses how to modify signed rental agreements and leases.)

How to Fill in Clause 27

You do not need to add anything to this clause.

Instructions for Signing the Lease or Rental Agreement

After all terms are final, you're ready to sign. Make two copies of the lease or rental agreement, including all attachments. You and each tenant should sign both copies in the space at the end. Include your signature, street address, phone number, and email, or that of the person you authorize as your agent, such as a property manager. There's also space for the tenants' signatures and phone numbers.

Again, as stressed in Clause 1, make sure all adults living in the rental unit, including both members of a married couple, sign the lease or rental agreement. And check that tenants' names and signatures match their driver's licenses or other government-issued identification.

If the tenant has a cosigner (see "About Cosigners," below), you'll need to add a line for the cosigner's signature.

If you alter our form by writing or typing in changes, be sure that you and all tenants initial the changes when you sign the document, so as to forestall any possibility that a tenant will claim you unilaterally inserted changes after the tenant signed.

 CAUTION
Don't sign a lease until all terms are final. All of your expectations should be written into the lease or rental agreement (or any attachments, such as tenant rules and regulations) before you and the tenant sign the document. Never sign an incomplete document assuming last-minute changes can be made later.

Signing the Lease or Rental Agreement Electronically

It's often more convenient to sign a lease or rental agreement electronically than to ask everyone to sign in person. Fortunately, in most situations electronic signatures (e-signatures) are just as valid and enforceable as in-person signatures. An e-signature is a digital file or symbol—such as a scanned pen-and-ink signature or a typed name— that someone attaches to or places on a contract or file to show that person's intent to sign the contract or file.

E-signatures are legal everywhere under the federal Electronic Signatures in Global and National Commerce Act (ESIGN). Additionally, all states have passed either the Uniform Electronic Transactions Act (UTEA) or their own e-signature laws, which recognize e-signatures in situations where federal law doesn't apply.

If you want to use e-signatures on your leases, rental agreements, and other rental documents that require signatures, follow these steps to make the e-signatures valid and enforceable:

1. Get consent from your tenants to discuss the rental and exchange documents electronically. The best practice—and one that's required in some places—is for the parties to agree to electronic communications in a written document (or email) that's separate from the lease or rental agreement.

2. Make sure your tenants know that they are agreeing to be bound to the terms of a document when they e-sign—they're not signing to indicate they merely received it or reviewed it. You can tell them in your email with the attached document, or require them to click a box that alerts them to the binding nature of their signature, which they must do before they sign (commercial programs, explained below, supply the alert box).

3. Give your tenants other options. Let them know they can sign documents in person if they prefer.

4. Follow up with hard copies. Provide all tenants and anyone else who signs (like a cosigner) with a paper copy of the signed document.

5. Retain copies (electronic or paper) of the fully executed documents.

6. Many landlords obtain e-signatures by emailing documents to the tenants and having them return scans of the signed documents. Most of the time, this is a valid and enforceable way of executing documents. This method has its downsides—for example, you must make sure you're sending the documents in a format that the receiver can't edit, and you can't be certain that the person who signs the document is the person you intended.

Perhaps the simplest way for landlords to avoid e-signature problems is to obtain "digital signatures"—electronic signatures that look like regular cursive writing and are unique and traceable to the signer. E-signature programs such as HelloSign, DocuSign, or SignNow, obtain the users' consent before allowing them to sign, authenticate the signatures, distribute copies of the signed documents to all the parties, and keep detailed records of the e-signing process. The cost of using these programs is fairly low—some even allow users to e-sign a few documents per month free of charge.

About Cosigners

Some landlords require cosigners on rental agreements and leases, especially when renting to students who are financially dependent on someone else. The cosigner signs a separate agreement or the rental agreement or lease, under which the cosigner agrees to cover any rent or damage-repair costs the tenant fails to pay.

In practice, a cosigner's promise to guarantee the tenant's rent obligation might have less legal value than you might think. This is because the threat of eviction is the primary factor that motivates a tenant to pay the rent, and, obviously, you cannot evict a cosigner. Also, because the cosigner must be sued separately in either a regular civil lawsuit or in small claims court—for example, when a tenant stiffs you for a month's rent—actually doing so might be more trouble than it's worth. This is especially true if the cosigner lives in another state, because the amount of money you are out will rarely justify hiring a lawyer and collecting a judgment.

In sum, the benefits of having a lease or rental agreement cosigned by someone who won't be living on the property are largely psychological. But these benefits could still be worth something: A tenant who thinks you can (and will) notify and sue a cosigning relative or friend might be less likely to default on the rent. Similarly, a cosigner asked to pay the tenant's debts might persuade the tenant to pay.

Because of the practical difficulties associated with cosigners, many landlords refuse to consider them, which is legal in every situation but one: If a tenant with a disability who has insufficient income (but is otherwise suitable) asks you to accept a cosigner who will cover the rent if needed, you must relax your blanket rule at least to the extent of investigating the suitability of the proposed cosigner. If that person is solvent and stable, federal law requires you to accommodate the applicant by accepting the cosigner, in spite of your general policy. (*Giebeler v. M & B Associates*, 343 F.3d 1143 (9th Cir. 2003).)

If you decide to accept a cosigner, you should have that person fill out a separate rental application and agree to a credit check—after all, a cosigner who has no resources or connection to the tenant will be completely useless. Should the tenant and the prospective cosigner object to these inquiries and the costs of a credit check, you might wonder how serious they are about the guarantor's willingness to stand behind the tenant. Once you are satisfied that the cosigner can genuinely back up the tenant, add a line at the end of the lease or rental agreement for the dated signature, phone, and address of the cosigner.

CAUTION
If you later amend the rental agreement or change the lease, have the cosigner sign the new version. Generally speaking, cosigners are bound only to the terms of the exact lease or rental agreement they cosign.

Give one copy of the signed lease or rental agreement to the tenant(s), and keep the other one for your files. (If you are renting to more than one tenant, you don't need to prepare a separate agreement for each cotenant. After all of you have signed the agreement, cotenants can make their own copies.)

TIP

Help tenants understand the lease or rental agreement before they sign it. Too many landlords thrust a lease or rental agreement at tenants and expect them to sign it unread. Far better to encourage tenants to ask questions about anything that's unclear, or to actually review each clause with new tenants. It will save you lots of hassles later on.

Some states require landlords who discuss the lease or rental agreement with tenants in a language other than English to provide a written translation. For example, California requires landlords who negotiate primarily in Spanish, Chinese, Tagalog, Vietnamese, or Korean to give the applicant an unsigned, translated version of the lease before asking the applicant to sign. This rule does not apply (that is, you may supply your English version only) if tenants supply their own translator who is not a minor and can fluently speak and read both languages.

Even if a translation is not legally required, you want your tenants to know and follow the rules. If most or all of your communications with the tenant about the lease or rental agreement are in a language other than English, you should give the tenant a written translation. (We include Spanish versions of our lease and rental agreement forms on Nolo's website. See Appendix B for the link to forms in this book.)

Lease-Option Contracts (Rent-to-Buy)

Occasionally, landlords of single-family houses will agree to rent to tenants who would like to eventually own the house. In periods of economic downturn, these arrangements are especially attractive to tenants who might not have the down payment money (or good credit required for a loan) to purchase the property outright, but expect their finances to improve over a period of one or more years. These tenants would like the option to buy their rented home, and would also like the opportunity to have some of their rent money applied toward the house purchase price.

Rent-to-buy can also be attractive for the landlord, who might intend to sell in the near future and would like to avoid the hassle and expense of putting the house on the market (selling to a resident tenant avoids staging costs and brokers' fees). In addition, a tenant who hopes to someday own the property will be motivated to take good care of it, and to honor other aspects of the lease.

When a landlord and tenant agree to a rent-to-buy (also called rent-to-own) arrangement, they sign an agreement (typically called a lease-option contract) that gives the tenant the right (the option) of buying the house in the future, providing certain conditions are met. The option agreement should be separate from the lease, but refer to it. The agreement covers issues like:

- the amount of the option fee and how it will be paid
- the date by which or the window of time in which the tenant has to exercise (or lose) the option
- how much (if any) of the monthly rent will be applied to the house purchase price, and
- the sale price of the home.

Many landlords are wary of rent-to-buy arrangements, for good reasons. The major drawback is that giving a tenant the option to buy the rental house ties the landlord down; you can't easily sell it to someone else, and you might find it difficult to use the property as collateral for a loan.

A second major disadvantage of agreeing to allow the tenant to buy the house is that in some states, purchase options trigger disclosures regarding the condition of the property and any defects, the same disclosures that sellers must make when engaging in a normal sale. Depending on the laws of your state, this might involve inspections and considerable work and expense.

When thinking about offering an option to buy, keep the following additional issues in mind.

Paying for the Option

An option curtails the ability of the owner to use the house for collateral. For example, if you want to finance your child's college education by getting a second mortgage on the property, you might have difficulty doing so. Because you are giving up a valuable right when granting the option, you can expect to be compensated. You'll need to negotiate how much the option right should cost; ideally, your tenant will pay you up front, though you could also agree to monthly payments, in addition to the rent.

Sales Price of the House

When you give a tenant an option to buy, you'll need to either name the price in your option contract or supply an objective way in which the price can be determined later. Naming the price now means that you risk misreading the market, and you could end up with a sale price that turns out to be less than actual market value at the time of sale.

You can avoid this risk by deferring the price, but you must set up a fail-safe method for arriving at it. For example, your contract might say, "Market value as determined by licensed brokers, one each chosen by landlord and tenant; and if the brokers cannot agree, the price to be

determined by a third who will be chosen by the two brokers." If you simply say, "Fair market value at the time the option is exercised," or "Price to be negotiated at the time," and you and the tenant cannot agree on a price, you won't be able to go to court and get a judge to settle it for you. In other words, the option will fall apart.

When the Tenant Must Exercise the Option, and Under What Circumstances

You'll want to give tenants a specific window of time, or a deadline, by which they must tell you that they're exercising the option. You can specify that the option be exercised within several months of the end of the underlying lease—this gives you time to begin planning for a sale or a successor tenant. Or, you could set a deadline (like the end of the first year of a multiyear lease), specifying that exercising the option will terminate the lease.

You'll also need to decide whether the tenant must have been "squeaky clean" in order to take advantage of the option—whether any prior lease defaults will bar the exercise (current lease violations should give you grounds to refuse to honor the option, as explained below). For instance, you might not want a tenant who has a history of late rent to exercise the option, because a tenant who has trouble making timely rent payments will probably have a hard time making mortgage payments, too. You might also want to insist on certain financial criteria, such as a minimum credit score.

The manner in which you will accept the tenant's decision should be spelled out. Written notification is preferable and personal delivery is the best method (certified mail is a good second choice).

Tenant Improvements and Rent

Many tenants will want the ability to begin improving "their" home, with the value of the improvements credited against the selling price. If you agree, be sure to consider what will happen if the tenant decides not to buy the home—will you reimburse the tenant?

Similarly, tenants might ask you to apply a portion of the rent toward a down payment. As with improvements, you'll need to address what will happen if the tenant does not exercise the option, or if the sale does not go through.

What Happens If You Need to Evict?

Your option contract should not, if drafted properly, curtail your ability to terminate the underlying lease if the tenant fails to pay the rent, causes damage, or otherwise gives you solid legal grounds for ending the tenancy. Option contracts should specify that the tenants may exercise the option only if they are in "good standing" with respect to the lease. A tenant who has been terminated or evicted is obviously not in good standing. Be sure you do not become obligated to return any option fees already paid.

"Right of Refusal" and "Right of Offer"

Instead of entering into a full-blown option contract, some landlords agree to give their tenants preferential treatment when and if the property goes on the market. In these situations, the landlord avoids some of the tricky issues mentioned above, but they are still not without drawbacks.

A "right of refusal" allows the tenant to match or improve on any deal the landlord hammers out with a third-party buyer. Once the landlord has secured a buyer, the landlord must give the tenant an opportunity to buy the property on the same or better terms. These arrangements are nothing but a headache for a seller, because it means that any potential buyer runs the risk of having the tenant trump the deal that the buyer has painstakingly hammered out. Knowing this, buyers won't bother negotiating with these sellers, and seasoned brokers (on both sides) avoid these situations like the plague.

A "right of first refusal" is much milder. With this right, the landlord promises to give the tenant the first opportunity to buy the home at the price named by the landlord. If the tenant declines, the home goes on the market. The landlord must not artificially inflate the offering price, in order to get rid of the tenant—the asking price must be commercially reasonable. But as many happy sellers find out, sometimes you don't really know what the house will go for, and selling at your named price might deprive you of a lucrative bidding war (which the tenant could always join, too).

Landlords do not give away rights of first refusal or offer—like options, these rights come at a price.

Get Legal Advice

Think long and hard about whether your interests would be served by giving tenants an option to buy, or even rights of first refusal or offer. If you decide to go ahead, be sure to consult an attorney who specializes in real estate law and a tax specialist before signing a lease-option contract. Remember, you're dealing with a very expensive investment—once the tenant exercises the option, it's the same as a sales contract. Structuring the option contract (or offer rights) in ways that do not protect your interests could be financially disastrous. You'll also need professional help in preparing a house sales contract.

Month-to-Month Residential Rental Agreement

Clause 1. Identification of Landlord and Tenant

This Agreement is between _____Marty Nelson_____ ("Tenant") and

___Alex Stevens_____ ("Landlord").

Each Tenant is jointly and severally liable for the payment of rent and performance of all other terms of this

Agreement.

Clause 2. Identification of Premises

Subject to the terms and conditions in this Agreement, Landlord rents to Tenant, and Tenant rents from

Landlord, for residential purposes only, the premises located at ___137 Howell St., Philadelphia, Pennsylvania___

_____("Premises").

Rental of the Premises also includes: _____

_____.

Rental of the Premises excludes: _____

_____.

Clause 3. Limits on Use and Occupancy

The Premises are to be used only as a private residence for Tenant(s) listed in Clause 1 of this Agreement, and

their minor children: ___N/A_____. Occupancy by guests

for more than ___ten days every six months_____ is prohibited without Landlord's written consent and will

be considered a breach of this Agreement.

Clause 4. Term of the Tenancy

The rental will begin on ___September 15, 20xx_____, and continue on a month-to-month

basis. Landlord may terminate the tenancy or modify the terms of this Agreement by giving the Tenant

_____30_____ days' written notice. Tenant may terminate the tenancy by giving the Landlord

_____30_____ days' written notice.

Clause 5. Payment of Rent

Regular monthly rent

Tenant will pay to Landlord a monthly rent of $___1,800_____, payable in advance on the first day of

each month, except when that day falls on a weekend or legal holiday, in which case rent is due on the next

business day. Rent will be paid as follows, or in another manner as Landlord designates from time to time:

Delivery of payment

Rent will be paid:

☑ by mail, to ___Alex Stevens, 28 Franklin Street, Philadelphia, Pennsylvania 19120___

☐ in person, at _____

☐ electronically, to _____

Form of payment

Landlord will accept payment in the form of:

☐ cash

☑ personal check made payable to ___Alex Stevens___

☑ certified funds or money order payable to ___Alex Stevens___

☐ credit or debit card

☐ other electronic funds transfer: _____

Prorated first month's rent

☑ On signing this Agreement, Tenant will pay to Landlord for the period of ___September 15, 20xx___

through ___September 30, 20xx___ the sum of $___900___ as rent, payable in advance of the start

of the tenancy.

☐ Upon move-in, Tenant will owe as rent the prorated rent specified above, plus one full month's rent in the

amount designated above, for a total of $_____ .

Clause 6. Late Charges

Because Landlord and Tenant agree that actual damages for late rent payments are very difficult or impossible

to determine, Landlord and Tenant agree to the following:

- Tenant will pay Landlord a late charge if Tenant fails to pay the rent in full within ___3___ days after

the date it is due.

- The late charge will be $___10___ plus $___5___ for each individual day that the rent continues

to be unpaid. The total late charge for any one month will not exceed $___45___ .

Landlord does not waive the right to insist on payment of the rent in full on the date it is due.

Clause 7. Returned Check and Other Bank Charges

If any check offered by Tenant to Landlord in payment of rent or any other amount due under this Agreement

is returned for lack of sufficient funds, a "stop payment," or any other reason, Landlord will make a demand for

payment and otherwise pursue remedies as allowed by law.

Clause 8. Security Deposit

On signing this Agreement, Tenant will pay to Landlord the sum of $ _1,800_ as a security deposit. Tenant may not, without Landlord's prior written consent, apply this security deposit to the last month's rent or to any other sum due under this Agreement. Within _30 days_ after Tenant has vacated the Premises, returned keys, and provided Landlord with a forwarding address, Landlord will return the deposit in full or give Tenant an itemized written statement of the reasons for, and the dollar amount of, any of the security deposit retained by Landlord, along with a check for any deposit balance.

The security deposit of $1,800 will be held at: _Federal Bank, 1 Federal Street, Philadelphia, Pennsylvania 19120_

Clause 9. Utilities

Tenant will pay all utility charges, except for the following, which will be paid by Landlord:

garbage and water

Clause 10. Prohibition of Assignment and Subletting

Tenant will not sublet any part of the Premises or assign this Agreement without the prior written consent of Landlord. Violating this clause is grounds for terminating the tenancy.

☑ a. Tenant will not sublet or rent any part of the Premises for short-term stays of any duration, including but not limited to vacation rentals.

☐ b. Short-stay rentals are prohibited except as authorized by law. Any short-stay rental is expressly conditioned upon the Tenant's following all regulations, laws, and other requirements as a condition to offering a short-stay rental. Failure to follow all laws, ordinances, regulations, and other requirements, including any registration requirement, will be deemed a material, noncurable breach of this Agreement and will furnish cause for termination.

Clause 11. Tenant's Maintenance Responsibilities

Tenant agrees to: (1) keep the Premises clean, sanitary, and in good condition and, upon termination of the tenancy, return the Premises to Landlord in a condition identical to that which existed when Tenant took occupancy, except for ordinary wear and tear; (2) immediately notify Landlord of any defects or dangerous conditions in and about the Premises of which Tenant becomes aware; and (3) reimburse Landlord, on demand by Landlord, for the cost of any repairs to the Premises, including Landlord's personal property therein, damaged by Tenant or Tenant's guests or business invitees through misuse or neglect.

Tenant has examined the Premises, including appliances, fixtures, carpets, drapes, and paint, and has found them to be in good, safe, and clean condition and repair, except as noted in the Landlord-Tenant Checklist.

Clause 12. Repairs and Alterations by Tenant

    a. Except as provided by law, or as authorized by the prior written consent of Landlord, Tenant will not make any repairs or alterations to the Premises, including nailing holes in the walls or painting the rental unit.

    b. Tenant will not, without Landlord's prior written consent, alter, rekey, or install any locks to the Premises or install or alter any security alarm system. Tenant will provide Landlord with a key or keys capable of unlocking all such rekeyed or new locks as well as instructions on how to disarm any altered or new security alarm system.

Clause 13. Violating Laws and Causing Disturbances

Tenant is entitled to quiet enjoyment of the Premises. Tenant and guests or invitees will not use the Premises or adjacent areas in such a way as to: (1) violate any law or ordinance, including laws prohibiting the use, possession, or sale of illegal drugs; (2) commit waste (severe property damage) or cause or tolerate a nuisance; or (3) annoy, disturb, inconvenience, or interfere with the quiet enjoyment and peace and quiet of any other tenant or nearby resident.

Clause 14. Damage to the Premises

In the event the Premises are partially or totally damaged or destroyed by fire or other cause, the following will apply:

    ☐ a. Premises totally damaged and destroyed. Landlord will have the option to: (1) repair such damage and restore the Premises, with this Agreement continuing in full force and effect, except that Tenant's rent will be abated while repairs are being made; or (2) give written notice to Tenant terminating this Agreement at any time within thirty (30) days after such damage, and specifying the termination date; in the event that Landlord gives such notice, this Agreement will expire and all of Tenant's rights pursuant to this Agreement will cease.

    ☐ b. Premises partially damaged by fire or other cause. Landlord will attempt to repair such damage and restore the Premises within thirty (30) days after such damage. If only part of the Premises cannot be used, Tenant must pay rent only for the usable part, to be determined by Landlord. If Landlord is unable to complete repairs within thirty (30) days, this Agreement will expire and all of Tenant's rights pursuant to this Agreement will terminate at the option of either party. Whether the Premises are totally or partially destroyed will be decided by Landlord, in the exercise of its sole discretion.

    ☐ c. In the event that Tenant, or Tenant's guests or invitees, in any way caused or contributed to the damage of the Premises, Landlord will have the right to terminate this Agreement at any time, and Tenant will be responsible for all losses, including, but not limited to, damage and repair costs as well as loss of rental income.

    ☐ d. Landlord will not be required to repair or replace any property brought onto the Premises by Tenant.

Clause 15. Renters' Insurance

Tenant acknowledges that Landlord's property insurance policy will not cover damage to or loss of Tenant's personal property. Tenant will obtain a renters' insurance policy that will:

- reimburse Landlord for cost of fire or water damage caused by Tenant or Tenant's guests, and vandalism to the Premises
- indemnify Landlord against liability to third parties for any negligence on the part of Tenant, Tenant's guests, or invitees; and
- cover damage to Tenant's personal possessions to a minimum of $100,000.

Tenant will provide Landlord with proof of such policy by giving Landlord a certificate of insurance issued by the insurance company within fifteen (15) days of _September 15, 20xx_. The policy will include Landlord as an "additional insured." Tenant will provide Landlord with a certificate of insurance upon every renewal. Tenant will not allow such policy to expire during the rental term. Failure to obtain and maintain a renters' insurance policy will be treated as a material breach of this Agreement.

Clause 16. Pets

No animal may be kept on the Premises without Landlord's prior written consent, except animals needed by tenants who have a disability, as that term is understood by law, and __one dog weighing less than 20 pounds__, under the following conditions: _Tenant complies with rules set out in "Attachment A, Addition to Clause 16, Pets,"_ _attached to this Agreement_.

Clause 17. Landlord's Right to Access

Landlord or Landlord's agents may enter the Premises in the event of an emergency, to make repairs or improvements, or to show the Premises to prospective buyers or tenants. Landlord may also enter the Premises to conduct an annual inspection to check for safety or maintenance problems. Except in cases of emergency, Tenant's abandonment of the Premises, court order, or where it is impractical to do so, Landlord will give Tenant __24 hours'__ notice before entering.

Clause 18. Extended Absences by Tenant

Tenant will notify Landlord in advance if Tenant will be away from the Premises for ____seven____ or more consecutive days. During such absence, Landlord may enter the Premises at times reasonably necessary to maintain the property and inspect for damage and needed repairs.

Clause 19. Possession of the Premises

a. *Tenant's failure to take possession.*

If, after signing this Agreement, Tenant fails to take possession of the Premises, Tenant will still be responsible for paying rent and complying with all other terms of this Agreement.

b. *Landlord's failure to deliver possession.*

If Landlord is unable to deliver possession of the Premises to Tenant for any reason not within Landlord's control, including, but not limited to, failure of prior occupants to vacate or partial or complete destruction of the Premises, Tenant will have the right to terminate this Agreement upon proper notice as required by law. In such event, Landlord's liability to Tenant will be limited to the return of all sums previously paid by Tenant to Landlord.

Clause 20. Tenant Rules and Regulations

☑ Tenant acknowledges receipt of, and has read a copy of, the Tenant Rules and Regulations, which are labeled Attachment ____B____ and attached to and incorporated into this Agreement by this reference. Tenant understands that serious or repeated violations of the rules may be grounds for termination.

Clause 21. Payment of Court Costs and Attorneys' Fees in a Lawsuit

In any action or legal proceeding to enforce any part of this Agreement, the prevailing party (*choose one:* ~~will not~~/will) recover reasonable attorneys' fees and court costs.

Clause 22. Disclosures

Tenant acknowledges that Landlord has made the following disclosures regarding the Premises:

☑ *Disclosure of Information on Lead-Based Paint and/or Lead-Based Paint Hazards* and the pamphlet *Protect Your Family From Lead in Your Home*

☐ Other disclosures: _____

_____

_____

_____.

Clause 23. Authority to Receive Legal Papers

The Landlord, any person managing the Premises, and anyone designated by the Landlord are authorized to accept service of process and receive other notices and demands, which may be delivered to:

☑ The Landlord, at the following address: __28 Franklin Street, Philadelphia, Pennsylvania 19120__

_____.

☐ The manager, at the following address: _____.

☐ The following person, at the following address: _____.

Clause 24. Additional Provisions

Additional provisions are as follows: _____N/A_____

_____

_____

_____

_____ .

Clause 25. Validity of Each Part

If a court holds any portion of this Agreement to be invalid, its invalidity will not affect the validity or enforceability of any other provision of this Agreement.

Clause 26. Grounds for Termination of Tenancy

The failure of Tenant or Tenant's guests or invitees to comply with any term of this Agreement, or the misrepresentation of any material fact on Tenant's Rental Application, is grounds for termination of the tenancy, with appropriate notice to Tenant and procedures as required by law.

Clause 27. Entire Agreement

This document constitutes the entire Agreement between the parties, and no promises or representations, other than those contained here and those implied by law, have been made by Landlord or Tenant. Any modifications to this Agreement must be in writing, signed by Landlord and Tenant.

Sept. 1, 20xx	Alex Stevens	Landlord
Date	Landlord or Landlord's Agent	Title

28 Franklin Street			
Street Address			

Philadelphia	Pennsylvania	19120	215-555-1578
City	State	Zip	Phone

alex@alex.com
Email

Sept. 1, 20xx	Marty Nelson	marty@marty.com	215-555-8751
Date	Tenant	email	Phone

Date	Tenant	email	Phone

Choosing Tenants: Your Most Important Decision

Choosing tenants is the most important decision any landlord makes. To do it well and stay out of legal trouble, you need a good system. Follow the steps in this chapter to maximize your chances of selecting tenants who will pay their rent on time, keep their units in good condition, and not cause legal or practical problems.

> TIP
> **Before you advertise your property for rent, make a number of basic decisions**—including how much rent to charge, whether to offer a fixed-term lease or a month-to-month tenancy, how many tenants can occupy each rental unit, how big a security deposit to require, and whether you'll allow pets. Making these important decisions should dovetail with writing your lease or rental agreement (see Chapter 1).

How to Advertise Rental Property

You can advertise rental property in many ways:
- posting a notice online (see "Online Services," below, for details)
- putting an "Apartment for Rent" sign in front of the building or in one of the windows
- taking out an ad in a local newspaper
- posting flyers on neighborhood bulletin boards
- listing with a local real estate broker that handles rentals
- buying ads in apartment rental guides or magazines, or
- hiring a property management company that will advertise your rentals as part of the management fee.

What will work best depends on a number of factors, including the characteristics of the rental property (such as rent, size, and amenities), its location, your budget, and how soon you need to find a tenant.

While large-scale landlords have great success with paid, nationally oriented advertising, many smaller landlords find marketing their rentals on a more personal level to be a better strategy. If you're renting only a few properties, you usually don't need (or want) to spend a lot of money on advertising—sometimes free is best. For example, you can spread the word about your rental through local social media and by word of mouth. Friends, colleagues, neighbors, and even current tenants can be great sources for finding tenants.

No matter how you let people know about the availability of your rental units, you want to follow these simple rules to stay out of legal hot water:

Describe the rental unit accurately. For practical reasons, avoid abbreviations and real estate jargon in your ad. Include basic details, such as:
- rent and deposit
- size—particularly number of bedrooms and baths
- location—either the general neighborhood or street address
- move-in date and term—fixed-term lease or month-to-month rental agreement
- special features—such as fenced-in yard, view, washer/dryer, fireplace, remodeled kitchen, furnished, garage parking, doorman, hardwood floors, or high-speed Internet
- pets (whether you allow them, and any restrictions, such as dog breeds that your insurance prohibits)
- phone number, email, or website for more details (unless you're going to show the unit only at an open house and don't want to take calls), and
- date and time of any open house.

If you have any important rules (legal and nondiscriminatory, of course), such as no smoking, put them in your ad. Letting prospective tenants know about important policies can save you from talking to a lot of unsuitable people.

Online Services

Countless online services exist to help you reach potential tenants. Do a bit of research to learn which sites are used most by people looking to rent in your area, as site usage varies by region. Here are some of the more established places renters look for listings:

Online community posting boards allow you to list your rentals at no or low charge and are a good place to start.

- **Craigslist.** Craigslist (Craigslist.org) has separate sites for every major metropolitan area. Visit the "Housing" section on your community's site to find the best place to post your listing.
- **Facebook.** Many communities form locally oriented "Groups" on Facebook where you can post rental listings. To find these local groups, search for your zip code, area code, or city's name in Facebook.
- **Online community groups**. Neighborhood groups, such as NextDoor, can be a good place to list your vacancy.

National apartment listing services are also available, with the largest ones representing millions of apartment units in the United States.

Some of the most established are:

- Rentals.com
- Doorsteps.com
- Apartments.com
- Zillow.com
- ForRent.com
- Zumper.com
- Rent.com, and
- ApartmentGuide.com.

These national sites offer a wide range of services, from simple text-only ads that provide basic information on your rental to full-scale virtual tours and floor plans of the rental property. Services typically include mobile apps, too. Prices vary widely depending on the type of ad, how long you want it to run, and any services you purchase (some websites provide tenant-screening services).

Before you use any online apartment rental service, make sure it's reputable. Find out how long the company has been in business and how they handle problems with apartment listings. Check for consumer complaints, and avoid paying a hefty fee without thoroughly checking out a company and its services.

Be sure your ad can't be construed as discriminatory. The best way to do this is to focus on only the rental property—not on any particular type of tenant. Specifically, ads should never mention sex, race, religion, disability, or age (unless yours is legally recognized senior citizens housing). And ads should never imply through words, photographs, or illustrations that you prefer to rent to people because of their age, sex, or race. (See "Avoiding Illegal Discrimination," below, for more on the subject.)

Quote an honest price in your ad. Or, put another way, if an applicant who is otherwise acceptable (has a good credit history and impeccable references and meets all the criteria explained below) shows up promptly and agrees to all the terms set out in your ad, that person should be able to rent your property for the price you have advertised. By contrast, if you suddenly find a reason why it will cost significantly more, you are likely to be in violation of your state's false advertising laws. This doesn't mean you are always legally required to rent at your advertised price, however. If a tenant asks for more services or significantly different lease terms that you feel justify more rent, it's fine to bargain and raise your price, as long as your proposed increase doesn't violate any rent control laws.

Don't advertise something you don't have.
Some large landlords, management companies, and rental services have advertised units that weren't really available in order to produce a large number of prospective tenants who could then be directed to higher-priced or inferior units. Such bait-and-switch advertising is illegal under consumer fraud laws, and many property owners have been prosecuted for such practices.

Don't overhype security measures. Don't exaggerate your written or oral description of security measures. Not only will you have begun the landlord-tenant relationship on a note of insincerity, but your descriptions of security might legally obligate you to actually provide what you have portrayed. Or, if you fail to do so, or fail to conscientiously maintain promised security measures in working order (such as outdoor lighting or an electronic gate on the parking garage), a court or jury could find your failure to be a material factor that allowed a crime to occur on the premises. And, if this happens, chances are good you will be held liable for a tenant's losses or injuries.

Ads That Invite Lawsuits

Advertisements like the following will come back to haunt you if a crime occurs on your rental property:

- "No one gets past our mega-security systems. A highly trained guard is on duty at all times."
- "We provide highly safe, highly secure buildings."
- "You can count on us. We maintain the highest apartment security standards in the business."

Again, the point is not that you shouldn't provide good security—or even that you shouldn't tell prospective tenants about it—but that it's best to do so in a calm, straightforward way.

Renting Property That's Still Occupied

It's always easier to wait until the old tenant moves out before showing a rental unit to prospective tenants. This gives you the chance to refurbish the unit and avoids problems such as promising the place to a new tenant, only to have the existing tenant not move out on time or leave the place a mess.

To eliminate any gap in rent, however, you might want to show a rental unit while current tenants are still there. This can create a conflict; in most states, you have a right to show the still-occupied property to prospective tenants, but your current tenants are still entitled to a reasonable level of privacy. (For details, see Clause 15 of the lease and rental agreement in Chapter 1.)

To minimize disturbing your current tenant, follow these guidelines:

- Before implementing your plans to find a new tenant, discuss them with outgoing tenants so you can be as accommodating as possible.
- Give current tenants as much notice as possible before entering and showing a rental unit to prospective tenants.
- Try to limit the number of times you show the unit in a given week, and make sure your current tenants agree to any evening and weekend visits.
- Consider reducing the rent slightly for the existing tenant if showing the unit really will be an imposition.
- If possible, avoid putting a sign on the rental property itself, because this almost guarantees that your existing tenants will be bothered by strangers. Or, if you can't avoid putting up a sign, make sure any sign clearly warns against disturbing the occupant and includes a telephone number for information. Something on the order of "For Rent: Shown by Appointment Only. Call 555-1700. Do Not Disturb Occupants" should work fine.

If, despite your best efforts to protect their privacy, the current tenants are uncooperative or hostile, it really is best to avoid hassles and wait until they leave before showing the unit. Also, if the current tenant is a complete slob or has damaged the place, you'll be far better off to apply paint and elbow grease before trying to rerent it.

Accepting Rental Applications

It's good business, as well as a sound way to protect yourself from future legal problems, to carefully screen prospective tenants. To avoid legal problems and choose the best tenant, ask all prospective tenants to fill out a written rental application that includes information on the applicant's employment, income, credit, and rental housing history, including up-to-date references. It's legal (and a good idea) to ask for the applicant's Social Security and driver's license numbers or, if the applicant doesn't have one of these, some other form of identifying information. For example, instead of a Social Security number, you could accept an ITIN (Individual Taxpayer Identification Number), which is issued by the IRS to persons who are required to file income taxes but who can't obtain a Social Security number (SSN). ITINs are issued to nonimmigrants (people who are in the United States legally but don't have the right to live here permanently). Almost anyone planning on staying in the United States long enough to rent an apartment (like someone with a student visa) will have an ITIN. If you refuse to rent to someone who has an ITIN but not an SSN, you might be courting a fair housing claim. You can also ask if the applicant has declared bankruptcy or been evicted. (You'll also get much of this information from a credit report, as discussed below.)

FORM

Rental Application form. You'll find a Rental Application in Appendix C of this book. You can also download this form on the Nolo website; the link is included in Appendix B of this book. A filled-in sample rental application is shown below.

Before giving prospective tenants a rental application, complete the box at the top, filling in the property address, the first month's rent, the rental term, and any deposit or credit check fee that tenants must pay before moving in. (Credit check fees are discussed later in this chapter.) If you're charging any other fee, such as a nonrefundable cleaning deposit, note this as well—if you are sure that the nonrefundable fee is legal in your state. (See "Don't Charge Nonrefundable Fees" in Chapter 1 for details.)

Here are some basic guidelines for accepting rental applications:

- Each prospective tenant—everyone age 18 or older—should completely fill out and sign a separate written application. This is true whether you're renting to a married couple or to unrelated roommates, a complete stranger, or the cousin of your current tenant.

- Always make sure that prospective tenants complete the entire rental application, including Social Security number, driver's license or other identifying information (such as a passport number), current employment, bank, and emergency contacts. You might need this information later to track down a tenant who skips town leaving unpaid rent or abandoned property. Also, you might need the Social Security number or other identifying information, such as a passport, to request an applicant's credit report.

Rental Application

A separate application is required from each applicant age 18 or older.

Date and time received by Landlord _____

THIS SECTION TO BE COMPLETED BY LANDLORD

Address of property to be rented: ___178 West 81st Street, Apt. 4F, NYC___

Rental term: ☐ month-to-month ☑ lease from ___March 1, 20xx___ to ___February 28, 20xx___

Amounts Due Prior to Occupancy

First month's rent: .... $ ___3,000___

Security deposit: .... $ ___3,000___

Credit check fee: .... $ ___38___

Other (specify): _____ $ _____

TOTAL $ ___6,038___

Applicant

Full Name—include all names you use or have used in the past: ___Hannah Silver___

Home Phone: ___609-555-3789___ Work Phone: ___609-555-4567___

Cell Phone: ___609-555-3790___ Email: ___hannah@coldmail.com___

Social Security Number: ___123-00-4567___ Driver's License Number/State: ___D123456/New Jersey___

Other Identifying Information: _____

Vehicle Make: ___Toyota___ Model: ___Corolla___ Color: ___White___ Year: ___2015___

License Plate Number/State: ___NJ1234567/New Jersey___

Additional Occupants

List everyone, including minor children, who will live with you:

Full Name	Relationship to Applicant
Dennis Olson	Husband

Rental History

FIRST-TIME RENTERS: INSTEAD ATTACH A DESCRIPTION OF YOUR HOUSING FOR THE PAST FIVE YEARS.

Current Address: ___39 Maple Street, Princeton, New Jersey 08540___

Dates Lived at Address: ___May 2011–date___ Rent $ ___2,000___ Security Deposit $ ___4,000___

Landlord/Manager: ___Jane Tucker___ Landlord/Manager's Phone: ___609-555-7523___

Reason for Leaving: ___New job in NYC___

Previous Address: _____1215 Middlebrook Lane, Princeton, New Jersey 08540_____

Dates Lived at Address: ____June 2008–May 2011____ Rent $ __1,800__ Security Deposit $ __1,000__

Landlord/Manager: ____Ed Palermo____ Landlord/Manager's Phone: __609-555-3711__

Reason for Leaving: ____Better apartment____

Previous Address: ___1527 Highland Drive, New Brunswick, New Jersey 08444___

Dates Lived at Address: ___Jan. 2007–June 2008___ Rent $ __800__ Security Deposit $ __800__

Landlord/Manager: ____Millie & Joe Lewis____ Landlord/Manager's Phone: __609-555-9999__

Reason for Leaving: ____Wanted to live closer to work____

Employment History

EMPLOYEES: ATTACH TAX RETURNS FROM THE MOST RECENT TWO YEARS, PLUS PAY STUBS FROM THE PAST SIX MONTHS.
SELF-EMPLOYED APPLICANTS: INSTEAD ATTACH TAX RETURNS FROM THE MOST RECENT TWO YEARS.

Name and Address of Current Employer: ___Argonworks, 54 Nassau Street, Princeton, New Jersey___

_____ Phone: (609) _555-2333_

Name of Supervisor: ___Tom Schmidt___ Supervisor's Phone: (609) _555-2333_

Dates Employed at This Job: __2008–date__ Position or Title: _Marketing Director_

Name and Address of Previous Employer: ____Princeton Times____

___13 Junction Rd., Princeton, NJ___ Phone: (609) _555-1111_

Name of Supervisor: ___Dory Krossber___ Supervisor's Phone: (609) _555-2366_

Dates Employed at This Job: __Jan. 2007–June 2008__ Position or Title: _Marketing Associate_

Income

1. Your gross monthly employment income (before deductions): $__8,000__

2. Average monthly amounts of other income (specify sources): $_____

    Note: This does not include my husband's income. See his application. $_____

_____ $_____

TOTAL: $__8,000__

Bank/Financial Accounts

	Account Number	Bank/Institution	Branch
Savings Account:	1222345	N.J. Federal	Trenton, NJ
Checking Account:	789101	Princeton S&L	Princeton, NJ
Money Market or Similar Account:	234789	City Bank	Princeton, NJ

Credit Card Accounts

Major Credit Card: ☑ VISA ☐ MC ☐ Discover Card ☐ Am Ex ☐ Other: _____

Issuer: _____City Bank_____ Account No. _____1234 5555 6666 7777_____

Balance $ _____1,000_____ Average Monthly Payment $ _____1,000_____

Major Credit Card: ☐ VISA ☐ MC ☐ Discover Card ☐ Am Ex ☑ Other: _____Dept. Store_____

Issuer: _____City Bank_____ Account No. _____2345 0000 9999 8888_____

Balance $ _____1,000_____ Average Monthly Payment $ _____1,000_____

Loans

Type of Loan (mortgage, car, student loan, etc.)	Name of Creditor	Account Number	Amount Owed	Monthly Payment

Other Major Obligations (such as child support, alimony, tax liens, etc.)

Type	Payee		Amount Owed	Monthly Payment

Pets

Type	Breed	Sex	Age	Neutered/spayed	Weight	Years owned
None now, but we might want to get a cat some time						
				None		

Miscellaneous

Describe water-filled furniture you want to have in the rental property: _____

Do you smoke? ☐ yes ☑ no

Have you ever:
Filed for bankruptcy? ☐ yes ☑ no   How many times _____
Been sued? ☐ yes ☑ no   How many times _____
Sued someone else? ☐ yes ☑ no   How many times _____
Been evicted? ☐ yes ☑ no   How many times _____

Explain (include dates) any "yes" listed above: _____

References and Emergency Contact

Personal Reference: _Joan Stanley_ Relationship: _Friend, coworker_

Address: _785 Spruce Street, Princeton, New Jersey 08540_

Email: _____ Phone: (609) _555-4578_

Personal Reference: _Marnie Swatt_ Relationship: _Friend_

Address: _82 East 59th Street, #12B, NYC_

Email: _____ Phone: (212) _555-8765_

Contact in Emergency: _Connie & Martin Silver_ Relationship: _Parents_

Address: _7852 Pierce Street, Somerset, New Jersey 08321_

Email: _____ Phone: (609) _555-7878_

Source

Where did you learn of this vacancy? _Ryan Cowell, Broker_

I certify that all the information given above is true and correct and understand that my lease or rental agreement may be terminated if I have made any material false or incomplete statements in this application. I authorize verification of the information provided in this application from my credit sources, credit bureaus, current and previous landlords and employers, and personal references. This permission will survive the expiration of my tenancy.

Hannah Silver February 15, 20xx

Applicant Date

Notes (Landlord/Manager): _____

- Request proof of identity and immigration status. Many landlords ask prospective tenants to show their driver's license or other photo identification as a way to verify that applicants are using their real names. Except in California (Cal. Civ. Code § 1940.3) and New York City (NYC Admin. Code § 8-107(5)(a)), you may also ask applicants for proof of identity and eligibility to work under U.S. immigration laws, such as a work permit, a passport, or a naturalization certificate, using Form I-9 (*Employment Eligibility Verification*) from the U.S. Citizenship and Immigration Services, or USCIS, a bureau of the U.S. Department of Homeland Security. This form (and instructions for completing it) are available from the USCIS website at www.uscis.gov/i-9, or by phone at 800-375-5283. Under federal fair housing laws, you may not selectively ask for such immigration information—that is, you must ask all prospective tenants, not just those you suspect might be in the country illegally. It is illegal to discriminate on the basis of race, color, or national origin, although you may reject someone on the basis of immigration status.

- Be sure all potential tenants sign the rental application, authorizing you to verify the information and references and to run a credit report. (Some employers and banks require written authorization before they will talk to you.) You might also want to prepare a separate authorization, signed and dated by the applicant, so that you don't need to copy the entire application and send it off every time a bank or employer wants proof that the tenant authorized you to verify the information.

Consent to Contact References and Perform Credit Check

I authorize _____ Jan Gold _____

to obtain information about me from my credit sources, current and previous landlords, employers, and personal references, to enable _____ Jan Gold _____ to evaluate my rental application.

I give permission for the landlord or its agent to obtain a consumer report about me for the purpose of this application, to ensure that I continue to meet the terms of the tenancy, for the collection and recovery of any financial obligations relating to my tenancy, or for any other permissible purpose.

Michael Clark
Applicant Signature

Michael Clark
Printed Name

123 State Street, Chicago, Illinois
Address

312-555-9876
Phone Number

February 2, 20xx
Date

Finally, note that this application does not ask applicants for their dates of birth (DOB). Many fair housing experts believe that doing so is risky, should a disappointed applicant attempt to challenge your rejection as an instance of age discrimination—having the date on the application at least establishes that you knew of the applicant's age. Some landlords still ask for the DOB, responding to credit reporting companies' requests for this information. You should be able to order a credit report and a screening report using the applicant's Social Security number; if vendors balk, you might want to ask for the DOB.

FORM

Reference and Credit Check Consent form. You'll find a copy of the Consent to Contact References and Perform Credit Check in Appendix C of this book. You can download this form on the Nolo website; the link is included in Appendix B of this book. A filled-in sample consent form is shown above.

Checking References, Credit History, and More

If an application looks good, your next step is to follow up thoroughly. The time and money you spend are some of the most cost-effective expenditures you'll ever make.

CAUTION

Be consistent in your screening. You risk a charge of illegal discrimination if you screen certain categories of applicants more stringently than others—for example, requiring credit reports only from minorities. (See "Avoiding Illegal Discrimination," below, for more on the subject.)

Here are six elements of a very thorough screening process. You should always go through at least the first three to check out the applicant's previous landlords and income and employment, and run a credit check.

Check With Current and Previous Landlords and Other References

Always call current and previous landlords or managers for references—even if you already have a written letter of reference from them. It's worth the time if it helps you weed out a tenant who might cause problems down the road. Also call employers and personal references listed on the application.

To organize the information you gather from these calls, use the Tenant References form, which lists key questions to ask landlords, employers, and other references.

TIP

Check out pets, too. If the prospective tenant has a dog or cat, be sure to ask previous landlords if the pet caused any damage or problems for other tenants or neighbors. It's also a good idea to meet the dog or cat, so you can make sure that it's well-groomed and well-behaved, before you make a final decision. You must, however, accommodate an applicant with a mental or physical disability whose dog serves as a support animal—no matter how mangy-looking the animal might be. (See the discussion of pet rules in Chapter 1, Clause 14.)

Take notes of all your conversations and keep them on file. You can indicate your reasons for refusing an individual on the Tenant References form—for example, negative credit information, bad references from a previous landlord, or your inability to verify information. You'll want a record of this information so that you can survive a fair housing challenge if a disappointed applicant files a discrimination complaint against you.

Tenant References

Name of Applicant: _____Michael Clark_____

Address of Rental Unit: _____123 State Street, Chicago, Illinois_____

Previous Landlord or Manager

Contact (name, property owner or manager, address of rental unit): _____Kate Steiner, 345 Mercer Street, Chicago, Illinois;_____

_____(312) 555-5432_____

Date: _____February 4, 20xx_____

Questions

When did tenant rent from you (move-in and move-out dates)? _____December 2012 to date_____

What was the monthly rent? _____$1,250_____   Did tenant pay rent on time?   ☐ Yes ☑ No

If rent was not paid on time, did you have to give tenant a legal notice demanding the rent?   ☐ Yes ☑ No

If rent was not paid on time, provide details _____He paid rent a week late a few times_____

Did you give tenant notice of any lease violation for other than nonpayment of rent?   ☐ Yes ☑ No

If you gave a lease violation notice, what was the outcome? _____

Was tenant considerate of neighbors—that is, no loud parties and fair, careful use of common areas?

_____Yes, considerate_____

Did tenant have any pets? ☑ Yes ☐ No   If so, were there any problems? _____He had a cat, contrary to_____

_____rental agreement_____

Did tenant make any unreasonable demands or complaints?   ☐ Yes ☑ No   If so, explain: _____

Why did tenant leave? _____He wants to live someplace that allows pets_____

Did tenant give the proper amount of notice before leaving?   ☑ Yes ☐ No

Did tenant leave the place in good condition? Did you need to use the security deposit to cover damage?

_____No problems_____

Any particular problems you'd like to mention? _____No_____

Would you rent to this person again? _____Yes, but without pets_____

Other comments: _____

Employment Verification

Contact (name, company, position): ___Brett Field, Manager, Chicago Car Company___

Date: ___February 5, 20xx___   Salary $ ___80,000 + bonus___

Dates of Employment: ___March 2011 to date___

Comments: ___No problems. Fine employee. Michael is responsible and hard working.___

Personal Reference

Contact (name and relationship to applicant): ___Sandy Cameron, friend___

Date: ___February 5, 20xx___   How long have you known the applicant? ___Five years___

Would you recommend this person as a prospective tenant? ___Yes___

Comments: ___Michael is very neat and responsible. He's reliable and will be a great tenant.___

Credit and Financial Information

___Mostly fine—see attached credit report.___

Notes, Including Reasons for Rejecting Applicant

___Applicant had a history of late rent payments and kept a cat, contrary to the rental agreement.___

FORM

Tenant References form. You'll find a copy of the Tenant References screening form in Appendix C of this book. You can also download this form on the Nolo website; the link is included in Appendix B of this book. A filled-in sample Tenant References form is shown above.

Verify Income and Employment

Obviously, you want to make sure that all tenants have the income to pay the rent each month. Call the prospective tenant's employer to verify income and length of employment. Make notes on the Tenant References form, discussed above.

Before providing this information, some employers require written authorization from the employee. You will need to send the employer a signed copy of the release included at the bottom of the rental application form or the separate Consent to Contact References and Perform Credit Check form. If for any reason you question the income information you get by telephone—for example, you suspect a buddy of the applicant is exaggerating on the applicant's behalf—you may also ask applicants for copies of recent paycheck stubs.

It's also reasonable to require documentation of other sources of income, such as Social Security, disability payments, workers' compensation, welfare, child support, or alimony.

How much income is enough? Think twice before renting to someone if the rent will take more than one-third of their gross income, especially if they have a lot of debts.

Obtain a Credit Report

Private credit reporting agencies collect and sell credit files and other information about consumers. Many landlords find it essential to check a prospective tenant's credit history with at least one credit reporting agency to see how responsible the person is about managing money. Jot your findings down on the Tenant References form, discussed above.

How to Get a Credit Report

A credit report contains a gold mine of information on a prospective tenant. You can find out, for example, if a particular person has a history of paying rent or bills late or has gone through bankruptcy, or ever been evicted. (Your legal right to get information on evictions, however, might vary from state to state.) Credit reports usually cover the past seven to ten years. Depending on the type of report you order, you might also get an applicant's credit score (the most popular being the "FICO"), a number that purports to indicate the risk that an individual will default on payments.

To run a credit check, you'll normally need a prospective tenant's name, address, and Social Security number, or ITIN (Individual Taxpayer Identification Number). Three credit bureaus have cornered the market on credit reports:

- Equifax, Equifax.com
- Experian, Experian.com, and
- TransUnion, TransUnion.com.

Although you generally cannot order a credit report directly from the big three bureaus, the bureaus have other options you might find helpful. For example, Experian has an option called "Experian Connect" (https://connect.experian.com) that allows prospective tenants to buy their credit report and credit score online, and give you access. This service provides you with a VantageScore, another type of credit score that's similar to FICO.

TransUnion also allows you to get credit information about potential tenants by creating a "SmartMove" account (MySmartMove.com). You send applicants an online invitation through the account. Once applicants receive the invite, they supply their personal information, and you can then view their credit report, a criminal report (subject to federal, state, and local laws that limit or restrict access to some records), an eviction report, a leasing recommendation, and a "ResidentScore." A ResidentScore is similar to a credit score, but TransUnion created it specifically for tenant screening purposes. ResidentScores range from 350 to 850, the same range that FICO and newer VantageScore models use. The higher the score, the better.

You can also get credit information about an applicant by going through a tenant screening service (type "tenant screening" into your browser's search box). Look for a company that is reputable (consider checking the company's rating with the Better Business Bureau along with any online customer reviews), has been in business for a while, and provides clear and informative reports.

Your state or local apartment association might also offer credit reporting services.

Tenant screening services and credit reporting agencies often provide reports the same day you request them. The costs of these reports depends on what type of and how many reports you order.

Tenants who are applying for more than one rental are understandably dismayed at the prospect of paying each landlord to pull the same credit report. They might obtain their own reports, make copies, and ask you to accept their copies. Federal law does not require you to accept an applicant's copy—you can require applicants to pay a credit check fee for you to run a new report. However, certain states—Wisconsin and Washington, for example—are exceptions: State law in Wisconsin forbids landlords from charging for a credit report if, before the landlord asks for a report, the applicant offers one from a consumer reporting agency and the report is less than 30 days old. (Wis. Adm. Code ATCP 134.05(4)(b).) In Washington, landlords must advise tenants whether they will accept a screening report done

by a consumer reporting agency (in which case the landlord may not charge the tenant a fee for a screening report). Landlords who maintain a website that advertises residential rentals must include this information on the home page. (Wash. Rev. Code Ann. § 59.18.257.)

Credit Check Fees

It's legal in most states to charge prospective tenants a fee for the cost of the credit report itself and for your time and trouble. Any credit check fee should be reasonably related to the cost of the credit check—$20 to $30 is common. Check your state law for any limits. California, for example, sets a maximum screening fee per applicant and requires landlords to provide an itemized receipt when accepting a credit check fee. (Cal. Civ. Code § 1950.6.)

Some landlords don't charge credit check fees, preferring to absorb the cost as they would any other cost of business. For low-end units, charging an extra fee can be a barrier to getting tenants in the first place, and a tenant who pays a fee, but is later rejected, is likely to be annoyed and possibly more apt to claim that your rejection was based on a discriminatory reason.

The rental application form in this book informs prospective tenants whether you charge a credit check fee. Be sure prospective tenants understand that paying a credit check fee does not guarantee the tenant will get the rental unit.

TIP

It's a mistake to collect a credit check fee from lots of people. If you expect a large number of applicants, you'd be wise not to accept fees from everyone. Instead, read over the applications first and do a credit check only on applicants you're seriously considering. That way, you won't waste your time (and prospective tenants' money) collecting fees from unqualified applicants.

CAUTION
It is illegal to charge a credit check fee if you do not use it for the stated purpose and pocket it instead. Return any credit check fees you don't use for that purpose.

What You're Looking for in a Credit Report

It makes sense to be leery of applicants with lots of debts—especially people whose monthly payments plus the rent obligation exceed 40% of their after-tax income. Also, look at the person's bill-paying habits, and, of course, pay attention to lawsuits and evictions.

Sometimes, your only choice is to rent to someone with poor or fair credit—or even no credit (for example, a student or recent graduate). If that's your situation, you should still adopt sensible screening requirements such as these:

- positive references from previous landlords and employers
- a creditworthy cosigner of the lease (see the discussion on cosigners at the end of Chapter 1)
- a good-sized deposit—as much as you can collect under state law and the market will bear (see Clause 8 of the form agreements in Chapter 1), and
- proof of specific steps taken to improve bad credit—for example, enrollment in a debt counseling group.

CAUTION
Take special care to store credit reports in a safe place, where only you and those who "need to know" have access to them. When you no longer need the reports, under the "Disposal Rule" of the Fair and Accurate Credit Transactions Act, you must destroy them. Use a shredder or burn the credit reports, and delete any reports kept on your computer or phone.

Verify Bank Account Information

If an individual's credit history raises questions about financial stability, you might want to double-check the bank accounts listed on the rental application. If so, you'll probably need an authorization form such as the one included at the bottom of the rental application, or the separate Consent to Contact References and Perform Credit Check form (discussed above). Banks differ as to the type of information they will provide over the phone. Generally, without a written authorization, banks will only confirm that an individual has an account there and that it is in good standing.

CAUTION
Be wary of an applicant who does not have a checking or savings account Tenants who offer to pay cash or with a money order should be viewed with extreme caution. Perhaps the individual bounced so many checks that the bank dropped the account or the income comes from a shady or illegitimate source —for example, from drug dealing.

Review Court Records

When prospective tenants have previously lived in your area, you might want to review local court records to see if collection or eviction lawsuits have been filed against them. Checking court records might seem like overkill—some of this information might be available on credit reports—but now and then it's a valuable tool. You won't violate antidiscrimination laws as long as you check the records of every applicant who reaches this stage of your screening process. Because court records are kept for many years, this kind of information can supplement references from recent landlords. Talk to the court clerk at the local court that handles eviction cases for information on how to check court records.

Use Megan's Law to Check State Databases of Sex Offenders

Not surprisingly, most landlords do not want tenants with criminal records, particularly convictions for violent crimes or crimes against children. Checking a prospective tenant's credit report, as recommended above, might be one way to find out about a person's criminal history.

"Megan's Law" can also be a useful source of information. This federal crime prevention law charges the FBI with keeping a nationwide database of persons convicted of sexual offenses against minors and violent sexual offenses against anyone. (42 U.S.C. §§ 14071 and following.) Every state has its own version of Megan's Law that requires certain convicted sexual offenders to register with local law enforcement officials who keep a database on their whereabouts.

For information on your access to this type of database, and restrictions on your use of information derived from a Megan's Law database, contact your local law enforcement agency. California landlords may not access their state's database unless they are doing so to protect a person "at risk." This means that routine checking is not legal. (Cal. Penal Code § 290.46(j)(1).) Massachusetts, Nevada, and New Jersey have some restrictions, too. To find out how to access your state's sex offender registry, you can also contact the Parents for Megan's Law (PFML) Hotline at 888-ASK-PFML, or check this organization's website at www.parentsformeganslaw.org.

Protect Personally Identifiable Information

When screening applicants, you'll collect a lot of personal and potentially sensitive information, including names, Social Security numbers, and more. Because the misuse of this personally identifiable information (known as "PII") can be so harmful to victims, many states require those who handle PII—including landlords—to follow security protocols and to report the unintended leaking of PII. Even if your state has not imposed specific requirements on use and handling, you should to take steps to protect the PII you obtain.

What Is PII?

PII is any information that someone could use to identify a particular person. For example, knowing a name and birthdate, someone might be able to tie that information to an actual person. Driver's license numbers, Social Security numbers, and email addresses are just a few examples of PII landlords often collect.

As a general rule, ask only for what's necessary to determine who will be a good tenant. The information we've suggested that you obtain during your screening process is the minimum amount you'll need to confidently evaluate your applicants.

Storing PII

Most landlords' records contain PII. (For information about what items should be in your records and how to maintain records, see "Organize Your Tenant Records" in Chapter 3.) State PII laws often require PII holders to take "reasonable steps" to protect PII. What's reasonable for your business depends on factors such as how you collect PII, how you store it, and how many people have access to it. At the very least, give others access to PII only when necessary, and consider developing a set of written rules for how to store PII. Whenever possible, password-protect PII, encrypt messages containing PII, and keep physical documents containing PII in one secured place with limited access.

Consumer Reports: A Special Form of PII

Consumer reports—any report you obtain from a consumer reporting company for purposes of screening potential tenants—require special handling. The consumer report used most often by landlords is a credit report. Under the "Disposal Rule" of the Fair and Accurate Credit Transactions Act, when you no longer need a consumer report, you must destroy it in a manner that is reasonable for your business and that prevents anyone from using or accessing the report without permission. The Federal Trade Commission (FTC)—the organization which enforces the Disposal Rule—suggests doing the following:

- burning, pulverizing, or shredding papers
- destroying or erasing electronic files or media so that the information cannot be reconstructed, and
- hiring a qualified document destruction contractor to dispose of consumer report material.

Destroying PII

Deciding when to destroy PII can be a tough call—you need to maintain thorough records, but you also don't want to hold on to PII longer than necessary. For most landlords, it's safe to destroy rental records four years after the tenancy ends. You'll also need to consider how long you should keep records for tax purposes. Beyond these basic recommendations, consider scheduling regular audits of your files to check for unneeded PII.

No matter how long you keep rental records, you should have written procedures on how to destroy PII. Some examples of PII destruction practices are:

- Destroy PII as soon as it's no longer needed.
- Black out and shred documents containing PII before throwing them away or recycling.

- Delete or overwrite unneeded electronic files. Hitting "delete" might not be enough to permanently delete files, so consult with an internet technology professional if you have any questions about permanently removing data.

What to Do If PII Is Stolen

Even if you take reasonable security measures, the PII of your applicants (and tenants) might become exposed. If this happens, check your state law—some states require you to report PII security breaches to affected consumers and even to the state itself, depending on the number of people affected by the breach. In any situation, you'll want to determine what PII was exposed, who was affected, and whether it's likely the PII will be misused. If you have any reason to believe the PII will be misused, contact the people whose information was taken as soon as possible. You should also evaluate how the PII was accessed, and take measures such as changing passwords or moving files to make sure it doesn't happen again.

RESOURCE

Stay current on the status of PII law in your state by going to The National Conference of State Legislatures' website (www.ncsl.org) and searching for "data security laws." For information on electronic record destruction, check out the Massachusetts Institute of Technology site (web.mit.edu) and search for "removing sensitive data." The FTC has a clear and thorough explanation of the Disposal Rule on its website (www.ftc.gov) as well as tips and advice on how to dispose of consumer reports. (On the FTC home page, search for the article's name: Disposing of Consumer Report Information? Rule Tells How.) Consider visiting this site on a regular basis to stay informed about any changes to or tips on complying with the Disposal Rule.

Avoiding Illegal Discrimination

Federal and state antidiscrimination laws limit what you can say and do in the tenant selection process. Basically, you need to keep in mind three important points:

1. You are legally free to choose among prospective tenants as long as your decisions are based on legitimate business criteria. You are entitled to reject people for the following reasons:
   - poor credit history
   - income that you reasonably regard as insufficient to pay the rent
   - negative references from previous land-lords indicating problems—such as property damage or consistently late rent payments—that make someone a bad risk
   - convictions for relevant criminal offenses
   - inability to meet the legal terms of a lease or rental agreement, such as someone who can't come up with the security deposit or who wants to keep a pet when your policy is no pets, or
   - more people than you want to live in the unit—assuming that your limit on the number of tenants is clearly tied to health and safety or legitimate business needs. (See Clause 3 discussion of occupancy limits in Chapter 1.)

2. Antidiscrimination laws specify clearly illegal reasons to refuse to rent to a tenant. The federal Fair Housing Act and Fair Housing Amendments Act (42 U.S.C. §§ 3601–3619, 3631) prohibit discrimination on the basis of race or color, religion, national origin, gender, age, familial status (pregnancy or children), and physical or mental disability (including recovering alcoholics and people with a past drug addiction). Many states and cities also prohibit discrimination based on marital status, source of income, military status, sexual orientation, or gender identity.

RESOURCE

More on housing discrimination rules. For more information on the rules and regulations of the Fair Housing Act, contact HUD's Housing Discrimination Hotline at 800-669-9777 or check the HUD website at www.HUD.gov. You can also contact a local HUD office.

For information on state and local housing discrimination laws, contact your state fair housing agency. HUD's website also contains a list of state agencies and contact information.

3. Consistency is crucial when dealing with prospective tenants. If you don't treat all tenants more or less equally—for example, if you arbitrarily set tougher standards for renting to a member of an ethnic minority (such as requiring a higher income level or proof of legal residence status), you are violating federal laws and opening yourself up to expensive lawsuits and the possibility of being hit with large judgments. On the other hand, if you require all prospective tenants to meet the same income standard and to supply satisfactory proof of their legal eligibility to work (as well as meet your other criteria), you will get the needed information, but in a nondiscriminatory way.

CAUTION

Show the property to and accept applications from everyone who's interested. Even if, after talking to someone on the phone, you doubt that a particular tenant can qualify, it's best to politely take all applications. Unless you can point to something in writing that clearly disqualifies a tenant, you are on shaky legal ground: Refusing to take an application might unnecessarily anger prospective tenants, and might make them more likely to look into the possibility of filing a discrimination complaint. Make decisions later about who will rent the property. Be sure to keep copies of all applications. (See discussion of record keeping in Chapter 3.)

The Rights of Tenants With Disabilities

The Fair Housing Acts require that landlords *accommodate* the needs of tenants with disabilities, at the landlord's own expense. (42 U.S.C. § 3604(f)(3)(B).) You are expected to adjust your rules, procedures, or services in order to give a person with a disability an equal opportunity to use and enjoy a dwelling unit or a common space. Accommodations include such things as providing a close-in, spacious parking space for a tenant who uses a wheelchair (assuming you provide parking). Your duty to accommodate tenants with disabilities does not mean that you must bend every rule and change every procedure at the tenant's request. You are expected to accommodate "reasonable" requests, but need not undertake changes that would seriously impair your ability to run your business.

The Fair Housing Acts also require landlords to allow tenants with disabilities to make reasonable *modifications* of their living unit at their expense if that is what is needed for the person to comfortably and safely live in the unit. (42 U.S.C. § 3604(f)(3)(A).) For example, a person with a disability has the right to modify the living space to the extent necessary to make the space safe and comfortable, as long as the modifications will not make the unit unacceptable to the next tenant or the tenant with a disability agrees to undo the modification when the tenant leaves. An example of a modification undertaken by a tenant with a disability is lowering countertops for a tenant who uses a wheelchair.

You are not obliged to allow a tenant with a disability to modify a unit at will, without your prior approval. You are entitled to ask for a reasonable description of the proposed modifications, proof that they will be done in a workmanlike manner, and evidence that the tenant is obtaining any necessary building permits. Moreover, if a tenant proposes to modify the unit in such a manner that will require restoration when the tenant leaves (such as the repositioning of lowered kitchen counters), you may require that the tenant pay into an interest-bearing escrow account the amount estimated for the restoration. (The interest belongs to the tenant.)

Choosing—and Rejecting— an Applicant

After you've collected applications and done some screening, you can start evaluating applicants, using the basic criteria discussed above. Start by eliminating the worst risks: people with negative references from previous landlords, a history of nonpayment of rent, or poor credit or recent and numerous evictions. Then make your selection.

Assuming you choose the best-qualified candidate (based on income, credit history, and references), you have no legal problem. But what if you have a number of more or less equally qualified applicants? Can you safely choose an older white man over a young black woman?

The answer is a qualified "yes." If two people rate equally, you can legally choose either one without legal risk in any particular situation. But be extra careful not to take the further step of always selecting a person of the same sex, age, or ethnicity. For example, if you are a larger landlord who is frequently faced with tough choices and who always avoids an equally qualified minority or disabled applicant, you are exposing yourself to charges of discrimination.

Information You Should Keep on Rejected Applicants

It is crucial that any tenant-screening system you implement documents how and why you chose a particular tenant.

Note your reasons for rejection— such as poor credit history, pets (if you don't accept pets), or a negative reference from a previous landlord—on the tenant references form or other document so that you have a paper trail if a tenant accuses you of illegal discrimination. You want to be able to back up your reason for rejecting the person. Keep organized files of applications and other materials and notes on prospective tenants for at least three years after you rent a particular unit. (See "Organize Your Tenant Records" in Chapter 3.) Keep in mind that if a rejected applicant files a complaint with a fair housing agency or files a lawsuit, your file will be made available to the applicant's lawyers. Knowing that, choose your words carefully, avoiding the obvious (slurs and exaggerations) and being scrupulously truthful.

Information You Must Provide Rejected Applicants

If you do not rent to someone because of an insufficient credit report or negative information in the report, you must give the applicant the name and address of the agency that reported the negative information or furnished the insufficient report. This is a requirement of the federal Fair Credit Reporting Act (FCRA). (15 U.S.C. §§ 1681 and following.) The notices are known as "adverse action reports."

In these cases, you must tell applicants that they have a right to obtain a copy of the file from the agency that reported the negative information, by requesting it within the next 60 days, or by asking within one year of having asked for their last free report. You must also tell rejected applicants that the credit reporting agency did not make the decision to reject them and cannot explain the reason for the rejection. Finally, you must tell applicants that they can dispute the accuracy of their credit report and add their own

consumer statement to their report. The law doesn't require you to communicate an applicant's right to disclosure in writing, but it's a good idea to do so (and to keep a copy of the rejection letter in your files). That way, you'll have irrefutable proof that you complied with the law if you're challenged in court. Use the Notice of Denial Based on Credit Report or Other Information form, shown below, to comply with the federal Fair Credit Reporting Act when you reject an applicant because of an insufficient credit report or negative information in the report.

FORM
Rejection letter form. You'll find a copy of the Notice of Denial Based on Credit Report or Other Information form in Appendix C of this book. You can also download this form on the Nolo website; the link is included in Appendix B of this book. A filled-in sample notice of denial form is shown below.

Exceptions: The federal requirements do not apply if you reject someone based on information that the applicant furnished or that you or an employee learned on your own.

Conditional Acceptances

You might want to make an offer to an applicant but condition that offer on the applicant paying more rent or a higher security deposit (one that's within any legal limits, of course), supplying a cosigner, or agreeing to a different rental term than you originally advertised. If your decision to impose the condition resulted from information you gained from a credit report or a report from a tenant screening service, you have to accompany the offer with an adverse action report (described in the section immediately above). Use the Notice of Conditional Acceptance Based on Credit Report or Other Information, shown below.

Notice of Denial Based on Credit Report or Other Information

To: __Ryan Paige_____
Applicant

__1 Mariner Square_____
Street Address

__Seattle, Washington 98101_____
City, State, and Zip Code

Your rights under the Fair Credit Reporting Act and Fair and Accurate Credit Transactions (FACT) Act of 2003.
(15 U.S.C. §§ 1681 and following.)

THIS NOTICE is to inform you that your application to rent the property at __75 Starbucks Lane, Seattle, WA 98108__
_____

been denied because of [*check all that apply*]:

☑ Insufficient information in the credit report provided by:

Credit reporting agency: __ABC Credit Bureau_____

Address, phone number, URL: __310 Griffey Way, Seattle, Washington 98140; Phone: 206-555-1212;__
__www.abccredit.com__

☐ Negative information in the credit report provided by:

Credit reporting agency: _____

Address, phone number, URL: _____
_____

☑ The credit score supplied on the credit report, __511__ , was used in whole or in part when making the selection.

☑ The consumer credit reporting agency noted above did not make the decision not to offer you this rental. It only provided information about your credit history. You have the right to obtain a free copy of your credit report from the consumer credit reporting agency named above, if your request is made within 60 days of this notice or if you have not requested a free copy within the past year. You also have the right to dispute the accuracy or completeness of your credit report. The agency must reinvestigate within a reasonable time, free of charge, and remove or modify inaccurate information. If the reinvestigation does not resolve the dispute to your satisfaction, you may add your own "consumer statement" (up to 100 words) to the report, which must be included (or a clear summary) in future reports.

☐ Information supplied by a third party other than a credit reporting agency or you and gathered by someone other than myself or any employee. You have the right to learn of the nature of the information if you ask me in writing within 60 days of the date of this notice.

_Jason McGuire_____   __10-01-20xx_____
Landlord/Manager   Date

Notice of Conditional Acceptance Based on Credit Report or Other Information

To: ___William McGee_____
Applicant

___1257 Bay Avenue_____
Street Address

___Anytown, Florida 12345_____
City, State, and Zip Code

Your application to rent the property at ___37 Ocean View Drive, #10-H, Anytown, Florida 12345_____

_____ [rental property address] has been accepted, conditioned on your

willingness and ability to: ___Supply a cosigner that is acceptable to the landlord_____

_____

Your rights under the Fair Credit Reporting Act and Fair and Accurate Credit Transactions (FACT) Act of 2003. (15 U.S.C. §§ 1681 and following.)

Source of information prompting conditional acceptance

My decision to conditionally accept your application was prompted in whole or in part by:

☑ Insufficient information in the credit report provided by

Credit reporting agency: _____Mountain Credit Bureau_____

Address, phone number, URL: ___75 Baywood Drive, Anytown, Florida 12345; 800-123-4567;_____
___www.mountaincredit.com_____

☐ Negative information in the credit report provided by:

Credit reporting agency: _____

Address, phone number, URL: _____

_____

☑ The consumer credit reporting agency noted above did not make the decision to offer you this conditional acceptance. It only provided information about your credit history. You have the right to obtain a free copy of your credit report from the consumer credit reporting agency named above, if your request is made within 60 days of this notice or if you have not requested a free copy within the past year. You also have the right to dispute the accuracy or completeness of your credit report. The agency must reinvestigate within a reasonable time, free of charge, and remove or modify inaccurate information. If the reinvestigation does not resolve the dispute to your satisfaction, you may add your own "consumer statement" (up to 100 words) to the report, which must be included (or a clear summary) in future reports.

☐ Information supplied by a third party other than a credit reporting agency or you and gathered by someone other than myself or any employee. You have the right to learn of the nature of the information if you ask me in writing within 60 days of the date of this notice.

*Jane Thomas*_____   *May 15, 20xx*_____
Landlord/Manager   Date

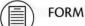 FORM

Conditional acceptance form. You'll find a copy of the Notice of Conditional Acceptance Based on Credit Report or Other Information in Appendix C of this book. You can also download this form on the Nolo website; the link is included in Appendix B of this book. A filled-in sample notice of conditional acceptance form is shown above.

Choosing a Tenant-Manager

Many landlords hire a manager to handle all the day-to-day details of running a rental property, including fielding tenants' routine repair requests and collecting the rent. If you hire a resident manager, make sure to get a completed rental application and check references and other information carefully. If you use a property management company, it will do this work for you. (See below.)

The person you hire as a manager will occupy a critical position in your business. Your manager will interact with every tenant and will often have access to their personal files and their homes. Legally, you have a duty to protect your tenants from injuries caused by employees you know (or should know) pose a risk of harm to others. If someone gets hurt or has property stolen or damaged by a manager whose dubious background you didn't check carefully, you could be sued, so it's crucial that you be especially vigilant when hiring a manager.

When you hire a manager, you should sign two separate agreements:

- an employment agreement that covers manager responsibilities, hours, and pay, and that can be terminated at any time for any reason by either party, and
- a month-to-month rental agreement that can be terminated by either of you with the amount of written notice (typically 30 days) required under state law.

Whether or not you compensate a manager with reduced rent or regular salary, be sure you comply with your legal obligations as an employer, such as following laws governing minimum wage and overtime.

 RESOURCE

More legal resources for landlords.
Every Landlord's Legal Guide, by Marcia Stewart, Janet Portman, and Ann O'Connell (Nolo), provides detailed advice on hiring a manager, including how to prepare a property manager agreement, and your legal obligations as an employer, such as following laws governing minimum wage and overtime.

The Manager's Legal Handbook, by Lisa Guerin and Sachi Barreiro (Nolo), is a complete guide to the latest workplace laws and regulations. It covers everything you need to know about hiring and firing employees, personnel policies, employee benefits, discrimination, and other laws affecting small business practices.

Property Management Companies

Owners of large apartment complexes often use property management companies, as do absentee owners. Some absentee owners hire property managers simply because they live too far away to be involved in everyday details; others hire property managers out of necessity—some states require owners who live out of state to hire local, licensed property managers. If you're considering renting out property you own in another state, be sure to research whether that state requires properties to have an in-state manager.

Property management companies generally take care of renting units, collecting rent, taking tenant complaints, arranging repairs and maintenance, and evicting troublesome tenants. Of course, some of these responsibilities can be shared with or delegated to resident managers who, in some instances, might work for the management company.

A variety of relationships between owners and management companies is possible, depending on your wishes and how the particular management company chooses to do business. For example, if you own one or more big buildings, the management company will probably recommend hiring a resident manager. But if your rental property has only a few units, or you own a number of small buildings spread over a good-sized geographical area, the management company will probably suggest simply responding to tenant requests and complaints from its central office.

One advantage of working with a management company is that you avoid all the legal hassles of being an employer: paying payroll taxes, buying workers' compensation insurance, and withholding income tax. The management company is an independent contractor, not an employee. It hires and pays the people who do the work. Typically, you sign a contract spelling out the management company's duties and fees. Most companies charge a fixed percentage—about 6% to 12%—of the total rent collected. (The salary of any resident manager is additional.) This gives the company a good incentive to keep the building filled with rent-paying tenants.

Another advantage is that good management companies are usually well informed about the law, keep thorough records, and are adept at staying out of legal hot water in such areas as discrimination, invasion of privacy, and returning deposits.

The primary disadvantage of hiring a management company is the expense. For example, if you pay a management company 10% of the $14,000 you collect in rent each month from tenants in a 12-unit building, this amounts to $1,400 a month and $16,800 per year. While many companies charge less than 10%, it's still quite an expense—even if you adjust for the fact that the property manager's fee is tax deductible. Also, if the management company works from a central office with no one on-site, tenants might feel that management is too distant and unconcerned with their day-to-day needs.

Management companies have their own contracts, which you should read thoroughly and understand before signing. Be sure you understand how you'll pay the company and its exact responsibilities.

Shop around for a management company—not all are created equal. A management company with a reputation for treating tenants poorly or ignoring service requests can hurt your chances of finding high-quality tenants. And, even though a management company is an independent entity, under certain circumstances a court could find you partially responsible for its misdeeds. Interview people at the company and ask them about past lawsuits or complaints. Ask other landlords in the area about their experiences with the company. In particular, try to learn the eviction rate in buildings they manage. Unusually large numbers of evictions might spell sloppiness in tenant screening or, worse, deliberate indifference. Keep in mind that many management companies get paid apart from their monthly fee every time they advertise and screen applicants, giving them an incentive to perform that task as often as possible.

And, finally, be sure to check online reviews. Online reviews will give you insight into what tenants think about the management company. Give the reviews whatever weight you think is appropriate, keeping in mind that most reviews are written either by people who the company asked for reviews or who had terrible experiences.

Getting the Tenant Moved In

Legal disputes between landlords and tenants can be almost as emotional as divorce court battles. While some might be inevitable, many disputes could be defused at the start if tenants were better educated as to their legal rights and responsibilities. A clearly written and easy-to-understand lease or rental agreement that details a tenant's obligations and is signed by all adult occupants of your rental unit is the best way to start a tenancy. (See Chapter 1.) But there's more that can be done to help establish a positive relationship when new tenants move in. Most important, you should:

- inspect the property, fill out a landlord-tenant checklist with the tenant, and photograph the rental unit, and
- prepare a move-in letter highlighting important terms of the tenancy and your expectations, such as how to report repair problems.

Inspect and Photograph the Unit

Using a landlord-tenant checklist that reflects the condition of the rental property at the beginning and end of the tenancy, with photos and video, is an excellent way to protect both you and your tenant when the tenant moves out and wants the security deposit returned. Without some record as to the condition of the unit, the tenant is all too likely to make unreasonable demands. For example, is there a landlord alive who has not been falsely told that a stained rug or a cracked mirror or broken stove was already damaged when the tenant moved in?

The checklist will provide good evidence as to why you withheld all or part of a security deposit. Coupled with a system to regularly keep track of the rental property's condition, the checklist will also be extremely useful to you if a tenant withholds rent, breaks the lease and moves out,

or sues you outright, claiming the unit needs substantial repairs.

 FORM

Landlord-Tenant Checklist form. You'll find a copy of the Landlord-Tenant Checklist in Appendix C. You can also download this form on the Nolo website; the link is included in Appendix B of this book. A filled-in sample Landlord-Tenant Checklist is shown below.

States That Require a Landlord-Tenant Checklist

A number of states require landlords to give new tenants a written statement on the condition of the rental premises at move-in time, including a comprehensive list of existing damages. Check "Required Landlord Disclosures" in Appendix A for the exact requirements in your state, including the type of inspection required at the end of the tenancy.

How to Fill Out the Checklist

You and the tenants should fill out the checklist together. If that's impossible, complete the form, make a copy, and give it to the tenants to review. Ask the tenants to note any disagreement promptly and return the checklist to you within a few days.

The checklist is in two parts: the General Condition of Rental Unit and Premises, and Checklist for Furnished Property. If your rental is not furnished, you can delete the second part.

You will be filling out the first column—*Move-In Condition*—on or before the tenant's move-in date. You'll fill out the second column—*Move-Out Condition*—when the tenant moves out and you inspect the unit again.

Landlord-Tenant Checklist

Property Address: 572 Fourth Street Apt. 11 Washington, D.C.

General Condition of Rental Unit and Premises

	Move-In Condition Date of Walk-Through: May 1, 20xx	Move-Out Condition Date of Walk-Through:
Living Room		
Flooring	OK, slight wearing from normal use	
Walls & Ceilings	OK	
Light Fixtures	OK	
Window Treatments	Miniblinds on both windows discolored	
Windows & screens	West window rattles, others OK	
Doors & handles/locks	OK	
Fireplace	OK	
Smoke detector & CO detector	Both present and OK	
Other	N/A	
Kitchen		
Flooring	Cigarette burn hole near island	
Walls & Ceilings	OK	
Light Fixtures	OK	
Window treatments	OK	
Windows & screens	OK	
Doors & handles/locks	N/A	
Cabinets	OK, a few knobs are loose	
Counters	Stained near stove	
Stove/oven/range	OK	
Refrigerator	OK	
Dishwasher	OK	
Garbage disposal	N/A	
Microwave	OK	
Stove hood	Burners filthy (grease)	
Sink & plumbing	OK	
Other appliances	N/A	
Smoke detector & CO detector	Smoke detector OK, no CO in kitchen	
Other	N/A	

	Move-In Condition Date of Walk-Through: May 1, 20xx	Move-Out Condition Date of Walk-Through:
Dining Room		
Flooring	OK	
Walls & Ceilings	Cracks in ceiling	
Light Fixtures	Dirty but works OK	
Window treatments	OK	
Windows & screens	OK	
Doors & handles/locks	OK	
Smoke detector & CO detector	N/A	
Other	N/A	
Bathroom		
Flooring	OK	
Walls & ceiling	Wallpaper peeling near ceiling, small patch of mildew. Landlord will clean mildew by 5/15	
Light fixtures	OK	
Window treatments	OK	
Windows & screens	OK	
Doors & handles/locks	OK	
Bathtub/shower (incl. attached door)	Tub chipped	
Sink, counters, & plumbing	OK, tenant notes discoloration of plastic faucet handle	
Cabinets & storage	OK	
Mirror(s)	Some blackening	
Toilet	Base of toilet dirty	
Ceiling fan/ventilation	OK	
Other	N/A	
Bedroom #1		
Flooring	OK	
Walls & ceiling	OK	
Lighting fixtures	OK	
Window treatments	Horizontal blinds don't go up all the way	
Windows & screens	OK	
Doors & handles/locks	Lock on door not working	
Closet	Water stain on closet floor	
Smoke detector & CO detector	Both OK	
Other	N/A	

	Move-In Condition Date of Walk-Through: May 1, 20xx	Move-Out Condition Date of Walk-Through:
Bedroom #2		
Flooring	OK	
Walls & ceiling	OK	
Lighting fixtures	Dented	
Window treatments	Horizontal blinds don't go up all the way	
Windows & screens	OK	
Doors & handles/locks	OK	
Closet	Piece of built-in shelf missing	
Smoke detector & CO detector	Both OK	
Other	N/A	
Other Areas		
Heating, A/C (mechanical room)	OK	
Lawn/garden	N/A	
Stairs and landings	N/A	
Patio, terrace, deck, etc.	Needs staining, otherwise OK	
Basement	N/A	
Garage	N/A	
Attic	N/A	
Entryway	N/A	
Laundry room	N/A	
Other	N/A	

☑ Tenants acknowledge that all smoke detectors were tested in their presence and found to be in working order, and that the testing procedure was explained to them. Tenants agree to promptly notify Landlord in writing should any smoke detector appear to be malfunctioning or inoperable. Tenants will not refuse Landlord access for the purpose of inspecting, maintaining, repairing, or installing legally-required smoke detectors.

☑ Tenants acknowledge that all carbon monoxide detectors were tested in their presence and found to be in working order, and that the testing procedure was explained to them. Tenants agree to promptly notify Landlord in writing should any carbon monoxide detector appear to be malfunctioning or inoperable. Tenants will not refuse Landlord access for the purpose of inspecting, maintaining, repairing, or installing legally-required carbon monoxide detectors.

Checklist for Furnished Property

	Move-Out Condition Date of Walk-Through: May 1, 20xx	Move-Out Condition Date of Walk-Through:
Living Room		
Coffee table	Two scratches on top	
End tables	OK	
Lamps	OK	
Chairs	OK	
Sofa	OK, a bit worn but no stains	
Decorative items (unattached mirrors, rugs, pictures, vases, etc.)	Rug has small tear	
Electronics	Modem and router in living room; both functioning well	
Other	N/A	
Kitchen		
No furnishings in kitchen		
Dining Room		
Chairs	4 dining room chairs, one wobbles	
Stools	N/A	
Table	OK	
Lamps	N/A	
Decorative items (unattached mirrors, rugs, pictures, vases, etc.)	1 framed painting, OK condition	
Electronics	N/A	
Other	One wooden buffet, scuffed and worn condition	
Bathroom		
Shelves & storage (unattached)	N/A	
Shower curtain & rod	Rod slightly rusted, no curtain	
Hamper	N/A	
Linens	N/A	
Decorative items (unattached mirrors, rugs, pictures, vases, etc.)	Two magnifying mirrors, good condition	
Other	Scale, working condition	

	Move-Out Condition Date of Walk-Through: May 1, 20xx	Move-Out Condition Date of Walk-Through:
Bedroom #1		
Bed(s)	1 queen size frame, box spring, mattress. All brand new.	
Chairs	N/A	
Bureau	N/A	
Chests	N/A	
Dressing table	N/A	
Bedside tables	2 small wooden, good condition	
Lamps	2 bedside lamps, good condition	
Linens	N/A	
Decorative items (unattached mirrors, rugs, pictures, vases, etc.)	Woven wall hanging, good condition	
Electronics	Flat screen TV, new	
Other	N/A	
Bedroom #2		
Bedroom #2 has no furnishings		
Other Areas		
Desks	N/A	
Shelves	Shoe shelf in entry	
Books, games, media	N/A	
Decorative items (unattached mirrors, rugs, pictures, vases, etc.)	N/A	
Electronics	Video doorbell, newly installed, located outside entry door	
Tools (yard and workshop)	N/A	
Trash & recycling bins	N/A	
Outdoor furniture	Metal café set on deck-small table and 2 chairs. Brand new.	
Recreational equipment	N/A	
Other	N/A	

Use this space to provide any additional explanation:

_____

_____

_____

_____

_____

_____

Landlord-Tenant Checklist completed on moving in on _____ May 1, 20xx _____
and approved by:

_____ *Bennie Cohen* _____ and _____ *Maria Crouse* _____
Landlord/Manager   Tenant

_____ *Sandra Martino* _____
Tenant

_____
Tenant

Landlord-Tenant Checklist completed on moving out on _____
and approved by:

_____ and _____
Landlord/Manager   Tenant

_____
Tenant

_____
Tenant

Each room has its own section in the Checklist. If you happen to be renting a one-bedroom, one-bath unit, our preprinted form will work just fine. However, chances are that your rental has a different number of rooms or elements in those rooms than those on the checklist form. Changes are no problem if you use the downloadable form. You can change the entries by adding or deleting rows and columns. For example, if you want to add a room, simply copy the Bedroom section, paste it into the table, and label it Bedroom #2. You may also delete sections and items if they are not included with your property.

General Condition of Rental Unit and Premises

In the *Move-In Condition* column, make detailed notes about items that aren't working or are dirty, scratched, or in poor condition. For example, don't simply note that the refrigerator "needs fixing" if the ice maker doesn't work—it's just as easy to write "ice maker broken, should not be used, expect to accomplish repair within a month of tenants' move-in." If the tenants use the ice maker anyway and cause water damage, they cannot claim that they weren't aware it wasn't working properly.

You should remedy any mold, pest, or other habitability issues before new tenants move in. However, if you aren't aware of the problem until the move-in inspection, describe it in the Checklist and note that you will be repairing it within a certain timeframe. (And don't forget to follow through on your promise to repair!)

Mark "OK" next to items that are in satisfactory condition—basically, clean, safe, sanitary, and in good working order.

Checklist for Furnished Property

If your rental is unfurnished or includes only a few furnishings that you can include in the first part of the Checklist, you can delete this part.

On the other hand, if your rental is fully or significantly furnished, you'll want to use this part of the Checklist to inventory and describe the included items.

You can delete items that aren't present in your rental, or you can place "N/A" in the applicable box. You can also add as many items or rooms to the Checklist as you need.

CAUTION
As part of your move-in procedures, make sure you test all smoke detectors, carbon monoxide (CO) detectors, and fire extinguishers in the tenant's presence and confirm they are in good working order. Clearly explain to the tenant how to test the smoke and CO detectors and point out the signs—for example, a beeping noise—of a failing detector. Alert tenants to their responsibility to regularly test smoke and CO detectors, and explain how to replace the battery when necessary. Be sure the tenants check the boxes at the end of the Checklist acknowledging that the smoke and CO detectors were tested in their presence and shown to be in working order. By doing this, you'll limit your liability if a detector fails and results in fire damage or injury. Testing and demonstrating the use of smoke and CO detectors at move-in is required in many cities and states.

Sign the Checklist

After you and the tenants agree on the matters covered in the Checklist, each of you should sign and date every page, as well as any attachments (such as a separate list of furnishings), on both sides. Keep the original checklist for yourself and attach a copy to the tenants' lease or rental agreement. (This Checklist is referred to in Clause 11 of the form agreements in Chapter 1.)

Be sure to keep the Checklist up to date if you repair, replace, add, or remove items or furnishings after the tenants move in. Both you and the tenants should initial and date any changes on the original, signed Checklist.

Photograph the Rental Unit

Taking photos or videos of the unit before new tenants move in is another excellent way to record the initial condition of the rental. You'll be able to compare your "after" pictures at the end of the tenancy with the "before" pictures, as well as refer to the written record you created via the Checklist. And, if tenants claim that damage was present when they moved in, you can show them the records to refresh their memory.

If you end up in mediation or court for not returning the full security deposit, having a visual record of the unit's condition will be invaluable. In addition, photos or a video can also help if you have to sue a former tenant for cleaning and repair costs that end up being more than the deposit amount.

Whether you take photos with your phone or use a separate camera, be sure that the photos are date- and time-stamped. If you make a video, clearly state the time and date when the video was made. Provide copies of the photos and videos to the tenants. Don't trust your phone to keep this evidence safe—upload the files to a secure place on the cloud.

You should repeat this process when the tenants leave, as part of your standard move-out procedure. (Chapter 4 discusses how to prepare a move-out letter.)

Send New Tenants a Move-In Letter

A move-in letter supplements the lease or rental agreement and provides basic information, such as the manager's phone number and office hours.

You can also use a move-in letter to explain any procedures and rules that are too detailed or numerous to include in your lease or rental agreement. (Alternatively, large landlords might want to use a set of tenant rules and regulations to cover some of these issues. See Clause 18 of the form agreements in Chapter 1.)

Here are some items you might want to cover in a move-in letter:

- how and where to report maintenance and repair problems
- any lock-out or rekey fees
- use of grounds and garage
- your policy regarding rent increases for additional roommates
- location of garbage cans, available recycling programs, and trash pickup days
- maintenance dos and don'ts, such as how to avoid overloading circuits and use the garbage disposal properly, and
- any other issues, such as pool hours, elevator operation, laundry room usage, and storage space.

Because every rental situation is unique, we can't supply you with a generic move-in letter that works for everyone. However, you can use the sample shown here as a model in preparing your own.

We recommend asking tenants to sign the last page of your move-in letter to indicate that they have read it. As an extra precaution, you can ask tenants to initial each page. After everyone has signed, keep a copy for your records and give one to the tenants.

Review your move-in letter before you provide it to a new tenant, and update it as needed.

FORM

Move-In Letter form. You'll find a copy of the Move-In Letter in Appendix C of this book. You can also download this form on the Nolo website; the link is included in Appendix B. A filled-in sample move-in letter is shown below.

Move-In Letter

Date ___September 1, 20xx___

Tenant ___Frank O'Hara___

Street Address ___139 Porter Street___

City and State ___Madison, Wisconsin 53704___

Dear ___Frank___ ,
_____ Tenant

Welcome to ___Apartment 45 B at Happy Hill Apartments___
_____ (address of rental unit). We hope you will enjoy living here. This letter is to explain what you can expect from the management and what we'll be looking for from you.

1. Rent: ___Rent is due on the first day of the month. There is no grace period for the payment of rent. (See Clauses 5 and 6 of your rental agreement for details, including late charges.) Also, we don't accept postdated checks.___

2. New Roommates: ___If you want someone to move in as a roommate, please contact us first. If your rental unit is big enough to accommodate another person, we will arrange for the new person to fill out a rental application. If it's approved, all of you will need to sign a new rental agreement. Depending on the situation, there might be a rent increase to add a roommate. Note that under our written agreement, you may not sublet without our prior approval. This includes short-term vacation rentals through Airbnb or similar services.___

3. Notice to End Tenancy: ___To terminate your month-to-month tenancy, you must give at least 28 days' written notice. We have a written form available for this purpose. We may also terminate the tenancy, or change its terms, on 28 days' written notice. If you give less than 28 days' notice, you will still be financially responsible for rent for the balance of the 28-day period.___

4. Deposits: ___Your security deposit will be applied to costs of cleaning, damages, or unpaid rent after you move out. You may not apply any part of the deposit toward any part of your rent in the last month of your tenancy. (See Clause 8 of your rental agreement.)___

5. Manager: ___Sophie Beauchamp (Apartment #15, phone 555-1234, email Sophie@sophie.com) is your resident manager. You should pay your rent to her at that address and promptly let her know of any maintenance or repair problems (see #7, below) and any other questions or problems. She's in her office every day from 8 a.m. to 10 a.m. and from 4 p.m. to 6 p.m. and can be reached by phone at other times.___

6. Landlord-Tenant Checklist: ___By now, Sophie Beauchamp should have taken you on a walk-through of your apartment to check the condition of all walls, drapes, carpets, and appliances and to test the smoke alarms and fire extinguisher. These are all listed on the Landlord-Tenant Checklist, which you should have reviewed carefully and signed. When you move out, we will ask you to check each item against its original condition as described on the Checklist.___

7. Maintenance/Repair Problems: We are determined to maintain a clean, safe building in which all systems are in good repair. To help us make repairs promptly, we will give you Maintenance/Repair Request forms to report to the manager any problems in your apartment, such as a broken garbage disposal, or on the building or grounds, such a burned-out light in the garage. (Extra copies are available from the manager.) In an emergency, or when it's not convenient to use this form, please call the manager at 555-1234.

8. Semiannual Safety and Maintenance Update: To help us keep your unit and the common areas in excellent condition, we'll ask you to fill out a form every six months updating any problems on the premises or in your rental unit. This will allow you to report any potential safety hazards or other problems that otherwise might be overlooked.

9. Annual Safety Inspection: Once a year, we will ask to inspect the condition and furnishings of your rental unit and update the Landlord-Tenant Checklist. In keeping with state law, we will give you reasonable notice before the inspection, and you are encouraged to be present for it.

10. Insurance: We highly recommend that you purchase renters' insurance. The building property insurance policy will not cover the replacement of your personal belongings if they are lost due to fire, theft, or accident. In addition, you could be found liable if someone is injured on the premises you rent as a result of your negligence. If you damage the building itself—for example, if you start a fire in the kitchen and it spreads—you could be responsible for large repair bills.

11. Moving Out: It's a little early to bring up moving out, but please be aware that we have a list of items that should be cleaned before we conduct a move-out inspection. If you decide to move, please ask the manager for a copy of our Move-Out Letter, explaining our procedures for inspection and returning your deposit.

12. Changes to Your Contact Information: Please notify us if your phone numbers change, so we can reach you promptly in an emergency.

Please let us know if you have any questions.

Sincerely,

Tom Guiliano
_____
Landlord/Manager

September 1, 20xx
_____
Date

I have read and received a copy of this statement.

Frank O'Hara
_____
Tenant

September 1, 20xx
_____
Date

Cash Rent and Security Deposit Checks

Every landlord's nightmare is a new tenant whose deposit or first rent check bounces.

To avoid this, never sign a lease or rental agreement, or let a tenant move furniture into your property or give the tenant a key, until you have the tenant's cash, certified check, or money order for the first month's rent and security deposit. Alternatively, deposit the tenant's check at the bank and make sure it clears before the move-in date. (While you have the tenant's first check, photocopy it for your records. The information on it can be helpful if you need to sue to collect a judgment from the tenant.) Be sure to give the tenant a signed receipt for the deposit.

Clause 5 of the form lease and rental agreements in Chapter 1 requires tenants to pay rent on the first day of each month. If the move-in date is other than the first day of the month, rent is prorated between that day and the end of that month.

Organize Your Tenant Records

Develop a system for recording all significant tenant complaints and repair requests, as well as your responses. This will provide a valuable paper trail should disputes develop later. Without good records, the outcome of a dispute could come down to your word against your tenant's—always a precarious situation.

Set up a file folder on each property with individual files for each tenant. Include the following documents in each tenant's file:

- tenant's rental application, credit report, and references, including information about any cosigners
- the signed lease or rental agreement, plus any changes or addenda

- the Landlord-Tenant Checklist plus photos or video made at move-in (or a note as to where to find these online), and
- a signed move-in letter.

After a tenant moves in, add these documents to the individual's file:

- your written requests for entry
- rent increase notices
- records of repair requests and details of how and when they were handled (if you keep repair records on the computer, you should regularly print out and save files from past months; if you have a master system to record all requests and complaints in one log, you would save that log separately, not necessarily put it in every tenant's file.)
- safety and maintenance updates and inspection reports, and
- correspondence (including copies of important emails and texts).

Your computer can also be a valuable tool to keep track of tenants. Set up a simple spreadsheet for each tenant with spaces for the following information:

- address or unit number
- move-in date
- phone number (cell, home, work)
- email
- name, address, and phone number of employer
- credit information and up-to-date banking information
- monthly rent amount and rent due date
- amount and purpose of deposits plus any information your state requires on location of deposit and interest payments
- details about the tenant's pet or service animal, if applicable
- vehicle make, model, color, year, and license plate number
- emergency contacts, and
- whatever else is important to you.

Once you enter the information into your spreadsheet, you'll be able to sort the list by address or other variables and easily print labels for rent increases or other notices.

If you own many rental properties, you should consider a property management software program that allows you to keep track of every aspect of your business, from the tracking of rents to the follow-up on repair requests.

Organize Income and Expenses for Schedule E

If you've been in the landlording business for any length of time, you will be used to reporting your income and expenses on Schedule E (assuming you file IRS Form 1040 to pay your taxes). The Schedule is relatively simple. For each address (which could include multiple rental units), you report the year's rent and list enumerated expenses (the first page of Schedule E is reproduced below). You can download a fillable version of Schedule E from www.IRS.gov.

Many landlords find it easiest to use *QuickBooks* or another accounting software package to track their income and expenses.

You can also use programs designed specifically for completing Schedule E, notably *Quicken Rental Property Manager,* which allows you to track income, expenses, and tax deductions and converts the information into a Schedule E at tax time. You can also design your own spreadsheet using *Excel* or a similar program to keep track of rental income and expenses. Finally, there's always the old-fashioned way of making your own paper ledger of income and expenses.

Of course, the system you use to track income and expenses is only as good as the information you enter. To maximize tax deductions, keep receipts and records of all rental-property–related expenses, such as interest payments on mortgage loans, property taxes, professional fees (your accountant, attorney, property management), insurance, repairs, advertising and tenant screening, and membership fees, plus all income from rent, late fees, and the like (including the cost of this book).

RESOURCE

For detailed information on completing Schedule E and valuable tax advice for landlords, see *Every Landlord's Tax Deduction Guide*, by Stephen Fishman (Nolo). For personalized advice, consult an accountant or tax professional (and remember, buying this book, or consulting with a tax pro, are both tax-deductible expenses).

SCHEDULE E (Form 1040)	**Supplemental Income and Loss**	OMB No. 1545-0074

SCHEDULE E
(Form 1040)

Department of the Treasury
Internal Revenue Service (99)

Supplemental Income and Loss

(From rental real estate, royalties, partnerships, S corporations, estates, trusts, REMICs, etc.)

▶ Attach to Form 1040, 1040-SR, 1040-NR, or 1041.

▶ Go to *www.irs.gov/ScheduleE* for instructions and the latest information.

OMB No. 1545-0074

20**20**

Attachment
Sequence No. **13**

Name(s) shown on return

Your social security number

Part I   **Income or Loss From Rental Real Estate and Royalties**   **Note:** If you are in the business of renting personal property, use **Schedule C.** See instructions. If you are an individual, report farm rental income or loss from **Form 4835** on page 2, line 40.

A Did you make any payments in 2020 that would require you to file Form(s) 1099? See instructions . . . . . ☐ **Yes** ☐ **No**

B If "Yes," did you or will you file required Form(s) 1099? . . . . ☐ **Yes** ☐ **No**

1a Physical address of each property (street, city, state, ZIP code)

A

B

C

1b	Type of Property (from list below)	**2**	For each rental real estate property listed above, report the number of fair rental and personal use days. Check the **QJV** box only if you meet the requirements to file as a qualified joint venture. See instructions.		Fair Rental Days	Personal Use Days	QJV
A				**A**			☐
B				**B**			☐
C				**C**			☐

Type of Property:

1 Single Family Residence   3 Vacation/Short-Term Rental   5 Land   7 Self-Rental

2 Multi-Family Residence   4 Commercial   6 Royalties   8 Other (describe)

Income:		**Properties:**		**A**	**B**	**C**
3	Rents received	**3**				
4	Royalties received	**4**				
Expenses:						
5	Advertising	**5**				
6	Auto and travel (see instructions)	**6**				
7	Cleaning and maintenance	**7**				
8	Commissions.	**8**				
9	Insurance	**9**				
10	Legal and other professional fees	**10**				
11	Management fees	**11**				
12	Mortgage interest paid to banks, etc. (see instructions)	**12**				
13	Other interest.	**13**				
14	Repairs.	**14**				
15	Supplies	**15**				
16	Taxes	**16**				
17	Utilities	**17**				
18	Depreciation expense or depletion	**18**				
19	Other (list) ▶	**19**				
20	Total expenses. Add lines 5 through 19	**20**				
21	Subtract line 20 from line 3 (rents) and/or 4 (royalties). If result is a (loss), see instructions to find out if you must file **Form 6198**	**21**				
22	Deductible rental real estate loss after limitation, if any, on **Form 8582** (see instructions)	**22**	(	)(	)(	)

23a	Total of all amounts reported on line 3 for all rental properties	**23a**	
b	Total of all amounts reported on line 4 for all royalty properties	**23b**	
c	Total of all amounts reported on line 12 for all properties	**23c**	
d	Total of all amounts reported on line 18 for all properties	**23d**	
e	Total of all amounts reported on line 20 for all properties	**23e**	
24	**Income.** Add positive amounts shown on line 21. **Do not** include any losses	**24**	
25	**Losses.** Add royalty losses from line 21 and rental real estate losses from line 22. Enter total losses here .	**25**	( )
26	**Total rental real estate and royalty income or (loss).** Combine lines 24 and 25. Enter the result here. If Parts II, III, IV, and line 40 on page 2 do not apply to you, also enter this amount on Schedule 1 (Form 1040), line 5. Otherwise, include this amount in the total on line 41 on page 2 .	**26**	

For Paperwork Reduction Act Notice, see the separate instructions.   Cat. No. 11344L   **Schedule E (Form 1040) 2020**

Changing or Ending a Tenancy

At some point after you've signed a lease or rental agreement, you might want to make changes—perhaps to increase the rent, or to let the tenant bring in a roommate or keep a pet. This chapter shows how to modify a signed lease or rental agreement. It also discusses how you—or your tenant—can end a tenancy, and offers tips on how to head off problems such as a tenant giving inadequate notice or breaking the lease. This chapter also summarizes the basic rules for returning security deposits.

How to Modify Signed Rental Agreements and Leases

All amendments to your lease or rental agreement should be in writing and signed by everyone who signed the original lease, including you, the tenants, and any cosigners.

Amending a Fixed-Term Lease

If you use a fixed-term lease, you cannot unilaterally alter the terms of the tenancy. You can't raise the rent or change the terms of the lease until the end of the lease period unless the lease allows it or the tenant agrees. If the tenant agrees to changes, however, simply follow the directions below for amending the rental agreement.

Amending a Month-to-Month Rental Agreement

If you want to change one or more clauses in a month-to-month rental agreement, no law requires that you get the tenant's consent. Legally, you simply send the tenant a notice of the change.

Most states require 30 days' advance notice (subject to any rent control laws) to change a month-to-month tenancy. (See the "State Rules on Notice Required to Change or Terminate a Month-to-Month Tenancy" chart in Appendix A

for a list of each state's notice requirements, and Clause 4 of the rental agreement in Chapter 1.) You'll need to consult your state statutes for the specific information on how you must deliver a notice to the tenant. (Most allow you to use first-class mail.)

Amending a Lease or Rental Agreement for COVID-Related Reasons

Many landlords are adjusting their rental practices to reflect new arrangements necessitated by coronavirus-related concerns. These changes often involve amending (at least temporarily) parts of the lease or rental agreement relating to:

Rent. Landlords are extending rent due dates, accepting rent in installments, reducing rent, and renouncing late fees

Guest policies. Landlords are being flexible with guest policies, and are amending or adding guest clauses to reflect the temporary presence of an additional person who has had to move due to health problems, job or housing loss, or the need to leave a household with an actively sick roommate, and

Security deposits. Landlords are agreeing to use the deposit to cover rent, and allowing it to be replenished over a set period of time.

You might need to address other issues with your tenants. Nolo offers an amendment form ($1.00) to guide you through possible variations. We caution all users to determine whether they are subject to a federal, state, or local eviction; and whether the moratorium imposes restrictions on items such as late fees, rent repayment plans, and security deposit use.

To purchase the amendment form, go to Nolo. com and type "Coronavirus-Related Amendment to Residential Lease" in the search box on the home page.

TIP

Contact the tenant and explain the changes. It makes good personal and business sense for you or your manager to contact the tenant personally and explain a rent increase or other changes before you follow up with a written notice. If the tenant is opposed to your proposal, your personal efforts will allow you to explain your reasons.

Generally, you don't need to redo the entire rental agreement in order to make a change or two. Just keep a copy of the amendment with the original rental agreement. If the change is small and simply alters part of an existing clause—such as increasing the rent or making the rent payable every 14 days instead of every 30 days—you can cross out the old language, write in the new (don't forget to indicate when the new rent kicks in), and sign in the margin next to the new words. Make sure the tenant also signs next to the change. Add the date that the two of you signed, in case a dispute later arises as to when everyone agreed to the new rent.

Preparing a New Lease or Rental Agreement

In some cases, however, you might want the tenant to sign a new rental agreement. For example, if you're adding a clause or making several changes to your lease or rental agreement, you will probably find it easiest to substitute a whole new agreement for the old one. If you prepare an entire new agreement, be sure that you and the tenant write "Canceled by mutual consent, effective (date)" on the old one, and sign it. In order to avoid the possibility of two inconsistent agreements operating at the same time, be sure that there is no time overlap between the old and new agreements. Similarly, so that the tenant is always subject to a written agreement, do not allow any gap between the cancellation date of the old agreement and the effective date of the new one.

TIP

A new tenant should mean a new agreement. Even when a new tenant is filling out the rest of a former tenant's lease term under the same conditions, it is never wise to allow the new resident to operate under the same lease or rental agreement. Start over and prepare a new agreement in the new tenant's name. (See Clause 10 of the form agreements in Chapter 2.)

Ending a Month-to-Month Tenancy

This section discusses a landlord's and a tenant's responsibilities when ending a month-to-month tenancy.

Giving Notice to the Tenant

You can end a month-to-month tenancy simply by giving the proper amount of notice. You don't usually have to state a reason, unless state or local law requires it. In most places, all you need to do is give the tenant a simple written notice that complies with your state's minimum notice requirement and states the date on which the tenancy will end. After that date, the tenant no longer has the legal right to occupy the premises.

In most states, and for most rentals, landlords who want to terminate a month-to-month tenancy must provide the same amount of notice as tenants—typically 30 days (discussed below). But this is not true everywhere. For example, in Georgia, landlords must give 60 days' notice to terminate a month-to-month tenancy, while tenants must give only 30 days' notice. (See the "State Rules on Notice Required to Change or Terminate a Month-to-Month Tenancy" chart in Appendix A.) State and local rent control laws can also impose notice requirements on landlords.

Different rules apply when you want a tenant to move because the tenant has violated a material term of the rental agreement—for example, by failing to pay rent. If so, the required notice periods are usually much shorter.

Restrictions to Ending a Tenancy

The general rules for terminating a tenancy described in this chapter often don't apply in the following situations:

- **Rent control ordinances.** Many rent control cities require "just cause" (a good reason) to end a tenancy, which typically includes moving in a close relative and refurbishing the unit. You will likely have to state your legal reason in the termination notice you give the tenant.
- **Discrimination.** It is illegal to end a tenancy because of a tenant's race, religion, or sex; because they have children; or for any other reason constituting illegal discrimination.
- **Retaliation.** You cannot legally terminate a tenancy to retaliate against a tenant for exercising any tenant-related right under the law, such as the tenant's right to complain to governmental authorities about defective housing conditions or, in many states, to withhold rent because of a health or safety problem the landlord has failed to correct. Chapter 16 of Nolo's *Every Landlord's Legal Guide* covers how to avoid tenant retaliation claims.

Each state (and even some cities) has its own detailed rules and procedures for preparing and serving termination notices, making it impossible to provide state-specific forms and instructions in this book. Consult a landlords' association or a local landlord-tenant organization along with your state statutes for information and sample forms. Once you find out how much notice you must give, how the notice must be delivered, and any other requirements, you'll be in good shape to handle this work yourself—usually with no lawyer needed.

How Much Notice the Tenant Must Give

In most states, a tenant who decides to move out must give you at least 30 days' notice. Some states allow less than 30 days' notice in certain situations—for example, when a tenant must leave early due to military orders or health problems. And, in some states, tenants who pay rent more frequently than once a month can give notice to terminate that matches their rent payment interval—for example, tenants who pay rent every two weeks would have to give 14 days' notice. Special rules apply to tenants in active military service. (See "Special Rules for Active Military Tenants," below.)

To educate your tenants, make sure your rental agreement includes your state's notice requirements for ending a tenancy. (See Clause 4 of the form agreements in Chapter 1.) It is also wise to list termination notice requirements in the move-in letter (discussed in Chapter 3) you send to new tenants.

For details about your state's requirements, see the "State Rules on Notice Required to Change or Terminate a Month-to-Month Tenancy" table in Appendix A.

Insist on a Tenant's Written Notice of Intent to Move

In many states, a tenant's notice must be in writing and give the exact date the tenant plans to move out. Even if it is not required by law, it's a good idea to insist that the tenant give you notice in writing (as does Clause 4 of the form agreements in Chapter 1).

Insisting on written notice will prove essential should your old tenants not move as planned after you have signed a lease or rental agreement with a new tenant. Not only will a written notice support your position if, at the last minute, the tenants try to claim that they didn't really set a firm move-out date, but it will also be invaluable if a new tenant sues you to recover the costs of temporary housing or storage fees because you could not deliver possession of the unit. In turn, you will want to sue the old (holdover) tenants for causing the problem by failing to move out. You will have a much stronger case against the holdover tenants if you can produce a written promise to move on a specific date, instead of your version of a conversation (which the tenants will undoubtedly dispute).

A sample tenant's notice of intent to move out form is shown below. Give a copy of this form to any tenant who announces a plan to move.

 FORM

Tenant's Intent to Move Out form.
You'll find a copy of the Tenant's Notice of Intent to Move Out in Appendix C of this book. You can also download this form on the Nolo website; the link is included in Appendix B of this book. A filled-in sample Tenant's Notice of Intent to Move Out form is shown below.

Special Rules for Active Military Tenants

Tenants who are in the active military, or who enter military service after signing a lease or rental agreement, may terminate when they receive permanent change of station orders or are deployed to a new location for 90 days or more. (Servicemembers Civil Relief Act, 50 App. U.S.C. §§ 3901 and following.) Tenants must mail written notice of their intent to terminate their tenancy for military reasons to the landlord or manager.

Rental agreements. Once the tenant mails or delivers the notice, the tenancy will terminate 30 days after the day that rent is next due. For example, if rent is due on the first of June and the tenant mails a notice on May 28, the tenancy will terminate on July 1. This rule takes precedence over any longer notice periods that might be specified in your rental agreement or by state law. If state law or your agreement provides for shorter notice periods, however, the shorter notice will control. Recently, many states have passed laws that offer the same or greater protections to members of the state defense force or National Guard.

Leases. A tenant who enters military service after signing a lease may terminate the lease by following the procedure for rental agreements, above. For example, suppose a tenant signs a one-year lease in April, agreeing to pay rent on the first of the month. The tenant enlists October 10 and mails you a termination notice on October 11. In this case, you must terminate the tenancy on December 1, 30 days after the first time that rent is due (November 1) following the mailing of the notice. This tenant will have no continuing obligation for rent past December 1, even though this is several months before the lease expires.

Tenant's Notice of Intent to Move Out

Date ___April 3, 20xx_____

Landlord ___Anne Sakamoto_____

Street Address ___888 Mill Avenue_____

City and State___Nashville, Tennessee 37126_____

Dear ___Ms. Sakamoto_____ ,
                          Landlord

This is to notify you that the undersigned Tenant(s), ___Patti and Joe Ellis_____

_____ , will be moving from

___999 Brook Lane, Apartment Number 11_____ ,

on ___May 3, 20xx_____ , ___30 days_____ from today. This

provides at least _____30 days'_____ written notice as required in the rental

agreement.

Sincerely,

_Patti Ellis_____
Tenant
_Joe Ellis_____
Tenant
_____
Tenant

Preparing a Move-Out Letter

Chapter 3 explains how a move-in letter can help get a tenancy off to a good start. Similarly, a move-out letter can also help reduce the possibility of disputes, especially over the return of security deposits. Send the letter as soon as you receive notice of the tenant's intent to leave. Your move-out letter should explain the following:

- how you expect the rental unit to be left, including specific cleaning requirements
- details on your final inspection procedures and how you will determine the level of cleaning and damage repair that you require
- the kinds of deposit deductions that you can legally make, and
- when and how you will send any refund.

See below for more detail on returning security deposits and on final inspection procedures.

FORM

Tenant's Move-Out Letter form. You'll find a copy of the Move-Out Letter in Appendix C of this book. You can also download this form on the Nolo website; the link is included in Appendix B of this book. A filled-in sample move-out letter form is shown below.

Accepting Rent After a Tenant Gives a 30-Day Notice

If you accept rent for any period beyond the date the tenants told you they are moving out, this likely cancels the termination notice and creates a new tenancy. Accepting (and documenting in writing) past-due rent from a tenant who has given notice will not cancel a termination notice, however.

Suppose, after giving notice, the tenant asks for a little more time in which to move out. Assuming no new tenant is moving in and you are willing to accommodate this request, prepare a written agreement setting out what you have agreed to in detail, and have the tenant sign it. See the sample letter, below, extending the tenant's move-out date.

CAUTION

If you collected the "last month's rent" when the tenant moved in, do not accept rent for the last month of the tenancy. You are legally obligated to use this money for the last month's rent. Accepting an additional month's rent might extend the tenant's tenancy.

When the Tenant Doesn't Give the Required Notice

All too often, tenants will send or give you a "too short" notice of intent to move. And it's not unheard of for tenants to move out with no notice or with a wave as they toss the keys on your desk.

Tenants who leave without giving enough notice have lost the right to occupy the premises but are still obligated to pay rent through the end of the required notice period. For example, when the notice period is 30 days, but the tenants move out 20 days after telling you of their plan to move, they still owe you rent for the remaining ten days.

In most states, you have a legal duty to try to rerent the property before you can charge tenants for giving you too little notice, but few courts expect a landlord to accomplish this in less than a month. (This rule, called the landlord's duty to mitigate damages, is discussed below.) You can also use the security deposit to cover unpaid rent (also discussed below).

Move-Out Letter

Date _____ July 5, 20xx _____

Tenant _____ Jane Wasserman _____

Street Address _____ 123 North Street, Apartment #23 _____

City and State _____ Atlanta, Georgia 30360 _____

Dear _____ Jane _____ ,
                              Tenant

We hope you have enjoyed living here. In order that we can mutually end our relationship on a positive note, this move-out letter describes how we expect your unit to be left and what our procedures are for returning your security deposit.

Basically, we expect you to leave your rental unit in the same condition it was when you moved in, except for normal wear and tear. To refresh your memory on the condition of the unit when you moved in, I've attached a copy of the Landlord-Tenant Checklist you signed at the beginning of your tenancy. I'll be using this same form to inspect your unit when you leave.

Specifically, here's a list of items you should thoroughly clean before vacating:

- ☑ Floors
    - ☑ sweep wood floors
    - ☑ vacuum carpets and rugs (shampoo if necessary)
    - ☑ mop kitchen and bathroom floors
- ☑ Walls, baseboards, ceilings, and built-in shelves
- ☑ Kitchen cabinets, countertops and sink, stove and oven—inside and out
- ☑ Refrigerator—clean inside and out, empty it of food, and turn it off, with the door left open
- ☑ Bathtubs, showers, toilets, and plumbing fixtures
- ☑ Doors, windows, and window coverings
- ☑ Other _____

Microwave oven—clean inside and out

_____

_____

_____

_____

If you have any questions as to the type of cleaning we expect, please let me know.

Please don't leave anything behind—that includes bags of garbage, clothes, food, newspapers, furniture, appliances, dishes, plants, cleaning supplies, or other items that belong to you.

Please be sure you have disconnected phone and utility services, changed your address for regular deliveries and subscriptions, and sent the post office a change of address form.

Once you have cleaned your unit and removed all your belongings, please call me at ___555-1234___ to arrange for a walk-through inspection and to return all keys. Please be prepared to give me your forwarding address where we may mail your security deposit.

It's our policy to return all deposits either in person or at an address you provide within ___one month___ _____ after you move out. If any deductions are made—for past-due rent or because the unit is damaged or not sufficiently clean—they will be explained in writing.

If you have any questions, please contact me at ___555-1234___ .

Sincerely,

Denise Parsons
Landlord/Manager

When You or Your Tenant Violates the Rental Agreement

If you seriously violate the rental agreement and fail to fulfill your legal responsibilities— for example, by not correcting serious health or safety problems—a tenant might legally be able to move out with no written notice or by giving less notice than is otherwise required. Called "constructive eviction," this doctrine typically applies only when living conditions are intolerable—for example, when a tenant has had no heat for an extended period in the winter, or when a tenant's use and enjoyment of the property has been substantially impaired because of drug dealing in the building.

The laws regarding constructive eviction vary slightly from state to state.

Generally, when a landlord is on notice that a rental unit has serious habitability problems for an extended time, the tenant is entitled to move out on short notice or, in extreme cases, without giving notice.

Along the same lines, landlords can evict tenants who violate a lease or rental agreement. For example, you may give a "notice to quit" to a tenant who fails to pay rent or damages the premises with less notice than is normally required to end a tenancy (typically three to five days, rather than 30 days). And, in the case of drug dealing, many states provide for expedited eviction procedures. Because state eviction rules and procedures vary greatly, the details of how to evict a tenant are beyond the scope of this book.

How Fixed-Term Leases End

A lease lasts for a fixed term, typically one year. As a general rule, neither you nor the tenant may unilaterally terminate the tenancy or change a material condition during the period of the lease, unless the other party has violated the terms of the lease. (There's an exception for tenants who join the military and want to terminate a lease,

as explained in "Special Rules for Active Military Tenants," above.)

When you and the tenant each live up to your promises, the lease simply ends of its own accord at the end of the lease term, and the tenant moves out. Alternatively, you could sign a new lease, with the same or different terms. As every landlord knows, however, life is not always so simple. Sooner or later, a tenant will stay beyond the end of the term without signing a new lease, or leave before the lease term ends without any legal justification for doing so.

Giving Notice to the Tenant

Because a lease specifies when it will end, you might not think it's necessary to remind the tenants of the expiration date. But doing so is a very good practice, and some states or cities (especially those with rent control) actually require it.

We suggest giving the tenant at least 60 days' written notice that the lease is going to expire. This reminder has several advantages. It can:

- **Get the tenants out on time.** Two months' notice allows plenty of time for the tenants to look for another place if they don't—or you don't—want to renew the lease.

- **Give you time to renegotiate the lease.** If you would like to continue renting to your present tenant but also want to change some lease terms or increase the rent, your notice serves to remind the tenant that the terms of the old lease will not automatically continue. Encourage the tenant to stay, but mention that you need to make some changes to the lease.

- **Allow you to find a new tenant quickly.** If you know a tenant is going to move, you can show the unit to prospective tenants ahead of time and minimize the time the space is vacant. You must still respect the current tenant's privacy. (Chapter 2 discusses showing the unit to prospective tenants.)

Sample Letter Extending Tenant's Move-Out Date

June 20, 20xx

Kalinda Blake
777 Broadway Terrace, Apartment #3
Richmond, Virginia 23233

Dear Kalinda:

On June 1, you gave me a 30-day notice of your intent to move out on July 1. You have since requested to extend your move-out to July 18 because of last-minute problems with closing escrow on your new house. This letter is to verify our understanding that you will move out on July 18, instead of July 1, and that you will pay prorated rent for 18 days (July 1 through July 18). Prorated rent for 18 days, based on your monthly rent of $1,200 or $40 per day, is $720.

Please sign below to indicate your agreement to these terms.

Sincerely,

Fran Moore, Landlord

Agreed to by Kalinda Blake, Tenant:

Signature ___*Kalinda Blake*_____

Date ___June 20, 20xx_____

RENT CONTROL

Your options might be limited in a rent control area. When your property is subject to rent or eviction controls, your ability to end your relationship with a current tenant might be limited. Many laws require "just cause" for refusing to renew a lease, which generally means that only certain reasons (such as the tenant's failure to pay rent, or your desire to move in a close relative) justify nonrenewal. If your law requires "just cause," and if your decision not to renew does not meet the law's "just clause" test, you might end up with a perpetual month-to-month tenant. Check your rent control laws carefully.

When the Tenant Remains After the Lease Expires

It's fairly common for a tenant to remain in a unit even though the lease has ended. If this happens, you have a choice: You can continue renting to the tenant, or you can take legal steps to get the tenant out.

When a tenant stays beyond the end of the lease, and you accept rent money without signing a new lease, in most states you will have created a new, month-to-month tenancy on the same terms that were in the old lease. In a few states, accepting rent might even have created a new lease for the same term—such as one year. In other words, you'll be stuck with the terms and rent in the old lease, for at least the first 30 days. If you want to change the terms in a new lease, you must abide by the law regarding giving notice for a month-to-month tenancy (discussed above). It will usually take you at least a month while you go about giving notice to your now month-to-month tenant.

To avoid the problem of tenants staying longer than you want, be sure to notify tenants that you expect them to leave no later than the lease expiration date, and don't accept rent after this date. If a tenant wants to stay a few days after a lease expires and you agree, it is wise to put your agreement in a letter. (See the sample letter extending the tenant's move-out date, above.)

When the Tenant Leaves Early

Tenants who leave (with or without notifying you beforehand) before a fixed-term lease expires and refuse to pay rent for the remainder of the lease have "broken the lease." Once the tenants leave for good, you have the legal right to take possession of the premises and rerent to another tenant.

A key question that arises is, how much do tenants with a lease owe when they break the lease? Let's start with the general legal rule. Tenants who sign a lease agree at the outset to pay a fixed amount of rent: the monthly rent multiplied by the number of months of the lease. The tenants are obligated to pay this amount in monthly installments over the term of the lease. The fact that payments are made monthly doesn't change the tenants' responsibility to pay rent for the entire lease term. And even when tenants give you notice of their intention to leave early, you are still owed the money for the rest of the term. As discussed below, depending on the situation, you can use the tenants' security deposit to cover part of the shortfall, or sue the tenants for rent owed.

TIP

Require tenants to notify you of extended absences. Clause 18 of the form lease and rental agreements (Chapter 2) requires tenants to inform you when they will be gone for an extended time, such as two or more weeks.

By requiring tenants to notify you of long absences, you'll know whether the rental has been abandoned or the tenant is simply on vacation. In addition, if you have such a clause and, under its authority, enter an apparently abandoned unit only to be confronted later by an indignant tenant, you can defend yourself by pointing out that the tenant violated the lease.

When Leaving Early Is Justified

There are some important exceptions to the blanket rule that a tenant who breaks a lease owes you the rent for the entire lease term. A tenant who leaves early might be off the hook for the remaining rent when:

- **The rental is unsafe or otherwise uninhabitable.** When you don't live up to your obligations to provide habitable housing, a court will conclude that you have "constructively evicted" the tenant. That releases the tenant from further obligations under the lease.

- **You have rented—or could rent—the unit to someone else.** Most courts require landlords to try to soften ("mitigate") the ex-tenant's liability for the remaining rent by attempting to find a new rent-paying tenant as soon as reasonably possible. The new tenant's rent is credited against what the former tenant owed. (This "mitigation of damages" rule is discussed below.)

- **The law allows the tenant to leave early.** A few states have laws that list allowable reasons to break a lease. For example, in Delaware, tenants need only give 30 days' notice to end a long-term lease if they need to move because their present employer relocated or because health problems (of the tenant or a family member) require

a permanent move. (Del. Code Ann. tit. 25 § 5314.) In many states, victims of domestic violence, sexual assault, or stalking may terminate a lease (with proper notice) early without penalty. In all states, tenants who enter active military duty after signing a lease must be released after delivering proper notice. (See "Special Rules for Active Military Tenants," above.) If your tenant has a good reason for a sudden move, you might want to research your state's law to see whether the tenant will still be on the hook for rent.

- **The rental is damaged or destroyed.** If a tenant's home is significantly damaged—by natural disaster or any other reason beyond the tenant's control—the tenant has the right to move out. State laws vary on the extent of the landlord's responsibility, depending on the cause of the damage. When a fire, flood, tornado, earthquake, or other natural disaster makes the dwelling unlivable; or when a third party is the cause of the destruction (for instance, a fire due to an arsonist), your best bet is to look to your insurance policy for help in repairing or rebuilding the unit and to assist your tenants in resettlement.

Your Duty to Mitigate Your Loss When the Tenant Leaves Early

When tenants break the lease without legal justification, in most states you can't just sit back and wait until the lease ends, and then sue the departed tenant for the total amount of your lost rent. Instead, you must try to rerent the property reasonably quickly and subtract the rent you receive from rent due on the remaining months of the lease (plus any past-due rent).

Even if this isn't the legal rule in your state, trying to rerent is a sound business strategy. It's much better to have rent coming in every month than to leave a rental unit vacant for months and hope that in the future you can sue and collect from a tenant who's probably long gone.

If you sue the tenant for the whole rent instead of making best efforts to rerent, you will collect only what the judge thinks is the difference between the fair rental value of the property and the original tenant's promised rent.

How much you can recover will be affected by the state of the rental market in your area; judges will usually account for the relative ease of finding new renters as well as any declines in rental rates. Even in areas where renters are easy to find, most judges will give you some time (probably at least 30 days) to find a new tenant.

How to Mitigate Your Damages

When you're sure that a tenant has moved out, you can turn your attention to rerenting the unit.

You do not need to relax your standards for acceptable tenants—for example, you are entitled to reject applicants with poor credit or rental histories. Also, you need not give the suddenly available property priority over other rental units that you would normally attend to first.

You are not required to rent the premises at a rate substantially below its fair market value. Keep in mind, however, that refusing to rent at less than the original rate might be foolish. If you are unable to ultimately collect from the former tenant, you will get *no* income from the property instead of less. You will have ended up hurting no one but yourself.

The Tenant's Right to Find a Replacement Tenant

Tenants who wish to leave before the lease expires might offer to find a suitable new tenant, in an effort to be off the hook for future rent payments. Unless you have a new tenant waiting, you have nothing to lose by cooperating. And refusing to cooperate could hurt you: When you refuse to accept an excellent new tenant and then withhold the lease-breaking tenant's deposit or sue for unpaid rent, you could wind up losing in court because, after all, you turned down the chance to reduce your losses (mitigate your damages).

Of course, in a really tight rental market, you might be able to lease the unit easily at a higher rent, or you might already have an even better prospective tenant on your waiting list. In that case, a tenant who breaks the lease benefits you, and you might not be interested in any new tenant provided by the old one.

Be sure to sign a new lease with any new tenant you accept.

Keep Good Records

When you sue a former tenant, you want to be able to show the judge that you acted reasonably in your attempts to rerent the property. Don't rely on your memory and powers of persuasion to convince the judge. Keep detailed records, including:

- the original lease
- receipts for cleaning and painting, with photos of the unit showing the need for repairs, if any
- your expenses for storing or properly disposing of any belongings the tenant left
- receipts for advertising the property and bills from credit reporting agencies investigating potential renters
- a log of the time you spent showing the property, and the value of that time
- a log of any potential renters you rejected, along with your reasons for rejecting them, and
- a copy of the new lease as documentation that you had to accept less rent than what the original tenant paid, if applicable.

When You Can Sue

When a tenant leaves prematurely, you should first use the tenant's deposit to cover your rerental costs and any shortfall between the original and replacement rent amounts. However, if the deposit isn't enough to cover your losses, you might need to sue the former tenant.

Deciding *where* to sue is usually easy: For most landlord-tenant disputes, small claims court is the court of choice, because it's fast, affordable, and doesn't require a lawyer. The only exception is when your former tenant owes you more than your small claims court's dollar limits.

Knowing *when* to sue is trickier. You might be eager to start legal proceedings as soon as the original tenant leaves, but, if you do, you won't know the extent of your losses, because you might find another tenant who will make up part of the lost rent. Must you wait until the end of the original tenant's lease? Or can you bring suit when you rerent the property?

The standard approach, and one that all states allow, is to go to court after you rerent the property. At this point, your losses—your expenses and the rent differential, if any—are known and final. The disadvantage is that you have had no income from that property since the original tenant left, and the original tenant might be long gone and not, practically speaking, worth chasing down.

 RESOURCE

Nolo's book on small claims court. *Everybody's Guide to Small Claims Court* (National Edition), by Cara O'Neill, provides detailed advice on bringing or defending a small claims court case, preparing evidence and witnesses for court, and collecting your court judgment when you win. *Everybody's Guide to Small Claims Court* will also be useful in defending yourself against a tenant who sues you in small claims court—for example, claiming that you failed to return a cleaning or security deposit.

Returning Security Deposits When a Tenancy Ends

Most states set very specific rules for the return of security deposits. A landlord's failure to return security deposits as legally required can result in substantial financial penalties.

Alerting Tenants to Final Inspection Procedures

Many landlords do a final inspection of the rental unit on their own and simply send the tenant an itemized statement with any remaining balance of the deposit. If at all possible, you should make the inspection with the tenant who's moving out, rather than by yourself (in fact, in some states the tenant must have notice and an opportunity to be present). Because state laws can be quite detailed as to rules and procedures for itemizing and returning security deposits, be sure to check your state statutes. (See "State Security Deposit Rules" in Appendix A.)

Inspecting the Unit When a Tenant Leaves

At the end of a tenancy, you will need to inspect the unit to assess any necessary cleaning and damage repair. At the final inspection, check the condition of each item on the Landlord-Tenant Checklist (described in Chapter 3) or a similar document that you and the tenant signed when the tenant moved in. If you did not use a Landlord-Tenant Checklist or a similar form to inventory the condition of the rental property at move-in, you should still do a walk-through inspection when the tenant moves out. You won't have the benefit of the "before" documentation, but you can still review the condition of the unit together and identify items that need cleaning, repair, or replacement. As explained earlier, it's a good idea (and the law in some states) to involve the tenants in the final inspection. (See "Alerting Tenants to Final Inspection Procedures," above.)

CAUTION

California has special rules and procedures for move-out inspections. California tenants are entitled to a pre–move-out inspection, when you tell the tenant what defects, if any, need to be corrected in order for the tenant to optimize the security deposit refund. California landlords must notify the tenant in writing of the right to request an initial inspection, at which the tenant has a right to be present. (Cal. Civ. Code § 1950.5 (f).) For details, see Nolo's *The California Landlord's Law Book: Rights & Responsibilities.*

Basic Rules for Returning Deposits

You are generally entitled to deduct from a tenant's security deposit the amount you need to fix damaged or dirty property (beyond "ordinary wear and tear") or to make up unpaid rent. But you must make your deductions and return deposits correctly. The specific rules vary from state to state, but landlords usually have between 14 and 30 days after the tenant leaves to return the deposit. (See "State Security Deposit Rules" in Appendix A.)

State security deposit statutes typically require you to mail the following within the time limit to the tenant's last known address (or forwarding address if you have one):

- a written itemized accounting of deductions, including back rent and costs of cleaning and damage repair, together with payment for any deposit balance, including any required interest
- the deposit that remains after any valid deductions, and
- any required interest.

Even if your state or law has no specific time limit for requiring itemization, promptly presenting the tenant with a written itemization of all deductions and a clear reason why each was made is an essential part of a savvy landlord's overall plan to avoid disputes with tenants. In general, we recommend 21 to 30 days as a reasonable time to return deposits.

Penalties for Violating Security Deposit Laws

If you don't follow state security deposit laws to the letter, you might pay a heavy price if a tenant sues you and wins. In addition to whatever amount you wrongfully withheld, you might have to pay the tenant punitive damages (penalties imposed when the judge feels that the defendant has acted especially outrageously) and court costs. In many states, if you "willfully" (deliberately and not through inadvertence) violate the security deposit statute, you could forfeit your right to retain any part of the deposit and could be liable for two or three times the amount wrongfully withheld, plus attorneys' fees and costs.

When the Deposit Doesn't Cover Damage and Unpaid Rent

If the security deposit doesn't cover what a tenant owes you for back rent, cleaning, or repairs, you might wish to file a lawsuit against the former tenant.

RESOURCE

More information on deposits. *Every Landlord's Legal Guide,* by Marcia Stewart, Janet Portman, and Ann O'Connell (Nolo), provides complete details on state laws and sample forms for returning and itemizing security deposits.

State Landlord-Tenant Law Charts

How to Use the State Landlord-Tenant Law Charts

The State Landlord-Tenant Law Charts are comprehensive 50-state charts that give you two kinds of information:

- the state rules, such as notice periods and deposit limits (what the statutes and cases say), and
- specific citations for key statutes and cases, which you can use if you want to read the law yourself or look for more information.

When you're looking for information for your state, simply find your state along the left-hand list on the chart, and read to the right—you'll see the statute or case, and the rule.

RESOURCE

How to find your state's laws. If you would like to read the actual statute that we summarize in these charts, you can easily find it online. Many times, when you type the citation itself (the letters and numbers that identify the law, such as Cal. Civ. Code Sec. 1954) right into your browser, you'll get a results list with a link to the law. Or, search for your state's statutes (such as "Arizona statutes"). That will usually result in a link to the state's entire set of laws, and you can search for your citation within the table of contents on that site.

COVID-19-Related Emergency Laws and Orders Might Affect These Statutes

Federal, state, and local governments have all passed emergency laws and orders in response to the COVID-19 pandemic. Many of these laws affect the landlord-tenant relationship by addressing issues such as evictions, late rent fees, and tenant screening.

Emergency laws passed by the federal government (such as the CARES Act and the Centers for Disease Control and Prevention's eviction moratorium) apply to landlords and tenants in all states. Along with federal laws, landlords and tenants must also follow the laws, orders, and regulations that apply in the state (and city or county) where their rental is located. Each state is handling the situation differently. In some states, governors are issuing emergency orders, while in others the state court or the state legislature (or a combination of any of these branches of government) are creating emergency rules.

As this book went to press, these COVID-inspired laws, regulations, and orders were changing daily. Printing in these charts what we know today would be misleading to you when you refer to the chart tomorrow. That's because even when you have a starting point (the first instance of the law or order), it can be very difficult to pin down the most recent version. For example, a governor might have issued an emergency order on April 1, 2020 that laid out details about when landlords can and cannot charge late fees for unpaid rent. However, that April 1, 2020 order might have been amended in October 2020. Most of the time, when you look at the April 1, 2020 order online, there is no indication that it has been amended or repealed.

Because of the rapidly changing nature of these COVID-19-related laws, there's no way we can accurately and fully address how they affect the charts we provide here in Appendix A. However, we can provide you with some tips and hints about how to find COVID-19-related emergency laws that might apply to your situation

- **Start by going to Nolo's article, *Emergency Bans on Evictions and Other Protections Related to Coronavirus,*** for state-by-state information on state responses, particularly in regards to evictions (type the article's name into the search box on the home page, or go directly to www.nolo.com/evictions-ban).

- **Go to your state's designated COVID-19 website.** Every state has one, and you can find it by searching the Internet for your state's name and "official COVID-19 website." From this page, you might be able to access quite a few official COVID-19-related emergency rules and regulations.

- **Read your state's emergency declaration.** Nearly every state has declared a state of emergency due to the pandemic. Even if the declaration doesn't address landlord-tenant matters, it can provide a launching point for additional research. Most states' emergency declarations can be found on the state's official COVID-19 website or on the governor's official website.

- **Visit your state governor's official website.** Governors' executive orders are the most likely source of regulations that will apply to the landlord-tenant relationship. Look for "emergency orders" or "executive orders." If your state governor's website has a separate category for COVID-19-related orders, look there first for applicable orders.

COVID-19-Related Emergency Laws and Orders Might Affect These Statutes (continued)

Regardless, to find relevant orders you should also use the website's search function to search for terms such as "rent," "landlord," "tenant,""evict," and "renter." Be creative with the terms you search for; not all states use the same terminology.

- Be warned: Many titles of executive orders consist of only a number or date when they were issued—the titles usually do not contain other information about the topic or substance of the order. Also, many executive orders are amended, extended, or repealed by subsequent orders that refer to the original order by nothing more than the original order's number or date— which means that a search of a keyword such as "rent" might not help in finding all the relevant orders. You might have to read through many orders to find any that apply to your situation.

- It's helpful to find the very first order that addresses your situation, then read subsequent ones to learn the current status of the original order. If you're still having difficulty, try searching the Internet for your governor's name and the topic you're interested in—many times, this will reveal a press release or news report that will indicate the date when your governor issued the relevant order (and might give you a link to the order itself).

- **Visit your state judicial branch's website.** If the state's highest court has issued orders relating to COVID-19, the information will likely be linked from the judicial branch's home page. Often, a state's judicial branch

will step in with landlord-tenant COVID-19 orders after being directed to do so by the governor. For example, at one point during the pandemic, Virginia's governor encouraged the state's highest court to extend the eviction moratorium, and the court issued an order doing so.

- **Visit your state legislature's website.** If your state's legislature has passed emergency COVID-19-related laws, you will most likely find them linked from the legislature's homepage. At press time, only a few states' legislatures have passed COVID-19 laws. However, the longer the pandemic drags on, the more likely it is that state legislatures will step in and pass more long-term COVID-19-related statutes.

- **Search the Internet for news on the issue.** Try searching for your exact question. Most search engines will recognize plain-language queries, and will display relevant results with dates. For example, if you're wondering whether landlords in your state can charge late fees during the pandemic, you could search for "Can landlords charge a late fee in [your state] during COVID-19?"—Look for the most recent posts. Attorney blogs, legal aid websites, news outlet articles, landlord organizations' websites, and tenant rights' groups' websites often have the most accurate and up-to-date information. As with any Internet research project, be sure to evaluate whether the source of the information is a reputable one, and try to find a second or third source to confirm the content.

State Landlord-Tenant Statutes

Here are some of the key statutes pertaining to landlord-tenant law in each state. In some states, important legal principles are contained in court opinions, not codes or statutes. Court-made law and rent stabilization—rent control—laws and regulations are not reflected in this chart. Note that because some states exempt certain occupancies from their general landlord-tenant statutes, such as rentals of mobile homes and short-term rentals, it's a good idea to confirm that these statutes apply to your rental situation. You'll find the details about each state's exemption statutes, if any, in the following chart titled "State Landlord-Tenant Law."

State	Statute
Alabama	Ala. Code §§ 35-9-1 to 35-9-100; 35-9A-101 to 35-9A-603
Alaska	Alaska Stat. §§ 34.03.010 to 34.03.380
Arizona	Ariz. Rev. Stat. Ann. §§ 12-1171 to 12-1183; 33-301 to 33-381; 33-1301 to 33-1381; 36-1637
Arkansas	Ark. Code Ann. §§ 18-16-101 to 18-16-306; 18-16-501 to 18-16-509; 18-17-101 to 18-17-913
California	Cal. Civ. Code §§ 789.3; 790 to 793; 827; 1925 to 1934; 1940 to 1954.05; 1954.50 to 1954.605; 1961 to 1995.340; 2079.10a; Cal. Health & Safety Code §§ 25400.28; 26147 to 26148; Cal. Bus. & Prof. Code § 8538; Cal. Govt. Code § 8589.45
Colorado	Colo. Rev. Stat. §§ 13-40-101 to 13-40-123; 13-40.1-101 to 13-40.1-102; 38-12-101 to 38-12-104; 38-12-301 to 38-12-1007; 38-12-1201 to 38-12-1205
Connecticut	Conn. Gen. Stat. Ann. §§ 47a-1 to 47a-74
Delaware	Del. Code Ann. tit. 25, §§ 5101 to 5907
District of Columbia	D.C. Code Ann. §§ 42-3201 to 42-3651.08; D.C. Mun. Regs., tit. 14, §§ 300 to 399
Florida	Fla. Stat. Ann. §§ 83.40 to 83.683; 404.056; 715.10 to 715.111
Georgia	Ga. Code Ann. §§ 44-1-16; 44-7-1 to 44-7-81
Hawaii	Haw. Rev. Stat. §§ 521-1 to 521-82
Idaho	Idaho Code §§ 6-301 to 6-324; 55-208 to 55-308
Illinois	425 Ill. Comp. Stat. § 60/3; 430 Ill. Comp. Stat. § 135/10; 735 Ill. Comp. Stat. §§ 5/9-201 to 5/9-321; 765 Ill. Comp. Stat. §§ 705/0.01 to 742/30; 750/1 to 750/35; 755/1 to 755/999
Indiana	Ind. Code Ann. §§ 8-1-2-1.2; 32-31-1-1 to 32-31-9-15; 36-1-24.2-1 to 36-1-24.2-4
Iowa	Iowa Code Ann. §§ 562A.1 to 562A.37
Kansas	Kan. Stat. Ann. §§ 58-2501 to 58-2573; 58-25,127; 58-25,137
Kentucky	Ky. Rev. Stat. Ann. §§ 224.1-410; 383.010 to 383.715; 902 Ky. Admin. Regs. 47:200
Louisiana	La. Rev. Stat. Ann. §§ 9:3251 to 9:3261.1; La. Civ. Code Ann. Art. 2002; 2668 to 2729
Maine	Me. Rev. Stat. Ann. tit. 14, §§ 6000 to 6046
Maryland	Md. Code Ann. [Real Prop.] §§ 8-101 to 8-604
Massachusetts	Mass. Gen. Laws Ann. ch. 111, § 127L; ch. 186, §§ 1A to 30; ch. 186a, §§ 1 to 6; ch. 239, § 8A
Michigan	Mich. Comp. Laws §§ 125.530; 554.131 to 554.201; 554.601 to 554.641; 600.2918
Minnesota	Minn. Stat. Ann. §§ 504B.001 to 504B.471
Mississippi	Miss. Code Ann. §§ 89-7-1 to 89-8-29
Missouri	Mo. Rev. Stat. §§ 441.005 to 441.920; 442.055; 535.010 to 535.300
Montana	Mont. Code Ann. §§ 70-24-101 to 70-27-117; 75-10-1305
Nebraska	Neb. Rev. Stat. §§ 69-2302 to 69-2314; 76-1401 to 76-1449
Nevada	Nev. Rev. Stat. Ann. §§ 40.215 to 40.425; 118A.010 to 118A.530
New Hampshire	N.H. Rev. Stat. Ann. §§ 477:4-g; 540:1 to 540:29; 540-A:1 to 540-A:8; 540-B:1 to 540-B:10
New Jersey	N.J. Stat. Ann. §§ 2A:18-51 to 2A:18-61.67; 2A:18-72 to 2A:18-84; 2A:42-1 to 2A:42-96; 46:8-1 to 46:8-51; 55:13A-7.14; 55:13A-7.18; N.J.A.C. §§ 5:10-5.1, 5:10-27.1
New Mexico	N.M. Stat. Ann. §§ 47-8-1 to 47-8-51; N.M. Admin. Code § 20.4.5.13
New York	N.Y. Real Prop. Law §§ 220 to 238; Real Prop. Acts. §§ 701 to 853; Mult. Dwell Law (all); Mult. Res. Law (all); Gen. Oblig. Law §§ 7-101 to 7-109; N.Y. Envtl. Conserv. Law § 27-2405; N.Y. Penal Law §§ 241.00 to 241.05; N.Y. Unconsol. Law §§ 8581 to 8597 (Emergency Housing Rent Control Law); 8601 to 8617 (Local Emergency Housing Rent Control Act); 8621 to 8634 (Emergency Tenant Protection Act)
North Carolina	N.C. Gen. Stat. §§ 42-1 to 42-14.2; 42-25.6 to 42-76
North Dakota	N.D. Cent. Code §§ 23-13-15; 47-06-04; 47-16-01 to 47-16-41; 47-17-01 to 47-17-05
Ohio	Ohio Rev. Code Ann. §§ 5321.01 to 5321.19

State Landlord-Tenant Statutes (continued)

Oklahoma	Okla. Stat. Ann. tit. 41, §§ 101 to 136; 201; tit. 74, § 324.11a	**Utah**	Utah Code Ann. §§ 57-17-1 to 57-17-5; 57-22-1 to 57-22-7; 57-27-201; 78B-6-801 to 78B-6-816
Oregon	Or. Rev. Stat. Ann. §§ 90.100 to 90.228; 90.243 to 90.265; 90.295 to 90.493; 105.005 to 105.168; 105.190; 479.270 to 479.280	**Vermont**	Vt. Stat. Ann. tit. 9, §§ 4451 to 4469a; 4471 to 4475
Pennsylvania	68 Pa. Cons. Stat. Ann. §§ 250.101 to 399.18	**Virginia**	Va. Code Ann. §§ 54.1-2108.1; 55.1-1200 to 55.1-1259
Rhode Island	R.I. Gen. Laws §§ 34-18-1 to 34-18-57	**Washington**	Wash. Rev. Code Ann. §§ 59.04.010 to 59.18.912
South Carolina	S.C. Code Ann. §§ 5-25-1330; 27-40-10 to 27-40-940	**West Virginia**	W.Va. Code §§ 37-6-1 to 37-6A-6; W.Va. Code St. R. § 64-92-6
South Dakota	S.D. Codified Laws §§ 43-32-1 to 43-32-36	**Wisconsin**	Wis. Stat. §§ 704.01 to 704.95; Wis. Admin. Code ATCP §§ 134.01 to 134.10
Tennessee	Tenn. Code Ann. §§ 66-7-101 to 66-7-102; 66-7-104; 66-7-106 to 66-7-107; 66-7-109 to 66-7-111; 66-28-101 to 66-28-521	**Wyoming**	Wyo. Stat. Ann. §§ 1-21-1001 to 1-21-1016; 1-21-1201 to 1-21-1211; 1-21-1301 to 1-21-1304; 34-2-128 to 34-2-129
Texas	Tex. Prop. Code Ann. §§ 91.001 to 92.355		

State Rules on Notice Required to Change or Terminate a Month-to-Month Tenancy

Except where noted, the amount of notice a landlord must give to increase rent or change another term of the rental agreement in month-to-month tenancy is the same as that required to end a month-to-month tenancy. Be sure to check state and local rent control laws, which might have different notice requirements.

State	Tenant	Landlord	Statute	Comments
Alabama	30 days	30 days	Ala. Code § 35-9A-441	No state statute on the amount of notice required to change rent or other terms.
Alaska	30 days	30 days	Alaska Stat. § 34.03.290(b)	No state statute on the amount of notice required to change rent or other terms.
Arizona	30 days	30 days	Ariz. Rev. Stat. Ann. §§ 33-1342, 33-1375	Landlords may adopt new rules and regulations that don't substantially modify the rental agreement after giving the tenant 30 days' notice.
Arkansas	30 days	30 days	Ark. Code Ann. § 18-17-704	No state statute on the amount of notice required to change rent or other terms.
California	30 days	30 days to terminate; 30-60+ days to change terms or increase rent, depending on size of increase	Cal. Civ. Code §§ 827, 1946	At least 30 days' notice to change rental terms, but if the change is a proposed rent increase of more than 10% of the rental amount charged to that tenant at any time during the 12 months prior to the effective date of the increase, either in and of itself or when combined with any other rent increases for the 12 months prior to the effective date of the increase, then an additional 30 days' notice is required.
Colorado	21 days	21 days	Colo. Rev. Stat. § 13-40-107	No state statute on the amount of notice required to change rent or other terms.
Connecticut		3 days	Conn. Gen. Stat. Ann. §§ 47a-9, 47a-23	Landlord must provide 3 days' notice to terminate tenancy. Landlord is not required to give a particular amount of notice of a proposed rent increase unless prior notice was previously agreed upon. If landlord makes a new rule or regulation resulting in a substantial modification of the rental agreement, it is not valid unless tenant agrees to it in writing.
Delaware	60 days	60 days	Del. Code Ann. tit. 25, §§ 5106, 5107	For termination, the 60-day notice period begins on the first day of the month following the day of actual notice. For change of terms, upon receiving notice of landlord's proposed change of terms tenant has 15 days to terminate tenancy. Otherwise, changes will take effect as announced.
District of Columbia	30 days	30-120 days, depending on reason for terminating the tenancy	D.C. Code Ann. §§ 42-3202, 42-3505.01, 42-3509.04(b)	No rent increases shall be effective until the first day on which rent is normally paid occurring more than 30 days after notice of the increase is given to the tenant. Landlords must have good reason (just cause) to terminate a month-to-month tenancy so long as the tenant is still paying rent.

State Rules on Notice Required to Change or Terminate a Month-to-Month Tenancy (continued)

State	Tenant	Landlord	Statute	Comments
Florida	15 days	15 days	Fla. Stat. Ann. § 83.57	No state statute on the amount of notice required to change rent or other terms.
Georgia	30 days	60 days	Ga. Code Ann. § 44-7-6 & -7	No state statute on the amount of notice required to change rent or other terms.
Hawaii	28 days	45 days	Haw. Rev. Stat. §§ 521-71, 521-21(d)	Landlord shall not increase rent without written notice given 45 consecutive days prior to the effective date of the increase. The landlord may terminate the rental agreement by notifying the tenant, in writing, at least 45 days in advance of the anticipated termination. The tenant may terminate the rental agreement by notifying the landlord, in writing, at least 28 days in advance of the anticipated termination.
Idaho	One month	15 or 30 days	Idaho Code §§ 55-208, 55-307	A "month" means a calendar month. For landlords: 30 days' notice to increase rent or end tenancy; 15 days' notice to change terms of lease other than rent.
Illinois	30 days	30 days	735 Ill. Comp. Stat. § 5/9-207	No state statute on the amount of notice required to change rent or other terms.
Indiana	One month	One month	Ind. Code Ann. §§ 32-31-1-1, 32-31-5-4	Unless agreement states otherwise, landlord must give 30 days' written notice to modify written rental agreement.
Iowa	30 days	30 days	Iowa Code Ann. §§ 562A.34, 562A.13(5)	To end or change a month-to-month agreement, landlord must give written notice at least 30 days before the next time rent is due (not including any grace period). Each tenant shall be notified, in writing, of any rent increase at least 30 days before the effective date. Such effective date shall not be sooner than the expiration date of original rental agreement or any renewal or extension thereof.
Kansas	30 days	30 days	Kan. Stat. Ann. §§ 58-2556, 58-2570	After the tenant enters into the rental agreement, if a rule or regulation that effects a substantial modification of the rental agreement is adopted, such rule or regulation isn't enforceable against the tenant unless the tenant consents to it in writing.
Kentucky	30 days	30 days	Ky. Rev. Stat. Ann. §§ 383.610, 383.695	If a rule or regulation is adopted after the tenant enters into the rental agreement, and that addition substantially modifies the original bargain, it is not valid unless the tenant consents to it in writing.
Louisiana	10 days	10 days	La. Civ. Code Art. 2728	No state statute on the amount of notice required to change rent or other terms.
Maine	30 days	30 days	Me. Rev. Stat. Ann. tit. 14, §§ 6002, 6015	Landlord must provide 45 days' notice to increase rent.
Maryland	One month	One month	Md. Code Ann. [Real Prop.] § 8-402(b)(3), (b)(4)	Two months' notice required in Montgomery County (single family rentals excepted) and Baltimore City.

State Rules on Notice Required to Change or Terminate a Month-to-Month Tenancy (continued)

State	Tenant	Landlord	Statute	Comments
Massachusetts	See comments	See comments	Mass. Gen. Laws Ann. ch. 186, § 12	Interval between days of payment or 30 days, whichever is longer.
Michigan	One month	One month	Mich. Comp. Laws § 554.134	No state statute on the amount of notice required to change rent or other terms.
Minnesota	See comments	See comments	Minn. Stat. Ann. § 504B.135	For terminations, interval between time rent is due or three months, whichever is less; no state statute on the amount of notice required to change rent or other terms.
Mississippi	30 days	30 days	Miss. Code Ann. § 89-8-19	No state statute on the amount of notice required to change rent or other terms.
Missouri	One month	One month	Mo. Rev. Stat. § 441.060	No state statute on the amount of notice required to change rent or other terms.
Montana	30 days	30 days	Mont. Code Ann. §§ 70-24-441, 70-26-109	Landlord may change terms of tenancy with 15 days' notice.
Nebraska	30 days	30 days	Neb. Rev. Stat. §§ 76-1422, 76-1437	A rule or regulation adopted after the tenant enters into the rental agreement is enforceable if the landlord gives reasonable notice to tenant of its adoption and if it doesn't substantially modify the rental agreement.
Nevada	30 days	30 days	Nev. Rev. Stat. Ann. §§ 40.251, 118A.300	Landlords must provide 45 days' notice to increase rent. Tenants 60 years old or older, or physically or mentally disabled, may request an additional 30 days' possession, but only if they have complied with basic tenant obligations as set forth in Nev. Rev. Stat. Chapter 118A (termination notices must include this information).
New Hampshire	30 days	30 days	N.H. Rev. Stat. Ann. §§ 540:2, 540:3, 540:11	Landlord may terminate only for just cause. Tenant's termination: If the date of termination given in the notice does not coincide with the rent due date, tenant is responsible for the rent for the entire month in which the notice expires, up to the next rent due date, unless the terms of the rental agreement provide otherwise.
New Jersey	One month	One month	N.J. Stat. Ann. §§ 2A:18-56, 2A:18-61.1	Landlord may terminate only for just cause. The landlord may increase the rent only at the beginning of the term of the agreement. The landlord cannot increase the rent while an agreement exists. The landlord must offer the tenant the option of entering into a new agreement, at the increased rental rate, after the old agreement expires. If the tenant doesn't sign the new agreement and doesn't move at the expiration of the old agreement, and has been given a valid notice to quit and notice of rent increase, a new tenancy is automatically created at the increased rental rate. New Jersey landlords should check local ordinances, as they might have different rules regarding rent increase notice.

State Rules on Notice Required to Change or Terminate a Month-to-Month Tenancy (continued)

State	Tenant	Landlord	Statute	Comments
New Mexico	30 days	30 days	N.M. Stat. Ann. §§ 47-8-37, 47-8-15(F)	Landlord must deliver rent increase notice at least 30 days before rent due date.
New York	One month, within NYC and statewide	Within NYC and statewide, 30 to 90 days for terminations and rent increases of 5% or more	N.Y. Real Prop. Law §§ 226-c, 232-b	Terminations and rent increases of 5% over existing rent: Tenants occupying for a year or having a lease of at least one year: 30 days' notice. Tenants occupying from one to two years and lease holders of one- to two-year leases: 60 days' notice. Tenants occupying more than two years or having leases of two years or more: 90 days' notice.
North Carolina	7 days	7 days	N.C. Gen. Stat. § 42-14	No state statute on the amount of notice required to change rent or other terms.
North Dakota	One calendar month	One calendar month	N.D. Cent. Code §§ 47-16-07, 47-16-15	Landlord may change the terms of the lease to take effect at the expiration of the month upon giving notice in writing at least 30 days before the expiration of the month. Tenant may terminate with 25 days' notice if landlord has changed the terms of the agreement.
Ohio	30 days	30 days	Ohio Rev. Code Ann. § 5321.17	No state statute on the amount of notice required to change rent or other terms.
Oklahoma	30 days	30 days	Okla. Stat. Ann. tit. 41, § 111	No state statute on the amount of notice required to change rent or other terms.
Oregon	30 days, or 72 hours (lack of bedroom exit only)	Termination: 30 days within the first year; 90 days after that, only for cause. Rent increase: See comments	Or. Rev. Stat. §§ 90.275, 90.323, 90.427, 90.460, 91.070	When the rental is in the same building or on the same property as the landlord's residence, and the property has no more than two dwelling units, unique termination periods and notice requirements apply. Temporary occupants are not entitled to notice. No rent increase during the first year of the tenancy. After that, 90 days, and rent cannot be increased more than 7% plus the consumer price index (CPI) above the existing rent during any 12-month period. Landlords are excepted from the 7%+CPI increase limit if either: the unit's first certificate of occupancy was issued less than 15 years from the date of the rent increase notice, or landlord accepts reduced rent as part of a federal, state, or local program or subsidy.
Pennsylvania		15 days	68 Pa. Stat. Ann. § 250.501	At the end of the term or due to a breach of the lease landlord must give 15 days' notice to terminate. If notice to terminate is due to tenant's failure to pay rent, notice required is 10 days.
Rhode Island	30 days	30 days	R.I. Gen. Laws §§ 34-18-16.1, 34-18-37	Landlord must provide 30 days' notice to increase rent if tenant is age 62 or younger; if tenant is more than 62 years old, landlord must provide 60 days' notice.

State Rules on Notice Required to Change or Terminate a Month-to-Month Tenancy (continued)

State	Tenant	Landlord	Statute	Comments
South Carolina	30 days	30 days	S.C. Code Ann. §§ 27-40-520, 27-40-770	Rules or regulations adopted after a tenant enters into a rental agreement do not apply to a tenant if the rules or regulations substantially modify the tenant's agreement with landlord and, after receiving notice upon adoption of the right to object, the tenant objects in writing to the landlord within 30 days after the rules are made.
South Dakota	One month	One month	S.D. Codified Laws Ann. §§ 43-8-8, 43-32-13	If tenant (or spouse or minor child) is in active duty in the military, landlord must give two months' notice (unless there is tenant misconduct, a sale of the property, or the property has passed into the landlord's estate). Landlord must give at least 30 days' notice to modify lease (including rent amount). Tenant may terminate lease within 15 days of receipt of the notice of modification.
Tennessee	30 days	30 days	Tenn. Code Ann. §§ 66-28-402, 66-28-512	A rule or regulation adopted after the tenant enters into the rental agreement is enforceable against the tenant if reasonable notice of its adoption is given to the tenant and the addition does not substantially modify the rental agreement.
Texas	One month	One month	Tex. Prop. Code Ann. §§ 91.001, 92.013	Landlord and tenant may agree in writing to different notice periods, or none at all. No state statute on the amount of notice required to change rent or other terms. A landlord shall give prior written notice to a tenant regarding a landlord rule or policy change that is not included in the lease agreement and that will affect any personal property owned by the tenant that is located outside the tenant's dwelling.
Utah		15 days	Utah Code Ann. § 78B-6-802	No state statute on the amount of notice required to change rent or other terms.
Vermont	One rental period, unless written lease says otherwise	30 days	Vt. Code Ann. tit. 9, §§ 4456(d), 4467	If there is no written rental agreement, for tenants who have continuously resided in the unit for two years or less, 60 days' notice to terminate; for those who have resided longer than two years, 90 days. If there is a written rental agreement, for tenants who have lived continuously in the unit for two years or less, 30 days; for those who have lived there longer than two years, 60 days.
Virginia	30 days	30 days	Va. Code Ann. §§ 55.1-1204, 55.1-1253	Rental agreement may provide for a different notice period. By operation of law, month-to-month tenant who does not have a written agreement has a 12-month lease, whose terms and conditions cannot be changed except by agreement of the parties.

State Rules on Notice Required to Change or Terminate a Month-to-Month Tenancy (continued)

State	Tenant	Landlord	Statute	Comments
Washington	20 days; tenants who are members of the armed forces (as well as their spouses and dependents) may give less than 20 days' notice if they receive permanent change of station or deployment orders that don't allow a 20-day written notice.	20 days; when landlord plans to convert apartments to condominiums that are separately owned—or plans to demolish, substantially remodel, or change the use of the premises—the landlord shall provide tenants with at least 120 days' written notice of termination.	Wash. Rev. Code Ann. §§ 59.18.140, 59.18.200	Landlord must give 60 days' notice to change rent, and any increase in rent may not become effective before the end of the term of the rental agreement, but if the rental is a subsidized tenancy, landlord can give 30 days' notice. If the landlord plans to change rental agreement to exclude children, the landlord shall give tenant at least 90 days' notice. All other changes require 30 days' written notice.
West Virginia	One month	One month	W.Va. Code § 37-6-5	No state statute on the amount of notice required to change rent or other terms.
Wisconsin	28 days	28 days	Wis. Stat. Ann. § 704.19	No state statute on the amount of notice required to change rent or other terms.
Wyoming			No statute	

State Rent Rules

Here are citations for statutes that set out rent rules in each state. When a state has no statute, the space is left blank. (See the "Notice Required to Change or Terminate a Month-to-Month Tenancy" chart in this appendix for citations to raising rent.)

State	When Rent Is Due	Grace Period	Where Rent Is Due	Late Fees
Alabama	Ala. Code § 35-9A-161(c)		Ala. Code § 35-9A-161(c)	
Alaska	Alaska Stat. § 34.03.020(c)		Alaska Stat. § 34.03.020(c)	
Arizona	Ariz. Rev. Stat. Ann. §§ 33-1314(C), 33-1368(B)		Ariz. Rev. Stat. Ann. § 33-1314(C)	Ariz. Rev. Stat. Ann. § 33-1368(B) [1]
Arkansas	Ark. Code Ann. § 18-17-401	Ark. Code Ann. §§ 18-17-701 & 18-17-901	Ark. Code Ann. § 18-17-401	
California	Cal. Civ. Code § 1947		Cal. Civ. Code § 1962	*Orozco v. Casimiro*, 121 Cal. App.4th Supp. 7 (2004) [2]
Colorado	No statute.			
Connecticut	Conn. Gen. Stat. Ann. § 47a-3a	Conn. Gen. Stat. Ann. § 47a-15a	Conn. Gen. Stat. Ann. § 47a-3a	Conn. Gen. Stat. Ann. §§ 47a-4(a)(8), 47a-15a [3]
Delaware	Del. Code Ann. tit. 25, § 5501(b)		Del. Code Ann. tit. 25, § 5501(b)	Del. Code Ann. tit. 25, § 5501(d) [4]
District of Columbia		D.C. Code Ann. § 42-3505.31		D.C. Code Ann. § 42-3505.31 [5]
Florida	Fla. Stat. Ann. § 83.46(1)			
Georgia	No statute. [6]			
Hawaii	Haw. Rev. Stat. § 521-21(b)		Haw. Rev. Stat. § 521-21(b)	Haw. Rev. Stat. § 521-21(f) [7]
Idaho	No statute.			
Illinois	735 Ill. Comp. Stat. Ann. § 5/9-218		735 Ill. Comp. Stat. Ann. § 5/9-218	
Indiana	*Watson v. Penn*, 108 Ind. 21 (1886), 8 N.E. 636 (1886)			
Iowa	Iowa Code Ann. § 562A.9(3)		Iowa Code Ann. § 562A.9(3)	Iowa Code Ann. § 562A.9(4) [8]

[1] Late fees must be set forth in a written rental agreement and be reasonable. (Arizona)

[2] Late fees will be enforced only if specified language is included in a written lease or rental agreement. (California)

[3] Landlords may not charge a late fee until 9 days after rent is due. (Connecticut)

[4] To charge a late fee, landlord must maintain an office in the county where the rental unit is located at which tenants can pay rent. If a landlord doesn't have a local office for this purpose, tenant has 3 extra days (beyond the due date) to pay rent before the landlord can charge a late fee. Late fee cannot exceed 5% of rent and cannot be imposed until the rent is more than 5 days late. (Delaware)

[5] Fee policy (including a statement of the maximum amount of late fees that may be charged) must be stated in the lease, and cannot exceed 5% of rent due or be imposed until rent is five days late (or later, if lease so provides). Landlord cannot evict for failure to pay late fee (may deduct unpaid fees from security deposit at end of tenancy). During a declared public emergency, landlords may not impose a late fee. (District of Columbia)

[6] Although there is no specific statute regarding late fees, Georgia law states that all contracts for rent bear interest from the time rent is due. (Georgia)

[7] Late charge cannot exceed 8% of the amount of rent due. (Hawaii)

[8] When rent is $700 per month or less, late fees cannot exceed $12 per day, or a total amount of $60 per month; when rent is more than $700 per month, fees cannot exceed $20 per day or a total amount of $100 per month. (Iowa)

State Rent Rules (continued)

State	When Rent Is Due	Grace Period	Where Rent Is Due	Late Fees
Kansas	Kan. Stat. Ann. § 58-2545(c)		Kan. Stat. Ann. § 58-2545(c)	
Kentucky	Ky. Rev. Stat. Ann. § 383.565(2)		Ky. Rev. Stat. Ann. § 383.565(2)	
Louisiana	La. Civ. Code Ann. art. 2703		La. Civ. Code Ann. art. 2703	
Maine		Me. Rev. Stat. Ann. tit. 14, § 6028		Me. Rev. Stat. Ann. tit. 14, § 6028 [9]
Maryland				Md. Code Ann. [Real Prop.] § 8-208(d)(3) [10]
Massachusetts		Mass. Gen. Laws Ann. ch. 186, § 15B(1)(c); ch. 239, § 8A		Mass. Gen. Laws Ann. ch. 186, § 15B(1)(c) [11]
Michigan	*Hilsendegen v. Scheich,* 21 N.W. 894 (1885)			
Minnesota				Minn. Stat. Ann. § 504B.177 [12]
Mississippi	No statute.			
Missouri	Mo. Rev. Stat. § 535.060			
Montana	Mont. Code Ann. § 70-24-201(2)(c)		Mont. Code Ann. § 70-24-201(2)(b)	
Nebraska	Neb. Rev. Stat. § 76-1414(3)		Neb. Rev. Stat. § 76-1414(3)	
Nevada	Nev. Rev. Stat. Ann. § 118A.210		Nev. Rev. Stat. Ann. § 118A.200	Nev. Rev. Stat. Ann. §§ 118A.200, 118A.210(4) [13]
New Hampshire	No statute.			N.H. Rev. Stat. § 540:8 [14]
New Jersey		N.J. Stat. Ann. § 2A:42-6.1	N.J. Stat. Ann. § 2A:42-6.1	N.J. Stat. Ann. § 2A:42-6.1 [15]
New Mexico	N.M. Stat. Ann. § 47-8-15(B)		N.M. Stat. Ann § 47-8-15(B)	N.M. Stat. Ann § 47-8-15(D) [16]

[9] Late fees cannot exceed 4% of the amount due for 30 days. Landlord must notify tenants, in writing, of any late fee at the start of the tenancy, and cannot impose it until rent is 15 days late. (Maine)

[10] Late fees cannot exceed 5% of the rent due. (Maryland)

[11] Late fees, including interest on late rent, may not be imposed until the rent is 30 days late. So long as the act providing for an eviction moratorium (Chapter 65 of the Acts of 2020) is in force, landlords may not impose late fees if, within 30 days of the rent due date, tenants provide documentation that the nonpayment was due to a financial impact from COVID-19. (Massachusetts)

[12] Late fee policy must be agreed to in writing, and may not exceed 8% of the overdue rent payment. The "due date" for late fee purposes does not include a date earlier than the usual rent due date, by which date a tenant earns a discount. (Minnesota)

[13] A court will presume that there is no late fee provision unless it is included in a written rental agreement, but the landlord can offer evidence to overcome that presumption. Landlord may charge a reasonable late fee as set forth in the rental agreement, but it cannot exceed 5% of the amount of the periodic rent, and the maximum amount of the late fee must not be increased based upon a late fee that was previously imposed. (Nevada)

[14] Landlord cannot demand an amount greater than the whole rent in arrears when rent is late. (New Hampshire)

[15] Landlord must wait 5 business days before charging a late fee, but only when the premises are rented or leased by senior citizens receiving Social Security Old Age Pensions, Railroad Retirement Pensions, or other governmental pensions in lieu of Social Security Old Age Pensions; or when rented by recipients of Social Security Disability Benefits, Supplemental Security Income, or benefits under Work First New Jersey. (New Jersey)

[16] Late fee policy must be in the lease or rental agreement and may not exceed 10% of the rent specified per rental period. Landlord must notify the tenant of the landlord's intent to impose the charge no later than the last day of the next rental period immediately following the period in which the default occurred. (New Mexico)

State Rent Rules (continued)

State	When Rent Is Due	Grace Period	Where Rent Is Due	Late Fees
New York	No statute.	N.Y. Real Prop. Law § 238-a		N.Y. Real Prop. Law § 238-a [17]
North Carolina		N.C. Gen. Stat. § 42-46		N.C. Gen. Stat. § 42-46 [18]
North Dakota	N.D. Cent. Code § 47-16-20			
Ohio	No statute.			
Oklahoma	Okla. Stat. Ann. tit. 41, § 109	Okla. Stat. Ann. tit. 41, § 132(B)	Okla. Stat. Ann. tit. 41, § 109	*Sun Ridge Investors, Ltd. v. Parker*, 956 P.2d 876 (1998) [19]
Oregon	Or. Rev. Stat. § 90.220	Or. Rev. Stat. § 90.260	Or. Rev. Stat. § 90.220	Or. Rev. Stat. § 90.260 [20]
Pennsylvania	No statute.			
Rhode Island	R.I. Gen. Laws § 34-18-15(c)	R.I. Gen. Laws § 34-18-35	R.I. Gen. Laws § 34-18-15(c)	
South Carolina	S.C. Code Ann. § 27-40-310(c)		S.C. Code Ann. § 27-40-310(c)	
South Dakota	S.D. Codified Laws Ann. § 43-32-12			
Tennessee	Tenn. Code Ann. § 66-28-201(c)	Tenn. Code Ann. § 66-28-201(d)	Tenn. Code Ann. § 66-28-201(c)	Tenn. Code Ann. § 66-28-201(d) [21]
Texas		Tex. Prop. Code Ann. § 92.019		Tex. Prop. Code Ann. §§ 92.019, 92.0191 [22]
Utah	No statute.			
Vermont	Vt. Stat. Ann. tit. 9, § 4455			
Virginia	Va. Code Ann. § 55.1-1204	Va. Code Ann. § 55.1-1204	Va. Code Ann. § 55.1-1204	Va. Code Ann. § 55.1-1204 [23]

[17] Landlord must wait five days after the rent due date before imposing a late fee. A late fee may not be more than $50 or 5% of the rent, whichever is less. (New York)

[18] Late fee when rent is due monthly cannot be higher than $15 or 5% of the rental payment, whichever is greater (when rent is due weekly, may not be higher than $4.00 or 5% of the rent, whichever is greater); and may not be imposed until the rent is 5 days late. A late fee may be imposed only one time for each late rental payment. A late fee for a specific late rental payment may not be deducted from a subsequent rental payment so as to cause the subsequent rental payment to be in default. (North Carolina)

[19] Preset late fees are invalid. (Oklahoma)

[20] Landlord must wait 4 days after the rent due date before imposing a late fee, and must disclose the late fee policy in the rental agreement. A flat fee must be "reasonable." A daily late fee may not be more than 6% of a reasonable flat fee, and cannot add up to more than 5% of the monthly rent. (Oregon)

[21] Landlord can't charge a late fee until the rent is 5 days late (the day rent is due is counted as the first day). If day five is a Sunday or legal holiday, landlord cannot impose a fee if the rent is paid on the next business day. Fee can't exceed 10% of the amount past due. (Tennessee)

[22] Late fee provision must be included in a written lease and cannot be imposed until the rent remains unpaid two full days after the date it is due. The fee must be reasonable: For properties that have four or fewer units, it cannot be more than 12% of the rent; for properties that have more than four units, it cannot be more than 10% of the rent; OR it must be related to the late payment of rent (such as expenses, costs, and overhead associated with the collection of late payment). Landlord may charge an initial fee and a daily fee for each day the rent is late--the combined fees are considered a single late fee. Tenants can ask landlords to provide a statement of whether they owe late fees. (Texas)

[23] Landlords cannot charge a tenant a late fee unless it is provided for in a written rental agreement or lease. No late charge shall exceed the lesser of 10% of the periodic rent or 10% of the remaining balance due and owed by the tenant. (Virginia)

	State Rent Rules (continued)			
State	**When Rent Is Due**	**Grace Period**	**Where Rent Is Due**	**Late Fees**
Washington	No statute.	Wash. Rev. Code Ann. § 59.18.170		Wash. Rev. Code Ann. § 59.18.285 [24]
West Virginia	No statute.			
Wisconsin	No statute.			Wis. Adm. Code § ATCP 134.09(8) [25]
Wyoming	No statute.			

[24] Nonrefundable fees must be described in lease or rental agreement; otherwise, they will be considered to be deposits. Landlords may not impose late fees until the rent is more than five days late. The fee may commence as of the first day the rent is overdue, and landlords may serve a notice to pay rent or quit as soon as the rent is overdue. If tenants can demonstrate in writing that their primary source of income is a regular, monthly source of governmental assistance that is not received until after the date rent is due in the rental agreement, landlords must adjust rental due date (to no more than five days after the date specified in the rental agreement). (Washington)

[25] Late fee policy must be in the rental agreement, landlord must first apply any prepaid rent (such as last month's rent) to the unpaid rent, and landlord may not charge a fee or impose a penalty for failure to pay the late rent fee. (Wisconsin)

State Security Deposit Rules

Here are the statutes and rules that govern a landlord's collection and retention of security deposits. Many states require landlords to disclose, at or near the time they collect the deposit, information about how deposits may be used, as noted in the Disclosure or Requirement section. Required disclosures of other issues, such as a property's history of flooding, are in the chart, "Required Landlord Disclosures."

Alabama

Ala. Code § 35-9A-201

Limit: One month's rent, except for pet deposits, deposits to cover undoing tenant's alterations, and deposits to cover tenant activities that pose increased liability risks.

Deadline for Landlord to Itemize and Return Deposit: 60 days after termination of tenancy and delivery of possession.

Alaska

Alaska Stat. § 34.03.070

Limit: Two months' rent, unless rent exceeds $2,000 per month. Landlord may ask for an additional month's rent as deposit for a pet that is not a service animal, but may use it only to remedy pet damage.

Disclosure or Requirement: Orally or in writing, landlord must disclose the conditions under which landlord may withhold all or part of the deposit.

Separate Account: Required (but may commingle prepaid rent with security deposits).

Advance Notice of Deduction: Not required.

Deadline for Landlord to Itemize and Return Deposit: 14 days if the tenant gives proper notice to terminate tenancy; 30 days if the tenant does not give proper notice or if landlord has deducted amounts needed to remedy damage caused by tenant's failure to maintain the property (Alaska Stat. § 34.03.120).

Arizona

Ariz. Rev. Stat. Ann. § 33-1321

Exemption: Excludes, among others, occupancy under a contract of sale of a dwelling unit or the property of which it is a part, if the occupant is the purchaser or a person who succeeds to his interest; occupancy by an employee of a landlord as a manager or custodian whose right to occupancy is conditional upon employment in and about the premises.

Limit: One and one-half months' rent.

Disclosure or Requirement: If landlord collects a nonrefundable fee, its purpose must be stated in writing. All fees not designated as nonrefundable are refundable.

Advance Notice of Deduction: Not required.

Deadline for Landlord to Itemize and Return Deposit: 14 days; tenant has the right to be present at final inspection.

Arkansas

Ark. Code Ann. §§ 18-16-301 to 18-16-305

Exemption: Security deposit rules do not apply to the following unless the management of the rental (including rent collection) is performed by a third party for a fee: Dwellings owned by an individual, if the individual, the individual's spouse and minor children—and any and all partnerships, corporations, or other legal entities formed for the purpose of renting dwelling units and of which they are officers, owners, or majority shareholders—own, or collectively own, five or fewer units.

Limit: Two months' rent.

Advance Notice of Deduction: Not required.

Deadline for Landlord to Itemize and Return Deposit: 60 days.

California

Cal. Civ. Code §§ 1940.5(g), 1950.5

Limit: Two months' rent (unfurnished); three months' rent (furnished). If the tenant is an active service member, no more than one month's rent (unfurnished) or two months' rent (furnished). Add extra one-half month's rent for waterbed.

Advance Notice of Deduction: Required.

Deadline for Landlord to Itemize and Return Deposit: 21 days.

State Security Deposit Rules (continued)

Colorado

Colo. Rev. Stat. §§ 38-12-102 to 38-12-104

Limit: No statutory limit.

Advance Notice of Deduction: Not required.

Deadline for Landlord to Itemize and Return Deposit: One month, unless lease agreement specifies longer period of time (which may be no more than 60 days); 72 hours (not counting weekends or holidays) if a hazardous condition involving gas equipment requires tenant to vacate.

Connecticut

Conn. Gen. Stat. Ann. § 47a-21

Limit: Two months' rent (tenant younger than 62 years of age); one month's rent (tenant 62 years of age or older). Tenants who paid a deposit in excess of one month's rent, who then turn 62 years old, are entitled, upon request, to a refund of the amount that exceeds one month's rent.

Separate Account: Required.

Interest Payment: Interest payments must be made annually (or credited toward rent, at the landlord's option) and no later than 30 days after termination of tenancy. The interest rate must be equal to the average rate paid on savings deposits by insured commercial banks, rounded to the nearest 0.1%, as published by the Federal Reserve Board Bulletin.

Advance Notice of Deduction: Not required.

Deadline for Landlord to Itemize and Return Deposit: 30 days, or within 15 days of receiving tenant's forwarding address, whichever is later.

Delaware

Del. Code Ann. tit. 25, §§ 5514, 5311

Limit: One month's rent on leases for one year or more. For month-to-month tenancies, no limit for the first year, but after that, the limit is one month's rent (at the expiration of one year, landlord must give tenant a credit for any deposit held by the landlord that is in excess of one month's rent). No limit for furnished units. Tenant may offer to supply a surety bond in lieu of or in conjunction with a deposit, which landlord may elect to receive.

Separate Account: Required. Orally or in writing, the landlord must disclose to the tenant the location of the security deposit account.

Advance Notice of Deduction: Not required.

Deadline for Landlord to Itemize and Return Deposit: 20 days.

District of Columbia

D.C. Code Ann. § 42-3502.17; D.C. Mun. Regs. tit. 14, §§ 308 to 310

Exemption: Landlords cannot demand or receive a security deposit from a tenant in a rental unit occupied by the tenant as of July 17, 1985, when no security deposit had been required prior to that date.

Limit: One month's rent.

Disclosure or Requirement: In the lease, rental agreement, or receipt, landlord must state the terms and conditions under which the security deposit was collected (to secure tenant's obligations under the lease or rental agreement).

Separate Account: Required.

Interest Payment: Required. Interest payments at the prevailing statement savings rate must be made at termination of tenancy.

Advance Notice of Deduction: Not required.

Deadline for Landlord to Itemize and Return Deposit: 45 days.

Florida

Fla. Stat. Ann. §§ 83.43(12), 83.49

Limit: No statutory limit.

Disclosure or Requirement: Within 30 days of receiving the security deposit, the landlord must disclose in writing whether it will be held in an interest- or non-interest-bearing account; the name of the account depository; and the rate and time of interest payments. Landlord who collects a deposit must include in the lease the disclosure statement contained in Florida Statutes § 83.49.

Separate Account: Required. Landlord may post a security bond securing all tenants' deposits instead.

State Security Deposit Rules (continued)

Interest Payment: Interest payments, if any (account need not be interest bearing) must be made annually and at termination of tenancy. However, no interest is due a tenant who wrongfully terminates the tenancy before the end of the rental term.

Advance Notice of Deduction: Required.

Deadline for Landlord to Itemize and Return Deposit: 15 to 60 days depending on whether tenant disputes deductions.

Georgia

Ga. Code Ann. §§ 44-7-30 to 44-7-37

Exemption: Landlord who owns ten or fewer rental units, unless these units are managed by an outside party, need not supply written list of preexisting damage, nor place deposit in an escrow account. Rules for returning the deposit still apply.

Limit: No statutory limit.

Disclosure or Requirement: Landlord must give tenant a written list of preexisting damage to the rental before collecting a security deposit.

Separate Account: Required. Landlord must place the deposit in an escrow account in a state- or federally regulated depository, and must inform the tenant of the location of this account. Landlord may post a security bond securing all tenants' deposits instead.

Advance Notice of Deduction: Required.

Deadline for Landlord to Itemize and Return Deposit: 30 days.

Hawaii

Haw. Rev. Stat. § 521-44

Limit: One month's rent. (Landlord may require an additional one month's rent as security deposit for tenants who keep a pet.)

Advance Notice of Deduction: Not required.

Deadline for Landlord to Itemize and Return Deposit: 14 days.

Idaho

Idaho Code § 6-321

Limit: No statutory limit.

Advance Notice of Deduction: Not required.

Deadline for Landlord to Itemize and Return Deposit: 21 days or up to 30 days if landlord and tenant agree.

Illinois

765 Ill. Comp. Stat. 710/1; 715/1 to 715/3

Limit: No statutory limit.

Disclosure or Requirement: If a lease specifies the cost for repair, cleaning, or replacement of any part of the leased premises; or the cleaning or repair of any component of the building or common area that will not be replaced, the landlord may withhold the dollar amount specified in the lease. Landlord's itemized statement must reference the specified dollar amount(s) and include a copy of the lease clause.

Interest Payment: Landlords who rent 25 or more units in either a single building or a complex located on contiguous properties must pay interest on deposits held for more than six months. The interest rate is the rate paid for minimum deposit savings accounts by the largest commercial bank in the state, as of December 31 of the calendar year immediately preceding the start of the tenancy. Within 30 days after the end of each 12-month rental period, landlord must pay any interest that has accumulated to an amount of $5 or more, by cash or credit applied to rent due, except when the tenant is in default under the terms of the lease. Landlord must pay all interest that has accumulated and remains unpaid, regardless of the amount, upon termination of the tenancy.

Advance Notice of Deduction: Not required.

Deadline for Landlord to Itemize and Return Deposit: For properties with 5 or more units, 30 to 45 days, depending on whether tenant disputes deductions or if statement and receipts are furnished.

Indiana

Ind. Code Ann. §§ 32-31-3-9 to 32-31-3-19

Exemption: Does not apply to rental agreements entered into before July 1, 1989.

Limit: No statutory limit.

Advance Notice of Deduction: Not required.

Deadline for Landlord to Itemize and Return Deposit: 45 days.

State Security Deposit Rules (continued)

Iowa

Iowa Code Ann. § 562A.12

Limit: Two months' rent.

Separate Account: Required.

Interest Payment: Interest payment, if any (account need not be interest bearing), must be made at termination of tenancy. Interest earned during first five years of tenancy belongs to landlord.

Advance Notice of Deduction: Not required.

Deadline for Landlord to Itemize and Return Deposit: 30 days.

Kansas

Kan. Stat. Ann. §§ 58-2548, 58-2550

Limit: One month's rent (unfurnished); one and one-half months' rent (furnished); for pets, add extra one-half month's rent.

Advance Notice of Deduction: Not required.

Deadline for Landlord to Itemize and Return Deposit: 30 days.

Kentucky

Ky. Rev. Stat. Ann. § 383.580

Limit: No statutory limit.

Disclosure or Requirement: Orally or in writing, landlord must disclose where the security deposit is being held and the account number.

Before accepting a security deposit, landlords must give tenants a list of preexisting damage that would justify a charge against the deposit, including the amount of the charge. Tenants have the right to inspect before taking possession. Both parties must sign the list, and if tenants disagree with its accuracy, they must state in writing the basis for their disagreement and sign the statement of dissent. A mutually signed listing is conclusive proof of the listed defects, but not as to latent (unobservable) defects.

Separate Account: Required.

Advance Notice of Deduction: Required.

Deadline for Landlord to Itemize and Return Deposit: 30 to 60 days depending on whether tenant disputes deductions.

Louisiana

La. Rev. Stat. Ann. § 9:3251

Limit: No statutory limit.

Advance Notice of Deduction: Not required.

Deadline for Landlord to Itemize and Return Deposit: One month.

Maine

Me. Rev. Stat. Ann. tit. 14, §§ 6031 to 6038

Exemption: Entire security deposit law does not apply to rental unit that is part of structure with five or fewer units, one of which is occupied by landlord

Limit: Two months' rent.

Disclosure or Requirement: Upon request by the tenant, landlord must disclose orally or in writing the account number and the name of the institution where the security deposit is being held.

Separate Account: Required.

Advance Notice of Deduction: Not required.

Deadline for Landlord to Itemize and Return Deposit: 30 days (if written rental agreement) or 21 days (if tenancy at will).

Maryland

Md. Code Ann. [Real Prop.] §§ 8-203, 8-203.1, 8-208

Limit: Two months' rent.

Exemption: Security deposit statutes do not apply to a tenancy arising after the sale of owner-occupied residential property where the seller and purchaser agree that the seller may remain in possession of the property for not more than 60 days after the settlement.

Separate Account: Required. Landlord may hold all tenants' deposits in secured certificates of deposit, or in securities issued by the federal government or the State of Maryland.

Interest Payment: For security deposits of $50 or more, when landlord has held the deposit for at least six months: Within 45 days of termination of tenancy, interest must be paid at the daily U.S. Treasury yield curve rate for 1 year, as of the first business day of each year, or 1.5% a year, whichever is greater, less any

State Security Deposit Rules (continued)

damages rightfully withheld. Interest accrues monthly but is not compounded, and no interest is due for any period less than one month. (See the Department of Housing and Community Development website for a calculator.) Deposit must be held in a Maryland banking institution.

Advance Notice of Deduction: Required.

Deadline for Landlord to Itemize and Return Deposit: 45 days.

Massachusetts

Mass. Gen. Laws Ann. ch. 186, § 15B

Limit: One month's rent.

Exemption: Security deposit rules do not apply to any lease, rental, occupancy, or tenancy of 100 days or less in duration, which lease or rental is for a vacation or recreational purpose.

Disclosure or Requirement: At the time of receiving a security deposit, landlord must furnish a receipt indicating the amount of the deposit; the name of the person receiving it and, if received by a property manager, the name of the lessor for whom the security deposit is received; the date on which it is received; and a description of the premises leased or rented. The receipt must be signed by the person receiving the security deposit.

Separate Account: Required. Within 30 days of receiving security deposit, landlord must disclose the name and location of the bank in which the security deposit has been deposited, and the amount and account number of the deposit.

Interest Payment: Landlord must pay tenant 5% interest per year or the amount received from the bank (which must be in Massachusetts) that holds the deposit. Interest should be paid yearly, and within 30 days of termination date. Interest will not accrue for the last month for which rent was paid in advance.

Advance Notice of Deduction: Not required.

Deadline for Landlord to Itemize and Return Deposit: 30 days.

Michigan

Mich. Comp. Laws §§ 554.602 to 554.616

Limit: One and one-half months' rent.

Disclosure or Requirement: Within 14 days of tenant's taking possession of the rental, landlord must furnish in writing the landlord's name and address for receipt of communications, the name and address of the financial institution or surety where the deposit will be held, and the tenant's obligation to provide in writing a forwarding mailing address to the landlord within 4 days after termination of occupancy. The notice shall include the following statement in 12-point boldface type that is at least 4 points larger than the body of the notice or lease agreement: "You must notify your landlord in writing within 4 days after you move of a forwarding address where you can be reached and where you will receive mail; otherwise your landlord shall be relieved of sending you an itemized list of damages and the penalties adherent to that failure."

Separate Account: Required. Landlord must place deposits in a regulated financial institution, and may use the deposits as long as the landlord deposits with the secretary of state a cash or surety bond.

Advance Notice of Deduction: Required. Tenants must dispute the landlord's stated deductions within 7 days of receiving the itemized list and balance, if any, or give up any right to dispute them.

Deadline for Landlord to Itemize and Return Deposit: 30 days.

Minnesota

Minn. Stat. Ann. §§ 504B.151, 504B.175, 504B.178, & 504B.195

Limit: No statutory limit. If landlord collects a "prelease deposit" and subsequently rents to tenant, landlord must apply the prelease deposit to the security deposit.

Disclosure or Requirement: Before collecting rent or a security deposit, landlord must provide a copy of all outstanding inspection orders for which a citation has been issued, pertaining to a rental unit or common

State Security Deposit Rules (continued)

area, specifying code violations that threaten the health or safety of the tenant, and all outstanding condemnation orders and declarations that the premises are unfit for human habitation. Citations for violations that do not involve threats to tenant health or safety must be summarized and posted in an obvious place. With some exceptions, landlord who has received notice of a contract for deed cancellation or notice of a mortgage foreclosure sale must so disclose before entering a lease, accepting rent, or accepting a security deposit; and must furnish the date on which the contract cancellation period or the mortgagor's redemption period ends.

Interest Payment: Landlord must pay 1% simple, noncompounded interest per year. (Deposits collected before 8/1/03 earn interest at 3%, up to 8/1/03, then begin earning at 1%.) Any interest amount less than $1 is excluded.

Advance Notice of Deduction: Not required.

Deadline for Landlord to Itemize and Return Deposit: Three weeks after tenant leaves and landlord receives forwarding address; five days if tenant must leave due to building condemnation.

Mississippi

Miss. Code Ann. § 89-8-21

Limit: No statutory limit.

Advance Notice of Deduction: Not required.

Deadline for Landlord to Itemize and Return Deposit: 45 days.

Missouri

Mo. Ann. Stat. § 535.300

Limit: Two months' rent.

Advance Notice of Deduction: Not required.

Deadline for Landlord to Itemize and Return Deposit: 30 days.

Montana

Mont. Code Ann. §§ 70-25-101 to 70-25-206

Limit: No statutory limit.

Disclosure or Requirement: Before signing a lease, landlords must give tenants a signed statement of the physical condition of the premises, including a statement (if applicable) that the premises have never been leased. Upon request, landlords must furnish a separate written statement of the damage and cleaning charges of the departing tenants. Landlords who fail to comply may not deduct any sums for damage or cleaning unless the landlord can establish by "clear and convincing evidence" that the tenant, tenant's family, licensees, or invitees were responsible.

Advance Notice of Deduction: Required. Tenant is entitled to advance notice of cleaning charges, but only if such cleaning is required as a result of tenant's negligence and is not part of the landlord's cyclical cleaning program.

Advance Notice of Deduction: Required.

Deadline for Landlord to Itemize and Return Deposit: 30 days; 10 days if no deductions.

Nebraska

Neb. Rev. Stat. § 76-1416

Limit: One month's rent (no pets); one and one-quarter months' rent (pets).

Advance Notice of Deduction: Not required.

Deadline for Landlord to Itemize and Return Deposit: 14 days.

Nevada

Nev. Rev. Stat. Ann. §§ 118A.240 to 118A.250

Exemption: Security deposit rules do not apply to the following, among others: (1) Occupancy under a contract of sale of a dwelling unit or the property of which it is a part, if the occupant is the purchaser or a person who succeeds to the purchaser's interest; (2) Occupancy by an employee of a landlord whose right to occupancy is conditional upon employment in and about the premises; (3) Occupancy by a person who is guilty of a forcible entry or forcible detainer.

Limit: Three months' rent; if both landlord and tenant agree, tenant may use a surety bond for all or part of the deposit.

State Security Deposit Rules (continued)

Disclosure or Requirement: Lease or rental agreement must explain the conditions under which the landlord will refund the deposit.

Deadline for Landlord to Itemize and Return Deposit: 30 days.

New Hampshire

N.H. Rev. Stat. Ann. §§ 540-A:5 to 540-A:8; 540-B:10

Exemption: Entire security deposit law does not apply to landlord who leases a single-family residence and owns no other rental property, or landlord who leases rental units in an owner-occupied building of five units or fewer (exemption does not apply to any individual unit in owner-occupied building that is occupied by a person 60 years of age or older).

Limit: One month's rent or $100, whichever is greater; when landlord and tenant share facilities, no statutory limit.

Disclosure or Requirement: Unless tenant has paid the deposit by personal or bank check, or by a check issued by a government agency, landlord must provide a receipt stating the amount of the deposit and the institution where it will be held. Regardless of whether a receipt is required, landlord must inform tenant that if tenant finds any conditions in the rental in need of repair, tenant may note them on the receipt or other written instrument, and return either within five days.

Separate Account: Required. Upon request, landlord must disclose the account number, the amount on deposit, and the interest rate. Landlord may post a bond covering all deposits instead of putting deposits in a separate account.

Interest Payment: Landlord who holds a security deposit for a year or longer must pay interest at a rate equal to the rate paid on regular savings accounts in the New Hampshire bank, savings & loan, or credit union where it's deposited. If a landlord mingles security deposits in a single account, the landlord must pay the actual interest earned proportionately to each tenant. A tenant may request the interest accrued every three years, 30 days before that year's tenancy expires. The landlord must comply with the request within 15 days of the expiration of that year's tenancy.

Advance Notice of Deduction: Not required.

Deadline for Landlord to Itemize and Return Deposit: 30 days; for shared facilities, if the deposit is more than 30 days' rent, landlord must provide written agreement acknowledging receipt and specifying when deposit will be returned—if no written agreement, 20 days after tenant vacates.

New Jersey

N.J. Stat. Ann. §§ 46:8-19 to 46:8-26

Exemption: Security deposit law does not apply to owner-occupied buildings with not more than two rental units where the tenant has failed to provide 30 days' written notice to the landlord invoking the law.

Separate Account: Required. Within 30 days of receiving the deposit and every time the landlord pays the tenant interest, landlord must disclose the name and address of the banking organization where the deposit is being held, the type of account, current rate of interest, and the amount of the deposit.

Interest Payment: Landlord with 10 or more units must invest deposits as specified by statute or place deposit in an insured money market fund account, or in another account that pays quarterly interest at a rate comparable to the money market fund. Landlords with fewer than 10 units may place deposit in an interest-bearing account in any New Jersey financial institution insured by the FDIC. All landlords may pay tenants interest earned on account annually or credit toward payment of rent due.

Advance Notice of Deduction: Not required.

Deadline for Landlord to Itemize and Return Deposit: 30 days; five days in case of fire, flood, condemnation, or evacuation.

New Mexico

N.M. Stat. Ann. § 47-8-18

Exemption: Security deposit rules do not apply to the following, among others: (1) Occupancy under a contract of sale of a dwelling unit or the property of

State Security Deposit Rules (continued)

which it is a part, if the occupant is the purchaser or a person who succeeds to the purchaser's interest; (2) Occupancy by an employee of an owner pursuant to a written rental or employment agreement that specifies that the employee's right to occupancy is conditional upon employment in and about the premises.

Limit: One month's rent (for rental agreement of less than one year); no limit for leases of one year or more.

Interest Payment: Landlord who collects a deposit larger than than one month's rent on a year's lease must pay interest, on an annual basis, equal to the passbook interest.

Advance Notice of Deduction: Not required.

Deadline for Landlord to Itemize and Return Deposit: 30 days.

New York

N.Y. Gen. Oblig. Law §§ 7-103 to 7-108

Limit: One month's limit for units other than those subject to the City Rent and Rehabilitation Law or the Emergency Housing Rent Control Law.

Disclosure or Requirement: If deposit is placed in a bank, landlord must disclose the name and address of the banking organization where the deposit is being held, and the amount of such deposit.

Separate Account: Statute requires that deposits not be commingled with landlord's personal assets, but does not explicitly require placement in a banking institution (however, deposits collected in buildings of six or more units must be placed in New York bank accounts).

Interest Payment: Landlord who rents out non-regulated units in buildings with five or fewer units need not pay interest. Interest must be paid at the prevailing rate on deposits received from tenants who rent units in buildings containing six or more units. The landlord in every rental situation may retain an administrative fee of 1% per year on the sum deposited. Interest can be subtracted from the rent, paid at the end of the year, or paid at the end of the tenancy according to the tenant's choice.

Advance Notice of Deduction: Required.

Deadline for Landlord to Itemize and Return Deposit: 14 days.

North Carolina

N.C. Gen. Stat. §§ 42-50 to 42-56

Exemption: Not applicable to rentals of single rooms.

Limit: One and one-half months' rent for month-to-month rental agreements; two months' rent if term is longer than two months; may also charge a reasonable, nonrefundable pet deposit.

Disclosure or Requirement: Within 30 days of the beginning of the lease term, landlord must disclose the name and address of the banking institution where the deposit is located or the name of the insurance company providing the bond.

Separate Account: The landlord may choose to furnish a bond from an insurance company licensed to do business in N.C. rather than deposit the security deposit in a trust account.

Advance Notice of Deduction: Not required.

Deadline for Landlord to Itemize and Return Deposit: 30 days; if landlord's claim against the deposit cannot be finalized within that time, landlord may send an interim accounting and a final accounting within 60 days of the tenancy's termination.

North Dakota

N.D. Cent. Code § 47-16-07.1

Limit: One month's rent. If tenant has a pet, an additional pet deposit of up to $2,500 or two months' rent, whichever is greater. To encourage renting to persons with records of felony convictions, landlords may charge these applicants up to two months' rent as security. Applicants who have had court judgments entered against them "for violating the terms of a previous rental agreement" can also be charged up to two months' rent (this appears to refer to prior evictions and might not apply to evictions based on conduct not prohibited by the rental agreement).

Separate Account: Required.

State Security Deposit Rules (continued)

Interest Payment: Landlord must pay interest if the period of occupancy is at least nine months. Money must be held in a federally insured interest-bearing savings or checking account for benefit of the tenant. Interest must be paid upon termination of the lease.

Advance Notice of Deduction: Not required.

Deadline for Landlord to Itemize and Return Deposit: 30 days.

Ohio

Ohio Rev. Code Ann. § 5321.16

Limit: No statutory limit.

Interest Payment: Any deposit in excess of $50 or one month's rent, whichever is greater, must bear interest on the excess at the rate of 5% per annum if the tenant stays for six months or more. Interest must be paid annually and upon termination of tenancy.

Advance Notice of Deduction: Not required.

Deadline for Landlord to Itemize and Return Deposit: 30 days.

Oklahoma

Okla. Stat. Ann. tit. 41, § 115

Limit: No statutory limit.

Separate Account: Required.

Advance Notice of Deduction: Not required.

Deadline for Landlord to Itemize and Return Deposit: 45 days.

Oregon

Or. Rev. Stat. § 90.300

Exemption: Security deposit rules do not apply to the following, among others: (1) Occupancy of a unit for no more than 90 days by a purchaser prior to the scheduled closing of a real estate sale or by a seller following the closing of a sale, in either case as permitted under the terms of an agreement for sale of a dwelling unit or the property of which it is a part (a tenant who holds but has not exercised an option to purchase the unit does not qualify for this exemption); (2) Vacation occupancy; (3) Occupancy by an employee of a landlord whose right to occupancy is conditional upon employment in and about the premises.

Limit: No statutory limit. Landlord may not impose or increase deposit within first year unless parties agree to modify the rental agreement to allow for a pet or other cause, and the imposition or increase relates to that modification.

Disclosure or Requirement: Landlord must provide a receipt for any security deposit the tenant pays.

Advance Notice of Deduction: Not required.

Deadline for Landlord to Itemize and Return Deposit: 31 days.

Pennsylvania

68 Pa. Cons. Stat. Ann. §§ 250.511a to 250.512

Limit: Two months' rent for first year of renting; one month's rent during second and subsequent years of renting.

Disclosure or Requirement: For deposits over $100, landlord must deposit them in a federally or state-regulated institution, and give tenant the name and address of the banking institution and the amount of the deposit.

Separate Account: Required. Instead of placing deposits in a separate account, landlord may purchase a bond issued by a bonding company authorized to do business in the state.

Interest Payment: Tenant who occupies rental unit for two or more years is entitled to interest beginning with the 25th month of occupancy. Landlord must pay tenant interest (minus 1% fee) at the end of the third and subsequent years of the tenancy.

Advance Notice of Deduction: Not required.

Deadline for Landlord to Itemize and Return Deposit: 30 days.

Rhode Island

R.I. Gen. Laws § 34-18-19

Exemption: Security deposit rules do not apply to the following, among others: (1) Occupancy under a contract of sale of a dwelling unit or the property of which it is a part, if the occupant is the purchaser or

State Security Deposit Rules (continued)

a person who succeeds to the purchaser's interest; (2) Occupancy by a paid employee of a landlord, whose right to occupancy is conditional upon employment substantially for services, maintenance, or repair of premises containing more than 11 units.

Limit: One month's rent (unfurnished); if furnished, separate furniture security deposit up to one month's rent if furnishings' replacement value at the start of the tenancy is $5,000 or more.

Advance Notice of Deduction: Not required.

Deadline for Landlord to Itemize and Return Deposit: 20 days.

South Carolina

S.C. Code Ann. § 27-40-410

Exemption: Security deposit rules do not apply to the following, among others: (1) Occupancy under a contract of sale of a dwelling unit or the property of which it is a part, if the occupant is the purchaser or a person who succeeds to the purchaser's interest; (2) Occupancy by an employee of a landlord whose right to occupancy is conditional upon employment in and about the premises; (3) Certain vacation rentals.

Limit: No statutory limit.

Advance Notice of Deduction: Not required.

Deadline for Landlord to Itemize and Return Deposit: 30 days.

South Dakota

S.D. Codified Laws Ann. §§ 43.32-6.1, 43-32-24

Limit: One month's rent (higher deposit may be charged if special conditions pose a danger to maintenance of the premises).

Advance Notice of Deduction: Not required.

Deadline for Landlord to Itemize and Return Deposit: Two weeks, and must supply reasons for withholding any portion; 45 days for a written, itemized accounting, if tenant requests it.

Tennessee

Tenn. Code Ann. § 66-28-301

Limit: No statutory limit.

Separate Account: Required. Orally or in writing, landlord must disclose the location of the separate account (but not the account number) used by landlord for the deposit.

Advance Notice of Deduction: Required.

Deadline for Landlord to Itemize and Return Deposit: No statutory deadline.

Texas

Tex. Prop. Code Ann. §§ 92.101 to 92.110

Limit: No statutory limit.

Disclosure or Requirement: If a security deposit isn't required by the lease or rental agreement, but the tenant is liable for damage or rent when they leave, the landlord must notify the tenant in writing about the claim before reporting the claim. Landlords who don't provide notice forfeit the right to collect damages and charges from the tenant.

Advance Notice of Deduction: Not required.

Deadline for Landlord to Itemize and Return Deposit: 30 days. If landlord wants to condition the refund of the security deposit on the tenant's giving advance notice of surrender, landlord must put this condition in the lease, and it must be either underlined or printed in conspicuous bold print.

Utah

Utah Code Ann. §§ 57-17-1 to 57-17-5

Limit: No statutory limit.

Disclosure or Requirement: For written leases or rental agreements only, if part of the deposit is nonrefundable, landlord must disclose this feature.

Advance Notice of Deduction: Not required.

Deadline for Landlord to Itemize and Return Deposit: 30 days.

Vermont

Vt. Stat. Ann. tit. 9, § 4461

Exemption: Security deposit rules do not apply to the following, among others: (1) Occupancy under a contract of sale of a dwelling unit or the property of which it is a part, if the occupant is the purchaser or a person who succeeds to the purchaser's interest;

State Security Deposit Rules (continued)

(2) Occupancy of a dwelling unit without right or permission by a person who is not a tenant.

Limit: No statutory limit.

Advance Notice of Deduction: Not required.

Deadline for Landlord to Itemize and Return Deposit: 14 days; 60 days if the rental is seasonal and not intended as the tenant's primary residence.

Virginia

Va. Code Ann. §§ 55.1-1204, 55.1-1206, 55.1-1208, 55.1-1226

Limit: Two months' rent. Alternatively, landlord may permit a tenant to provide damage insurance coverage in an amount not more than two months' rent in lieu of the payment of a security deposit. (Landlord may also require a mix of a deposit and insurance.) The damage insurance coverage must meet the requirements listed in Virginia Code Annotated sections 55.1-1226(I)-(K).

Advance Notice of Deduction: Not required.

Deadline for Landlord to Itemize and Return Deposit: 45 days; 30 days to itemize any deductions to be made during the course of the tenancy (45 days if the deductions exceed the amount of the security deposit). Lease can provide for expedited processing at the end of the tenancy and specify an administrative fee for such processing, which will apply only if tenant requests it with a separate written document. Landlord must give tenant written notice of tenant's right to be present at a final inspection.

Washington

Wash. Rev. Code Ann. §§ 59.18.260 to 59.18.285; 59.18.610

Limit: Landlords must allow tenants to pay the deposit and fees in installments (does not apply if the deposit and any nonrefundable fees are less than 25% of the monthly rent, or the landlord has not demanded the last month's rent). Tenants with tenancies of three months or more may pay in three equal and consecutive installments, beginning at the start of the tenancy; two installments for shorter tenancies. Installment schedules must be written and signed. Does not apply to holding deposits (which may not be more than 25% of the first month's rent).

Disclosure or Requirement: In the lease, landlord must disclose the circumstances under which all or part of the deposit may be withheld. No deposit may be collected unless the rental agreement is in writing and a written checklist or statement specifically describing the condition and cleanliness of or existing damages to the premises and furnishings is provided to the tenant at the start of the tenancy.

The landlord must provide tenant with a written receipt for the deposit and provide the name, address, and location of where the deposit will be kept; if location changes, landlord must notify tenant. Nonrefundable fees must be identified as such in a written rental agreement. If landlords fail to provide a written agreement, tenants are entitled to the return of the fee. If the written agreement does not specify that the fee is refundable, it must be treated as a refundable deposit.

Separate Account: Required.

Advance Notice of Deduction: Not required.

Deadline for Landlord to Itemize and Return Deposit: 21 days.

West Virginia

W.Va. Code §§ 37-6A-1 to 37-6A-6

Exemption: Agreements for the payment of security deposits entered into before June 10, 2011.

Limit: No statutory limit.

Deadline for Landlord to Itemize and Return Deposit: 60 days from the date the tenancy has terminated, or within 45 days of the occupancy of a subsequent tenant, whichever is shorter. If the damage exceeds the amount of the security deposit and the landlord has to hire a contractor to fix it, the notice period is extended 15 days.

Wisconsin

Wis. Admin. Code ATCP 134.04, 134.06; Wis. Stat. § 704.28

Exemption: Security deposit rules do not apply to the following, among others: (1) A dwelling unit occupied, under a contract of sale, by the purchaser of the dwelling unit or the purchaser's successor in interest; (2) A dwelling unit which the landlord provides free of charge to any person; (3) A dwelling unit which

State Security Deposit Rules (continued)

the landlord provides as consideration to a person whom the landlord currently employs to operate or maintain the premises.

Limit: No statutory limit.

Disclosure or Requirement: Before accepting the deposit, landlord must inform tenant of tenant's inspection rights, disclose all habitability defects and show tenant any outstanding building and housing code violations, inform tenant of the means by which shared utilities will be billed, and inform tenant if utilities are not paid for by landlord.

Advance Notice of Deduction: Not required.

Deadline for Landlord to Itemize and Return Deposit: 21 days.

Wyoming

Wyo. Stat. §§ 1-21-1207, 1-21-1208

Limit: No statutory limit.

Disclosure or Requirement: Lease or rental agreement must state whether any portion of a deposit is nonrefundable, and landlord must give tenant written notice of this fact when collecting the deposit.

Advance Notice of Deduction: Not required.

Deadline for Landlord to Itemize and Return Deposit: 30 days, when applying it to unpaid rent (or within 15 days of receiving tenant's forwarding address, whichever is later); additional 30 days allowed for deductions due to damage.

Required Landlord Disclosures

Many states require landlords to inform tenants of important state laws or individual landlord policies, either in the lease or rental agreement or in another writing. Common disclosures include a landlord's imposition of nonrefundable fees (where permitted), tenants' rights to move-in checklists, and the identity of the landlord or landlord's agent or manager. Disclosures concerning the security deposit are in the chart, "State Security Deposit Rules."

Also, keep in mind that landlords in *all* states must disclose information about lead-based paint to tenants if the building they are renting was built before 1978. See Chapter 1, "Lead Disclosures," for details.

Alabama

Ala. Code § 35-9A-202

Owner or agent identity: Landlord must disclose to the tenant in writing at or before the commencement of the tenancy the name and address of the person authorized to manage the premises, and an owner of the premises or a person authorized to act for and on behalf of the owner for the purpose of service of process and for the purpose of receiving notices and demands. (Exception: does not apply to resident purchaser under a contract of sale (but does apply to a resident who has an option to buy), nor to the continuation of occupancy by the seller or a member of the seller's family for a period of not more than 36 months after the sale of a dwelling unit or the property of which it is a part.)

Alaska

Alaska Stat. §§ 34.03.080, 34.03.150

Owner or agent identity: Landlord must disclose to the tenant in writing at or before the commencement of the tenancy the name and address of the person authorized to manage the premises, and an owner of the premises or a person authorized to act for and on behalf of the owner for the purpose of service of process and for the purpose of receiving notices and demands. (Alaska Stat. § 34.03.080)

Extended absence: The rental agreement must require that the tenant notify the landlord of an anticipated extended absence from the premises in excess of seven days; however, the notice maybe given as soon as reasonably possible after the tenant knows the absence will exceed seven days. (Alaska Stat. § 34.03.150)

Arizona

Ariz. Rev. Stat. Ann. §§ 33-1314, 33-1314.01,33-1319, 33-1321, 33-1322, 36-1637

Nonrefundable fees permitted? Yes. The purpose of all nonrefundable fees or deposits must be stated in writing. Any fee or deposit not designated as nonrefundable is refundable. (Ariz. Rev. Stat. Ann. § 33-1321)

Move-in checklist required? Yes. Tenants also have the right to be present at a move-out inspection. (Ariz. Rev. Stat. Ann. § 33-1321)

Separate utility charges: If landlord charges separately for gas, water, wastewater, solid waste removal, or electricity by installing a submetering system, landlord may recover the charges imposed on the landlord by the utility provider, plus an administrative fee for the landlord for actual administrative costs only, and must disclose separate billing and fee in the rental agreement. If landlord uses a ratio utility billing system, the rental agreement must contain a specific description of the ratio utility billing method used to allocate utility costs. (Ariz. Rev. Stat. Ann. § 33-1314.01)

Owner or agent identity: Landlord must disclose to the tenant in writing at or before the commencement of the tenancy the name and address of the person authorized to manage the premises, and an owner of the premises or a person authorized to act for and on behalf of the owner for the purpose of service of process and for the purpose of receiving notices and demands. (Ariz. Rev. Stat. Ann. § 33-1322)

Business tax pass-through: If the landlord pays a local tax based on rent and that tax increases, landlord may pass through the increase by increasing the rent upon 30 days' notice (but not before the new tax is effective), but only if the landlord's right to adjust the rent is disclosed in the rental agreement. (Ariz. Rev. Stat. Ann. § 33-1314)

Required Landlord Disclosures (continued)

Availability of landlord and tenant act: Landlord must inform tenant in writing that the Residential Landlord and Tenant Act is available on the Arizona department of housing's website. (Ariz. Rev. Stat. Ann. § 33-1322)

Bed bug information: Landlords must provide existing and new tenants with educational materials on bed bugs, including information and physical descriptions, prevention and control measures, behavioral attraction risk factors, information from federal, state, and local centers for disease control and prevention, health or housing agencies, nonprofit housing organizations, or information developed by the landlord. (Ariz. Rev. Stat. Ann. § 33-1319)

Smoke detectors: Landlords must install smoke detectors and give tenant written notification of tenant's responsibilities (tenant must maintain it unless tenant gives written notification to the landlord of its malfunction, at which point landlord must maintain it). (Ariz. Rev. Stat. Ann. § 36-1637)

Arkansas

No disclosure statutes.

California

Cal. Civ. Code §§ 1710.2, 1940.6, 1940.7, 1940.8, 1940.9, 1946.2, 1947.5, 1947.12, § 1950.5(m), 1954.603, 2079.10a; Cal. Bus. & Prof. Code § 8538; Cal. Health & Safety Code §§ 25400.28, 26147, 26148; Cal. Gov't. Code § 8589.45

Nonrefundable fees permitted? No. (Cal. Civ. Code § 1950.5(m))

Move-in checklist required? No.

Registered sexual offender database: Landlords must include this notice in every lease or rental agreement: "Notice: Pursuant to Section 290.46 of the Penal Code, information about specified registered sex offenders is made available to the public via an Internet Web site maintained by the Department of Justice at www.meganslaw.ca.gov. Depending on an offender's criminal history, this information will include either the address at which the offender resides or the community of residence and ZIP Code in which the offender resides." (Cal. Civ. Code § 2079.10a)

Tenant paying for others' utilities: Prior to signing a rental agreement, landlord must disclose whether gas or electric service to tenant's unit also serves other areas, and must disclose the manner by which costs will be fairly allocated. (Cal. Civ. Code § 1940.9)

Ordnance locations: Prior to signing a lease, landlord must disclose known locations of former federal or state ordnance in the neighborhood (within one mile of rental). (Cal. Civ. Code § 1940.7)

Mold: Prior to signing a rental agreement, landlord must provide written disclosure when landlord knows, or has reason to know, that mold exceeds permissible exposure limits or poses a health threat. Landlords must distribute a consumer handbook, developed by the State Department of Health Services, describing the potential health risks from mold. (Cal. Health & Safety Code §§ 26147, 26148)

Pest control service: When the rental agreement is signed, landlord must provide tenant with any pest control company disclosure landlord has received, which describes the pest to be controlled, pesticides used and their active ingredients, a warning that pesticides are toxic, and the frequency of treatment under any contract for periodic service. (Cal. Civ. Code § 1940.8; Cal. Bus. & Prof. Code § 8538)

Intention to demolish rental unit: Landlords or their agents who have applied for a permit to demolish a rental unit must give written notice of this fact to prospective tenants, before accepting any deposits or screening fees. (Cal. Civ. Code § 1940.6)

No-smoking policy: For leases and rental agreements signed after January 1, 2012: If the landlord prohibits or limits the smoking of tobacco products on the rental property, the lease or rental agreement must include a clause describing the areas where smoking is limited or prohibited (does not apply if the tenant has previously occupied the dwelling unit). For leases and rental agreements signed before January 1, 2012: A newly adopted policy limiting or prohibiting smoking is a change in the terms of the tenancy (will not apply to lease-holding tenants until they renew their leases; tenants renting month-to-month must be given

Required Landlord Disclosures (continued)

30 days' written notice). Does not preempt any local ordinances prohibiting smoking in effect on January 1, 2012. (Cal. Civ. Code § 1947.5)

Flooding: In leases or rental agreements signed after July 1, 2018, landlord must disclose, in at least eight-point type, that the property is in a special flood hazard area or an area of potential flooding if the landlord has actual knowledge of this fact. Actual knowledge includes receipt from a public agency so identifying the property; the fact that the owner carries flood insurance; or that the property is in an area in which the owner's mortgage holder requires the owner to carry flood insurance. Disclosure must advise tenant that additional information can be had at the Office of Emergency Services' website, and must include the Internet address for the MYHazards tool maintained by the Office. Disclosure must advise tenant that owner's insurance will not cover loss to tenant's property, and must recommend that tenant consider purchasing renter's insurance that will cover loss due to fire, flood, or other risk of loss. Disclosure must note that the owner is not required to provide additional information. (Cal. Govt. Code § 8589.45)

Bed bug information: Before signing a lease or rental agreement, landlord must give potential tenants information about bed bugs, including information about their behavior and biology, the importance of cooperation for prevention and treatment, and the importance of prompt written reporting of suspected infestations to the landlord. (Cal. Civ. Code § 1954.603)

Methamphetamine or Fentanyl: If a property has been contaminated and is subject to a remediation order, landlord must provide written notice of and a copy of the order to all prospective tenants who have submitted an application. The tenant has to acknowledge receipt of the notice in writing before signing a rental agreement, and the landlord must attach the notice to the rental agreement. If a landlord fails to provide this notice, the prospective tenant can void the rental agreement.

For the rental of mobile homes and manufactured homes, the landlord must notify prospective tenants, in writing, of all methamphetamine or fentanyl laboratory activities that have taken place in the mobile home or manufactured home, and any remediation of the home or vehicle, and the property can't be rented until the prospective tenant is provided with a copy of the order. If there is already a tenant, the landlord must attach the notice and order to the rental agreement. (Cal. Health & Safety Code § 25400.28)

Death on the premises within the past three years: If an occupant died on the property within three years of the landlord's offer to rent, the landlord must disclose this fact. Landlords are not required to disclose that an occupant of that property was living with human immunodeficiency virus (HIV) or died from AIDS-related complications. (Cal. Civ. Code § 1710.2)

Single-family tenancy subject to the Tenant Protection Act of 2019: Single-family rentals that are subject to the Tenant Protection Act must advise tenants as of January 1, 2020 with the following notice (notice must be in the lease or rental agreement as of July 1, 2020): "This property is not subject to the rent limits imposed by Section 1947.12 of the Civil Code and is not subject to the just cause requirements of Section 1946.2 of the Civil Code. This property meets the requirements of Sections 1947.12 (c)(5) and 1946.2 (e)(7) of the Civil Code and the owner is not any of the following: (1) a real estate investment trust, as defined by Section 856 of the Internal Revenue Code; (2) a corporation; or (3) a limited liability company in which at least one member is a corporation." (Cal. Civ. Code §§ 1946.2, 1947.12)

Single-family tenancy subject to the Tenant Protection Act of 2019, owner move-in: For tenancies subject to the Tenant Protection Act, landlord may terminate the lease in order to move in the owner or a specified relative if the lease includes the following provision: "This lease will terminate before the termination date if the owner or owner's spouse, domestic partner, children, grandchildren, parents, or grandparents decide to occupy the premises." (Cal. Civ. Code § 1946.2)

Required Landlord Disclosures (continued)

Colorado

Colo. Rev. Stat. Ann. §§ 38-12-801, 38-12-903, 38-12-904, 38-12-1005

Disclosure of landlord: Written rental agreements and leases must include a statement of the name and address of the person who is the landlord or the landlord's authorized agent. If this person's identity changes, the tenants must be notified of the new contact person within one business day after the change, and the landlord must post the identity of the new landlord or authorized agent in a conspicuous location on the rental premises. (Colo. Rev. Stat. Ann. § 38-12-801)

Bed bugs: Upon request from prospective tenants, landlords must disclose whether the unit for rent contained bed bugs within the previous eight months. If requested, landlords must also disclose the last date (if any) the unit being rented was inspected for, and found to be free of, bed bugs. (Colo. Rev. Stat. Ann. § 38-12-1005)

Rental application fee: Landlords who collect a rental application fee must disclose the anticipated expenses for which the fee will be used or itemize the actual expenses incurred. When landlords charge application fees based on the average cost of processing rental applications, they must explain how they determined the average rental application fee. (Colo. Rev. Stat. Ann. § 38-12-903)

Rental application denial: Landlords who deny rental applications must give rejected applicants a written notice of the denial that states the reasons for the denial. If a landlord cannot site the specific screening criteria because of the use of a proprietary screening system, the landlord must instead provide the rejected applicant with a copy of the report from the screening company. Landlords can provide electronic versions of the denial notice, but must provide a paper denial notice upon request. Landlords must make a good-faith effort to provide the notice within 20 calendar days of the denial. (Colo. Rev. Stat. Ann. § 38-12-904)

Connecticut

Conn. Gen. Stat. Ann. §§ 47a-3e, 47a-3f, 47a-6, 47a-7a

Common interest community: When rental is in a common interest community, landlord must give tenant written notice before signing a lease. (Conn. Gen. Stat. Ann. § 47a-3e)

Owner or agent identity: Before the beginning of the tenancy, landlord must disclose the name and address of the person authorized to manage the premises and the person who is authorized to receive all notices, demands, and service of process. (Conn. Gen. Stat. Ann. § 47a-6)

Bed bug information: Landlords may not advertise a unit that the landlord knows or reasonably suspects is infested with bed bugs. Before signing a lease, landlords must tell prospective tenants whether the unit (or any contiguous unit owned or subleased by the landlord) is infested. If asked by tenants or prospective tenants, landlords must disclose the last date on which the rental unit was inspected for bed bugs and found to be free of any infestation. (Conn. Gen. Stat. Ann. § 47a-7a)

Fire system information: When renting a dwelling unit in a building required to be equipped with a fire sprinkler system pursuant to any statute or regulation, the landlord of such dwelling unit must include notice in the rental agreement as to the existence or nonexistence of an operative fire sprinkler system in such building, and such notice shall be printed in not less than twelve-point boldface type of uniform font. If there is an operative fire sprinkler system in the building, the rental agreement will also state the last date of maintenance and inspection, in not less than twelve-point boldface type of uniform font. (Conn. Gen. Stat. Ann. § 47a-3f)

Delaware

Stoltz Management Co. v. Phillip, 593 A.2d 583 (1990); Del. Code Ann. tit. 25, § 5311, 25 Del. Code Ann. 5105, 25 Del. Code Ann. 5118, 25 Del. Code Ann. § 5312

Nonrefundable fees permitted? No, except for an optional service fee for actual services rendered, such

Required Landlord Disclosures (continued)

as a pool fee or tennis court fee. Tenant may elect, subject to the landlord's acceptance, to purchase an optional surety bond instead of or in combination with a security deposit. (Stoltz Management Co. v. Phillip, 593 A.2d 583 (1990); Del. Code Ann. tit. 25, § 5311)

Owner or agent identity: On each written rental agreement, the landlord must prominently disclose the names and usual business addresses of all persons who are owners of the rental unit or the property of which the rental unit is a part, or the names and business addresses of their appointed resident agents. (25 Del. Code Ann. § 5105)

Summary of landlord-tenant law: A summary of the Landlord-Tenant Code, as prepared by the Consumer Protection Unit of the Attorney General's Office or its successor agency, must be given to the new tenant at the beginning of the rental term. If the landlord fails to provide the summary, the tenant may plead ignorance of the law as a defense. (25 Del. Code Ann. § 5118)

Separate utility metering: Landlords may install meters for the purposes of separately charging individual units for utility services, but can only bill tenants according to these measurements if the rental agreement discloses the existence and use of meters. (25 Del. Code Ann. § 5312)

District of Columbia

D.C. Code Ann. §§ 42-3502.22, 42-3505.31; DC ST §§ 42-3502.22, 42-3531.01 and following; 12 D.C. Mun. Regs. § PM-704G; 14 D.C. Mun. Regs. § 300

Nonrefundable fees permitted? Yes. (D.C. Code Ann. § 42-3502.22

General disclosures: Upon receiving a rental application, landlords must provide on a disclosure form published by the Rent Administrator (or in another suitable format until a form is published) along with supporting documents each of the following: (a) the units rental rate; (b) any pending petitions filed that could affect the rental unit, including petitions for rent increases during the following 12 months; (c) any surcharges on the rent (including capital improvement surcharges) and the date they expire; (d) the frequency of possible rent increases; (e) the rent-controlled or exempt status of the rental, its business license, and a copy of the registration or claim of exemption (and any recent related filings); (f) all copies of code violation reports for the rental within the last 12 months, or previously issued reports for violations which have not been abated; (g) the Rent Administrator's pamphlet that explains rent increases and petitions that can be filed; (h) the amount of any nonrefundable application fee; (i) the amount of the security deposit, the interest rate on the security deposit, and how the security deposit will be returned when the tenant vacates the unit; (j) ownership information; (k) information about the presence of mold in the rental unit or common areas in the previous three years, unless the mold has been remediated by certified and licensed indoor mold remediation professional; (l) the voter registration packet developed by the D.C. Board of Elections (this packet should be part of the Rent Administrator's disclosure form, but if it has not been included in the form, the landlord should provide the packet if one exists); and (m) a copy of the current Tenant Bill of Rights published by the Office of the Tenant Advocate. (14 D.C. Mun. Regs. § 300)

Landlords must give written notice to each tenant, on a form published by the Rent Administrator (or in another suitable format until a form is published), that the disclosure forms and documents for the tenant's rental unit are available for inspection. The written notice must include the location of the disclosure forms and a table of contents laying out the categories of information included in the disclosure forms. (DC ST § 42-3502.22)

Upon a tenant's written request not more than once per calendar year, the landlord, within 10 business days of the request, must also disclose the amount of, and the basis for, each rent increase for the prior three years. If applicable, the disclosure must identify any substantially identical rental unit on which a vacancy increase was based. (D.C. Code Ann. § 42-3502.22)

Required Landlord Disclosures (continued)

Rental regulations: At the start of every new tenancy, landlord must give tenant a copy of the District of Columbia Municipal Regulations, CDCR Title 14, Housing, Chapter 3, Landlord and Tenant; and a copy of Title 14, Housing, Chapter 1, § 101 (Civil Enforcement Policy) and Chapter 1, § 106 (Notification of Tenants Concerning Violations). (14 D.C. Mun. Regs. § 300)

Late fees: Landlords can charge late rent fees only if the maximum amount of the late fee that may be charged is disclosed in the written lease or rental agreement. (D.C. Code Ann. § 42-3505.31)

Fire alarms: In buildings with four or more rental, rooming, or sleeping units (including condominium or cooperative units), owners must conspicuously post (and give to each tenant) written information on the following: How to operate manual alarm boxes, how to respond when smoke detectors activate (including abandoning the dwelling unit, closing its door, and activating the nearest alarm box), information on whether the building is monitored by a supervising station, and instructions on calling 911. (12 D.C. Mun. Regs. § PM-704G)

Florida

Fla. Stat. Ann. §§ 83.50, 404.056

Nonrefundable fees permitted? Yes, no statute directly on point, but by custom, nonrefundable fees are allowed.

Landlord identity: The landlord, or a person authorized to enter into a rental agreement on the landlord's behalf, must disclose in writing to the tenant, at or before the commencement of the tenancy, the name and address of the landlord or a person authorized to receive notices and demands on the landlord's behalf. (Fla. Stat. Ann. § 83.50)

Radon: In all leases, landlord must include this warning: "RADON GAS: Radon is a naturally occurring radioactive gas that, when it has accumulated in a building in sufficient quantities, may present health risks to persons who are exposed to it over time. Levels of radon that exceed federal and state guidelines have been found in buildings in

Florida. Additional information regarding radon and radon testing may be obtained from your county health department." (Fla. Stat. Ann. § 404.056)

Georgia

Ga. Code Ann. §§ 44-1-16, 44-7-20, 44-7-3, 44-7-30, 44-7-33

Nonrefundable fees permitted? Yes. Landlord and tenant may agree that certain prepaid sums, covering future rent or services or utilities supplied to the tenant, will not be returned to the tenant at the end of the tenancy. (Ga. Code Ann. § 44-7-30)

Move-in checklist required? Yes. Landlords cannot collect a security deposit unless they have given tenants a list of preexisting damages. Landlord must provide tenant with a comprehensive list of any existing damage to the premises before the tenant gives landlord a security deposit. (Ga. Code Ann. § 44-7-33)

Flooding: Before signing a lease, if the living space or attachments have been damaged by flooding three or more times within the past five years, landlord must so disclose in writing. (Ga. Code Ann. § 44-7-20)

Owner or agent identity: When or before a tenancy begins, landlord must disclose in writing the names and addresses of the owner of record (or a person authorized to act for the owner) for purposes of service of process and receiving and receipting demands and notices; and the person authorized to manage the premises. If such information changes during the tenancy, landlord must advise tenant within 30 days in writing or by posting a notice in a conspicuous place. (Ga. Code Ann. § 44-7-3)

Former residents, crimes: Unless asked by a prospective tenant, landlord does not have to disclose whether the rental was the site of a homicide or other felony, or a suicide or a death by accidental or natural causes; or whether it was occupied by a person who was infected with a virus or any other disease that has been determined by medical evidence as being highly unlikely to be transmitted through the occupancy of a dwelling place presently or previously occupied by such an infected person. However, if a prospective

Required Landlord Disclosures (continued)

tenant asks about any of these things, landlord must answer truthfully to the best of the landlord's individual knowledge. (Ga. Code Ann. § 44-1-16)

Hawaii

Haw. Rev. Stat. §§ 521-42, 521-43

Nonrefundable fees permitted? No.

Other fees: The landlord may not require or receive from or on behalf of a tenant at the beginning of a rental agreement any money other than the money for the first month's rent and a security deposit as provided in this section.

Move-in checklist required? Yes. (Haw. Rev. Stat. § 521-42)

Owner or agent identity: Landlord must disclose name of owner or agent; if owner lives in another state or on another island, landlord must disclose name of agent on the island. (Haw. Rev. Stat. § 521-43)

Tax excise number: Landlord must furnish its tax excise number so that tenant can file for a low-income tax credit. (Haw. Rev. Stat. § 521-43)

Idaho

No disclosure statutes.

Illinois

Utilities: *765 Ill. Comp. Stat. § 740/5*
Rent concessions: *765 Ill. Comp. Stat. §§ 730/0.01 to 730/6*
Radon: *720 Ill. Comp. Stat. §§ 46/15, 46/25*
Smoke detectors: *425 Ill. Comp. Stat. § 60/3(d)*
Carbon monoxide alarms: *430 Ill. Comp. Stat. § 135/10(c)*

Utilities: Where tenant pays a portion of a master metered utility, landlord must give tenant a copy in writing either as part of the lease or another written agreement of the formula used by the landlord for allocating the public utility payments among the tenants. (765 Ill. Comp. Stat. § 740/5)

Rent concessions: Any rent concessions must be described in the lease, in letters not less than one-half inch in height consisting of the words "Concession Granted," including a memorandum on the margin or across the face of the lease stating the amount or

extent and nature of each such concession. Failure to comply is a misdemeanor. (765 Ill. Comp. Stat. §§ 730/0.01 to 730/6)

Radon: Landlords are not required to test for radon, but if the landlord tests and learns that a radon hazard is present in the dwelling unit, landlord must disclose this information to current and prospective tenants. If a tenant notifies a landlord that a radon test indicates the existence of a radon hazard in the rental unit, landlord must disclose that risk to any prospective tenant of that unit, unless a subsequent test by the landlord shows that a radon hazard does not exist. Requirements do not apply if the dwelling unit is on the third or higher story above ground level, or when the landlord has undertaken mitigation work and a subsequent test shows that a radon hazard does not exist. (720 Ill. Comp. Stat. §§ 46/15, 46/25)

Smoke detectors: Landlord must give one tenant per dwelling written information about smoke detector testing and maintenance. (425 Ill. Comp. Stat. § 60/3(d))

Carbon monoxide alarms: Landlord must give one tenant per dwelling written information regarding CO alarm testing and maintenance. (430 Ill. Comp. Stat. § 135/10(c))

Indiana

Ind. Code Ann. § 8-1-2-1.2, 32-31-1-21, 32-31-3-18, 32-31-5-7

Agent identity: Landlord's agent must disclose in writing the name and address of a person living in Indiana who is authorized to manage the property and to act as the owner's agent. (Ind. Code Ann. § 32-31-3-18)

Smoke detectors: Landlord must require the tenant to acknowledge in writing that the rental unit is equipped with a functional smoke detector. (Ind. Code Ann. § 32-31-5-7)

Floodplain disclosure: If the lowest floor of a rental structure (including a basement) is at or below the 100-year frequency flood elevation, the landlord must disclose in the lease that the structure is located in a floodplain. (Ind. Code Ann. § 32-31-1-21)

Required Landlord Disclosures (continued)

Water or sewage disposal services: A landlord who pays for water, sewage disposal, or both, and who passes the costs on to tenants must describe the following in the lease, the tenants' first bill, or in a writing before signing the lease: A description of the water or sewage disposal services to be provided, and an itemized statement of the fees that will be charged. The disclosure must be printed using a font that is at least as large as the largest font used in the document in which the disclosure is included. The disclosure must include a description of the water or sewage disposal services to be provided, an itemized statement of the fees that will be charged, and this statement: "If you believe you are being charged in violation of this disclosure or if you believe you are being billed in excess of the utility services provided to you as described in this disclosure, you have a right under Indiana law to file a complaint with the Indiana Utility Regulatory Commission. You may contact the Commission at (insert phone number for the tenant to contact the Commission)." (Ind. Code Ann. § 8-1-2-1.2)

Iowa

Iowa Code § 562A.13

Owner or agent identity: Landlord must disclose to the tenant in writing at or before the commencement of the tenancy the name and address of the person authorized to manage the premises, and an owner of the premises or a person authorized to act for and on behalf of the owner for the purpose of service of process and for the purpose of receiving notices and demands. (Iowa Code § 562A.13)

Utilities: For shared utilities, landlord must fully explain utility rates, charges, and services to the prospective tenant before the rental agreement is signed. (Iowa Code § 562A.13)

Contamination: The landlord or a person authorized to enter into a rental agreement on behalf of the landlord must disclose to each tenant, in writing before the commencement of the tenancy, whether the property is listed in the comprehensive environmental response compensation and liability information

system maintained by the federal Environmental Protection Agency. (Iowa Code § 562A.13)

Kansas

Kan. Stat. Ann. §§ 58-2548, 58-2551

Move-in checklist required? Yes. Within 5 days of move-in, landlord and tenant must jointly inventory the rental. (Kan. Stat. Ann. § 58-2548)

Owner or agent identity: Landlord must disclose to the tenant in writing at or before the commencement of the tenancy the name and address of the person authorized to manage the premises, and an owner of the premises or a person authorized to act for and on behalf of the owner for the purpose of service of process and for the purpose of receiving notices and demands. (Kan. Stat. Ann. § 58-2551)

Kentucky

Ky. Rev. Stat. Ann. §§ 224.1-410, 383.580, 383.585, 902 Ky. Admin. Regs. 47:200

Move-in checklist required? Yes. Landlord and tenant must complete a checklist before landlord can collect a security deposit. (Ky. Rev. Stat. Ann. § 383.580)

Owner or agent identity: Landlord must disclose to the tenant in writing at or before the commencement of the tenancy the name and address of the person authorized to manage the premises, and an owner of the premises or a person authorized to act for and on behalf of the owner for the purpose of service of process and for the purpose of receiving notices and demands. (Ky. Rev. Stat. Ann. § 383.585)

Methamphetamine contamination disclosure: An owner of contaminated property who rents a property where the local health department has posted a methamphetamine contamination notice must disclose in writing to potential tenants that the property is contaminated and has not been decontaminated pursuant to the state's requirements. The disclosure must contain the physical address of the property, the location within the posted property that was used in the production

Required Landlord Disclosures (continued)

of methamphetamine, and a copy of the Notice of Methamphetamine Contamination. If a prospective tenant asks, the owner must provide a copy of any documents related to the methamphetamine contamination provided to the owner by law enforcement, the Energy and Environment Cabinet, the Department for Public Health, or the local health department. (Ky. Rev. Stat. Ann. § 224.1-410; 902 Ky. Admin. Regs. 47:200)

Louisiana

La. Rev. Stat. Ann. § 9:3260.1

Foreclosure: Before entering into a lease or rental agreement, landlord must disclose to potential tenants their right to receive notification of any future foreclosure action. If the premises are currently subject to a foreclosure action, landlord must also disclose this in writing. (La. Rev. Stat. Ann. § 9:3260.1)

Maine

Me. Rev. Stat. Ann. tit. 14, §§ 6024, 6030-C, 6030-D, 6021-A, 6030-E

Utilities: No landlord may lease or offer to lease a dwelling unit in a multiunit residential building where the expense of furnishing electricity to the common areas or other area not within the unit is the sole responsibility of the tenant in that unit, unless both parties to the lease have agreed in writing that the tenant will pay for such costs in return for a stated reduction in rent or other specified fair consideration that approximates the actual cost of electricity to the common areas. (Me. Rev. Stat. Ann. tit. 14, § 6024)

Energy efficiency: Landlord must provide to potential tenants who will pay for energy costs (or upon request from others) a residential energy efficiency disclosure statement in accordance with Title 35-A, section 10006, subsection 1 that includes, but is not limited to, information about the energy efficiency of the property. Before a tenant enters into a contract or pays a deposit to rent or lease a property, the landlord must provide the statement to the tenant, obtain the tenant's signature on the statement, and sign the statement. The landlord must retain the

signed statement for at least 3 years. Alternatively, the landlord may include in the application for the residential property the name of each supplier of energy that previously supplied the unit, if known, and the following statement: "You have the right to obtain a 12-month history of energy consumption and the cost of that consumption from the energy supplier." (Me. Rev. Stat. Ann. tit. 14, § 6030-C)

Radon: Unless a mitigation system has been installed, starting in 2014 and every 10 years after when requested by a tenant, the landlord shall test for radon in the rental. If the building was constructed after March 1, 2014, the landlord shall test for radon within 12 months of the occupancy of the building by a tenant. Within 30 days of receiving test results, the landlord shall provide written notice to existing tenants that includes the date of the test, the results, whether mitigation has been performed, the risk associated with radon, and notice that the tenant has the right to conduct a test. The same written notice must also be given to any new tenants before they sign a lease or pay a deposit to rent. The notice must include an acknowledgment that the tenant has received the disclosure. (Me. Rev. Stat. Ann. tit. 14, § 6030-D)

Bed bugs: Before renting a dwelling unit, landlord must disclose to a prospective tenant if an adjacent unit or units are currently infested with or are being treated for bed bugs. Upon request from a tenant or prospective tenant, landlord must disclose the last date that the dwelling unit the landlord seeks to rent or an adjacent unit or units were inspected for a bed bug infestation and found to be free of a bed bug infestation. (Me. Rev. Stat. Ann. tit. 14, § 6021-A)

Smoking policy: Landlord must give tenant written disclosure stating whether smoking is prohibited on the premises, allowed on the entire premises, or allowed in limited areas of the premises. If the landlord allows smoking in limited areas on the premises, the notice must identify the areas on the premises where smoking is allowed. Disclosure must be in the lease or a separate written notice,

Required Landlord Disclosures (continued)

and landlord must disclose before tenant signs a lease or pays a deposit and must obtain a written acknowledgment of notification from the tenant. (Me. Rev. Stat. Ann. tit. 14, § 6030-E)

Maryland

Md. Code Ann., [Real Prop.] § 8-203.1
Habitation: *Md. Code Ann., [Real Prop.] § 8-208*
Owner disclosure: *Md. Code Ann., [Real Prop.] § 8-210*

Move-in checklist required? Yes. Before collecting a deposit, landlord must supply a receipt with details on move-in and move-out inspections, and the receipt must be part of the lease. (Md. Code Ann., [Real Prop.], § 8-203.1)

Habitation: A lease must include a statement that the premises will be made available in a condition permitting habitation, with reasonable safety, if that is the agreement, or if that is not the agreement, a statement of the agreement concerning the condition of the premises; and the landlord's and the tenant's specific obligations as to heat, gas, electricity, water, and repair of the premises. (Md. Code Ann. [Real Prop.], § 8-208)

Owner or agent identity: The landlord must include in a lease or post the name and address of the landlord; or the person, if any, authorized to accept notice or service of process on behalf of the landlord. (Md. Code Ann. [Real Prop.], § 8-210)

Montgomery County: Before a prospective tenant signs a lease for 125 days or more, the landlord of a rental within a condominium or development must provide to the prospective tenant, if applicable, a copy of the rules, declaration, and recorded covenants and restrictions that limit or affect the use and occupancy of the property or common areas and to which the owner of the rental is obligated. The written lease must, if applicable, include a statement that the obligations of the owner that limit or affect the use and occupancy of the property are enforceable against the tenant. (Md. Code Ann. [Real Prop.], § 8-210)

Massachusetts

Mass. Gen. Laws ch. 186, §§ 21, 15C, 22(f), 15B(2)(c)

Move-in checklist required? Yes, if landlord collects a security deposit. (Mass. Gen. Laws ch. 186, § 15B(2)(c))

Insurance: Upon tenant's request and within 15 days, landlord must furnish the name of the company insuring the property against loss or damage by fire and the amount of insurance provided by each such company and the name of any person who would receive payment for a loss covered by such insurance. (Mass. Gen. Laws ch. 186, § 21)

Tax escalation: If real estate taxes increase, landlord may pass on a proportionate share of the increase to the tenant only if the lease discloses that in the event of an increase, the tenant will be required to pay only the proportion of the increase as the tenant's leased unit bears to the property being taxed (that proportion must be disclosed in the lease). In addition, the lease must state that if the landlord receives a tax abatement, landlord will refund a proportionate share of the abatement, minus reasonable attorneys' fees. (Mass. Gen. Laws ch. 186, § 15C))

Utilities: Landlord may not charge for water unless the lease specifies the charge and the details of the water submetering and billing arrangement. (Mass. Gen. Laws ch. 186, § 22(f))

Michigan

Stutelberg v. Practical Management Co., 245 N.W.2d 737 (1976); Mich. Comp. Laws §§ 554.601b, 554.608, 554.634

Nonrefundable fees permitted? Yes. (Stutelberg v. Practical Management Co., 245 N.W.2d 737 (1976))

Move-in checklist required? Yes. However, the requirement does not need to be included in the rental agreement. (Mich. Comp. Laws § 554.608)

Owner or agent identity: A rental agreement must include the name and address at which notice can be given to the landlord. (Mich. Comp. Laws § 554.634)

Truth in Renting Act: A rental agreement must also state in a prominent place in type not smaller than the size of 12-point type, or in legible print

Required Landlord Disclosures (continued)

with letters not smaller than 1/8 inch, a notice in substantially the following form:

"NOTICE: Michigan law establishes rights and obligations for parties to rental agreements. This agreement is required to comply with the Truth in Renting Act. If you have a question about the interpretation or legality of a provision of this agreement, you may want to seek assistance from a lawyer or other qualified person." (Mich. Comp. Laws § 554.634)

Rights of domestic violence victims: A rental agreement or lease may contain a provision stating, "A tenant who has a reasonable apprehension of present danger to him or her or his or her child from domestic violence, sexual assault, or stalking may have special statutory rights to seek a release of rental obligation under MCL 554.601b." If the rental agreement or lease does not contain such a provision, the landlord must post an identical written notice visible to a reasonable person in the landlord's property management office, or deliver written notice to the tenant when the lease or rental agreement is signed. (Mich. Comp. Laws § 554.601b)

Minnesota

Minn. Stat. Ann. §§ 504B.151, 504B.171, 504B.173, 504B.181, 504B.195

Owner or agent identity: Landlord must disclose to the tenant in writing at or before the commencement of the tenancy the name and address of the person authorized to manage the premises, and an owner of the premises or a person authorized to act for and on behalf of the owner for the purpose of service of process and for the purpose of receiving notices and demands. (Minn. Stat. Ann. § 504B.181)

Outstanding inspection orders, condemnation orders, or declarations that the property is unfit: The landlord must disclose the existence of any such orders or declarations before the tenant signs a lease or pays a security deposit. (Minn. Stat. Ann. § 504B.195)

Buildings in financial distress: Once a landlord has received notice of a deed cancellation or notice of foreclosure, landlord may not enter into a periodic tenancy where the tenancy term is more than two

months, or a lease where the lease extends beyond the redemption period (other restrictions may apply). (Minn. Stat. Ann. § 504B.151)

Landlord and tenant mutual promises: This mutual promise must appear in every lease or rental agreement: "Landlord and tenant promise that neither will unlawfully allow within the premises, common areas, or curtilage of the premises (property boundaries): controlled substances, prostitution or prostitution-related activity; stolen property or property obtained by robbery; or an act of domestic abuse, criminal sexual conduct, or harassment, as defined by MN Statute Section 504B.206(1)(a), against a tenant, licensee, or any authorized occupant. They further promise that the aforementioned areas will not be used by themselves or anyone acting under their control to manufacture, sell, give away, barter, deliver, exchange, distribute, purchase, or possess a controlled substance in violation of any criminal provision of chapter 152." (Minn. Stat. Ann. § 504B.171)

Screening fee: Before accepting an applicant's screening fee, landlords must disclose in writing: The name, address, and phone number of the tenant screening service (if landlord uses such a service), and the landlord's acceptance criteria. Landlords must notify rejected applicants within 14 days, identifying the criteria the applicant did not meet. (Minn. Stat. Ann. § 504B.173)

Mississippi

No disclosure statutes.

Missouri

Mo. Rev. Stat. §§ 441.236, 442.055, 535.185

Methamphetamine contamination: Landlord who knows that the premises were used to produce methamphetamine must disclose this fact to prospective tenants, regardless of whether the people involved in the production were convicted for such production. (Mo. Rev. Stat. § 441.236)

Owner or agent identity: Landlord must disclose to the tenant in writing at or before the commencement of the tenancy the name and address of the person

Required Landlord Disclosures (continued)

authorized to manage the premises, and an owner of the premises or a person authorized to act for and on behalf of the owner for the purpose of service of process and for the purpose of receiving notices and demands. (Mo. Rev. Stat. § 535.185)

Radioactive or hazardous material: Landlords who know that the rental property is or was contaminated with radioactive or other hazardous material must disclose this fact to prospective tenants. Landlords have knowledge when they've received a report stating that the property is or was contaminated. Failure to disclose when required is a Class A misdemeanor. (Mo. Rev. Stat. § 442.055)

Montana

Mont. Code Ann. §§ 70-16-703, 70-24-301, 70-25-101(4), 70-25-206, 75-10-1305

Nonrefundable fees permitted? No. A fee or charge for cleaning and damages, no matter how designated, is presumed to be a security deposit. (Not a clear statement that such a fee isn't nonrefundable, but by implication it must be.) (Mont. Code Ann. § 70-25-101(4))

Move-in checklists required? Yes, checklists are required when landlords collect a security deposit. (Mont. Code Ann. § 70-25-206)

Owner or agent identity: Landlords or people authorized to enter into a rental agreement on their behalf shall disclose to the tenant in writing at or before the commencement of the tenancy the name and address of the person authorized to manage the premises; and the owner of the premises or a person authorized to act for the owner for the purpose of service of process and receiving notices and demands. (Mont. Code Ann. § 70-24-301)

Mold: Before signing a lease, if a landlord has knowledge that mold is present in the rental, the landlord must disclose its presence; and if the landlord knows that the building has been tested for mold, the landlord must advise the tenant that testing has occurred and provide a copy of the results (if available), as well as any evidence of subsequent treatment. Landlords can avoid liability for damages resulting from mold if they comply with these rules, provide tenants with a mold disclosure statement in the form prescribed by statute, and obtain the tenants' written acknowledgment of receipt of the statement. (Mont. Code Ann. § 70-16-703)

Methamphetamine contamination: Before signing a lease or rental agreement, a landlord who knows that the property was used as a meth lab must disclose this history to a potential tenant. Disclosure is not required if the property has been remediated to the states standards by a contractor who is certified by the state. Landlords who themselves did not cause the contamination, and who have obtained documentation of decontamination that they have provided to tenants, will not be liable in a tenant's lawsuit for damages. (Mont. Code Ann. § 75-10-1305)

Nebraska

Neb. Rev. Stat. § 76-1417

Owner or agent identity: The landlord or any person authorized to enter into a rental agreement on his or her behalf must disclose to the tenant in writing at or before the commencement of the tenancy the name and address of the person authorized to manage the premises, and an owner of the premises or a person authorized to act for and on behalf of the owner for the purpose of service of process and receiving notices and demands.

Nevada

Nev. Rev. Stat. Ann. §§ 118A.200, 118A.275

Nonrefundable fees permitted? Yes. Lease must explain fees that are required and the purposes for which they are required. (Nev. Rev. Stat. Ann. § 118A.200)

Move-in checklist required? Yes. Lease must include tenants' rights to a checklist and a signed record of the inventory and condition of the premises under the exclusive custody and control of the tenant. (Nev. Rev. Stat. Ann. § 118A.200)

Nuisance and flying the flag: Lease must include a summary of the provisions of NRS 202.470 (penalties for permitting or maintaining a nuisance);

Required Landlord Disclosures (continued)

information regarding the procedure a tenant may use to report to the appropriate authorities a nuisance, a violation of a building, safety, or health code or regulation; and information regarding the right of the tenant to engage in the display of the flag of the United States, as set forth in NRS 118A.325. (Nev. Rev. Stat. Ann. § 118A.200)

Foreclosure proceedings: Landlord must disclose to any prospective tenant, in writing, whether the premises to be rented is the subject of a foreclosure proceeding (disclosure need not be in the lease). (Nev. Rev. Stat. Ann. § 118A.275)

Lease signed by an agent of the landlord who does not hold a property management permit: In single-family rentals only, unless the lease is signed by an authorized agent of the landlord who holds a current property management permit, the top of the first page of the lease must state, in font that is at least twice the size of any other size in the agreement, that the tenant might not have valid occupancy unless the lease is notarized or signed by an authorized agent of the owner who holds a management permit. The notice must give the current address and phone number of the landlord. In addition, it must state that even if the foregoing has not been provided, the agreement is enforceable against the landlord. (Nev. Rev. Stat. Ann. § 118A.200)

New Hampshire

N.H. Rev. Stat. Ann. § 477:4-g, 540-A:6

Move-in checklist required? Yes. Landlord must inform tenant that if tenant finds any conditions in the rental in need of repair, tenant may note them on the security deposit receipt or other writing. Not a true checklist. (N.H. Rev. Stat. Ann. § 540-A:6)

Methamphetamine disclosure: If methamphetamine was produced on a property and the department of environmental sciences has not determined that the property meets remediation cleanup standards, the landlord must disclose in writing to the tenant that methamphetamine production has occurred. (N.H. Rev. Stat. § 477:4-g)

New Jersey

N.J. Stat. Ann. §§ 46:8-44, 46:8-45, 46:8-46, 46:8-50, 55:13A-7.14, 55:13A-7.18, N.J. Admin. Code §§ 5:10-27.1, 5:10-27 App. 27A

Flood zone: Prior to move-in, landlord must inform tenant if rental is in a flood zone or area (does not apply to properties containing two or fewer dwelling units, or to owner-occupied properties of three or fewer units). (N.J. Stat. Ann. § 46:8-50)

Truth in Renting Act: Except in buildings of two or fewer units, and owner-occupied premises of three or fewer units, landlord must distribute to new tenants at or prior to move-in the Department of Community Affairs' statement of legal rights and responsibilities of tenants and landlords of rental dwelling units (Spanish also). (N.J. Stat. Ann. §§ 46:8-44, 46:8-45, 46:8-46)

Child protection window guards: Landlords of multi-family properties must include information in the lease about tenants' rights to request window guards. The Legislature's Model Lease and Notice clause reads as follows: "The owner (landlord) is required by law to provide, install and maintain window guards in the apartment if a child or children 10 years of age or younger is, or will be, living in the apartment or is, or will be, regularly present there for a substantial period of time if the tenant gives the owner (landlord) a written request that the window guards be installed. The owner (landlord) is also required, upon the written request of the tenant, to provide, install and maintain window guards in the hallways to which persons in the tenant's unit have access without having to go out of the building. If the building is a condominium, cooperative or mutual housing building, the owner (landlord) of the apartment is responsible for installing and maintaining window guards in the apartment and the association is responsible for installing and maintaining window guards in hallway windows. Window guards are only required to be provided in first floor windows where the window sill is more than six feet above grade or there are other hazardous conditions that make installation of window guards necessary to protect the

Required Landlord Disclosures (continued)

safety of children." The notice must be conspicuous and in boldface type. (N.J. Stat. Ann. § 55:13A-7.14; N.J. Admin. Code §§ 5:10-27.1, 5:10-27 App. 27A)

Water quality: Owners of multifamily properties who must prepare a Consumer Confidence Report, or who receive such a report from a public community water system, must post the report in every routinely used common area (if the property has no such area, owners must give copies to each rental unit). Owners of multifamily properties who supply water, who are not required to prepare a Consumer Confidence Report, but who must test its water, must post a chart containing the results of the tests. Charts must be posted in every routinely used common area (if the property has no such area, owners must give copies to each rental unit). (N.J. Stat. Ann. § 55:13A-7.18)

New Mexico

N.M. Stat. Ann. § 47-8-19, N.M. Admin. Code § 20.4.5.13

Owner or agent identity: Landlord must disclose to the tenant in writing at or before the commencement of the tenancy the name and address of the person authorized to manage the premises, and an owner of the premises or a person authorized to act for and on behalf of the owner for the purpose of service of process and for the purpose of receiving notices and demands. (N.M. Stat. Ann. § 47-8-19)

Illegal drug lab on premises: Landlord cannot rent a property where controlled substances were manufactured or located unless landlord provides written notice to tenant of these facts. The tenant must acknowledge receipt of the notice in writing, and the landlord must provide a copy of the notice and acknowledgement to the New Mexico environment department. (N.M. Admin. Code § 20.4.5.13)

New York

N.Y. Envtl. Conserv. Law § 27-2405, N.Y. Real Prop. Law § 235-bb, N.Y. Mult. Res. Law §§ 4, 15, N.Y. Exec. Law § 296

Refundable fees: No, not needed to be stated in rental agreement (N.Y. Gen. Oblig. Laws § 7-108)

Move-in checklist: Yes, rights not needed to be stated in rental agreement (N.Y. Gen. Oblig. Laws § 7-108)

Checklists, other details: Tenants are entitled to a pre-move out inspection unless tenant terminates with less than two weeks' notice.

Air contamination: Landlord who receives a government report showing that air in the building has, or may have, concentrations of volatile organic compounds (VOCs) that exceed governmental guidelines must give written notice to prospective and current tenants. The notice must appear in at least 12-point bold face type on the first page of the lease or rental agreement. It must read as follows: "NOTIFICATION OF TEST RESULTS: The property has been tested, for contamination of indoor air: **test results and additional information are available upon request**." (N.Y. Envtl. Conserv. Law § 27-2405)

Certificate of occupancy: In structures with three or fewer dwelling units, where a certificate of occupancy is required by law, landlords must provide prospective tenants proof of a current certificate prior to signing a lease or rental agreement. Landlords may provide prospective tenants with a copy of the actual certificate, or provide notice of said certificate in bold face type. Waivers of this requirement are void. (N.Y. Real Prop. Law § 235-bb)

Smoke detectors: In multifamily buildings of three or more units, condominiums, and cooperatives located in towns, villages, and cities with populations less than 325,000, landlord must notify tenants in writing, individually or by posting a notice in a common area, of owners' and tenants' duties regarding smoke detectors. (N.Y. Mult. Res. Law §§ 4, 15)

Reasonable accommodation: Landlords must give all tenants and prospective tenants a written notice of their right to request reasonable modifications and accommodations for their disability. The notice must be posted in all vacant available rentals and given to all current tenants within 30 days of the beginning of their tenancy. The notice must contain information about where to file complaints and any other information the Division of Human Rights requires. (N.Y. Exec. Law § 296)

Required Landlord Disclosures (continued)

North Carolina

N.C. Gen. Stat. Ann. § 42-46

Nonrefundable fees permitted? Landlord may collect only one of the following, when specific conditions are met: Complaint filing fee, court appearance fee, and second trial fee. Failure to pay the fees cannot support a termination notice. (N.C. Gen. Stat. Ann. § 42-46)

Eviction fees: If landlords wish to collect fees relating to eviction, they must specify certain types of fees in a written lease. Landlords must disclose their right to collect reasonable attorneys' fees, which cannot exceed 15% of the amount owed by the tenant, or 15% of the monthly rent stated in the lease if the eviction is based on a default other than the nonpayment of rent. Landlords must also disclose the fees they will charge for filing a complaint, to appear in court, and for their second trial (landlord can charge and retain only one of these fees). (N.C. Gen. Stat. Ann. § 42-46)

North Dakota

N.D. Cent. Code § 47-16-07.2

Move-in checklist required? Yes. Landlord must give tenant a statement describing the condition of the premises when tenant signs the rental agreement. Both parties must sign the statement. (N.D. Cent. Code § 47-16-07.2)

Ohio

Ohio Rev. Code Ann. § 5321.18

Owner or agent identity: Every written rental agreement must contain the name and address of the owner and the name and address of the owner's agent, if any. If the owner or the owner's agent is a corporation, partnership, limited partnership, association, trust, or other entity, the address must be the principal place of business in the county in which the residential property is situated. If there is no place of business in such county, then its principal place of business in this state must be disclosed, including the name of the person in charge thereof.

Oklahoma

Okla. Stat. Ann. tit. 41, §§ 113a, 116, 118, and Okla. Stat. Ann. tit. 74, § 324.11a

Flooding: If the premises to be rented has been flooded within the past five (5) years and such fact is known to the landlord, the landlord shall include such information prominently and in writing as part of any written rental agreements. (Okla. Stat. Ann. tit. 41, § 113a)

Owner information: As a part of any rental agreement the lessor shall prominently and in writing identify what person at what address is entitled to accept service or notice under this act. Landlord must disclose to the tenant in writing at or before the commencement of the tenancy the name and address of the person authorized to manage the premises, and an owner of the premises or a person authorized to act for and on behalf of the owner for the purpose of service of process and receiving notices and demands. (Okla. Stat. Ann. tit. 41, § 116)

Smoke detectors: Landlord must explain to tenant how to test the smoke detector to ensure that it is in working order. (Okla. Stat. Ann. tit. 74, § 324.11a)

Methamphetamine disclosure: Before signing a rental agreement, if the landlord knows or has reason to know that the unit or any part of the premises was used in the manufacture of methamphetamine, the landlord must disclose this information to a prospective tenant. Does not apply when the landlord has tested the unit or premises and the results show that the level of contamination is less than 0.1 mcg per 100cm^2 of surface materials in the affected part. (Okla. Stat. Ann. tit. 41, § 118)

Tenant repairs, maintenance, alterations, or remodeling: When landlord and tenant agree that the tenant will perform specified repairs, maintenance tasks, alterations, or remodeling, they must put this agreement in writing, independent of the rental agreement, and presented in a manner that will make it hard to overlook (using ample font size, for example). (Okla. Stat. Ann. tit. 41, § 118)

Required Landlord Disclosures (continued)

Oregon

Ore. Rev. Stat. Ann. §§ 90.220, 90.222, 90.228, 90.295, 90.302, 90.305, 90.310, 90.315, 90.316, 90.317, 90.318, 90.367, 479.270

Nonrefundable fees permitted? Landlords' written rules may not provide for tenant fees, except for specified events as they arise, including a late rent payment; tenant's late payment of a utility or service charge; a dishonored check, pursuant to Or. Rev. Stat. Ann. § 30.701(5); failure to clean up pet waste in areas other than tenant's unit; failure to clean up garbage and rubbish (outside tenant's dwelling unit); failure to clean pet waste of a service or companion animal from areas other than the dwelling unit; parking violations and improper use of vehicles within the premises; smoking in a designated nonsmoking area; keeping an unauthorized pet capable of inflicting damage on persons or property; tampering or disabling a smoke detector. (Or. Rev. Stat. Ann. § 90.302)

Owner or agent identity: Landlord must disclose to the tenant in writing at or before the commencement of the tenancy the name and address of the person authorized to manage the premises, and an owner of the premises or a person authorized to act for and on behalf of the owner for the purpose of service of process and for the purpose of receiving notices and demands. (Or. Rev. Stat. Ann. § 90.305)

Legal proceedings: If at the time of the execution of a rental agreement for a dwelling unit in premises containing no more than four dwelling units the premises are subject to any of the following circumstances, the landlord must disclose that circumstance to the tenant in writing before the execution of the rental agreement: (a) Any outstanding notice of default under a trust deed, mortgage, or contract of sale, or notice of trustee's sale under a trust deed; (b) Any pending suit to foreclose a mortgage, trust deed, or vendor's lien under a contract of sale; (c) Any pending declaration of forfeiture or suit for specific performance of a contract of sale; or (d) Any pending proceeding to foreclose a tax lien. (Or. Rev. Stat. Ann. § 90.310)

Utilities: The landlord must disclose to the tenant in writing at or before the commencement of the tenancy any utility or service that the tenant pays directly to a utility or service provider that directly benefits the landlord or other tenants. A tenant's payment for a given utility or service benefits the landlord or other tenants if the utility or service is delivered to any area other than the tenant's dwelling unit.

A landlord may require a tenant to pay to the landlord a utility or service charge that has been billed by a utility or service provider to the landlord for utility or service provided directly to the tenant's dwelling unit or to a common area available to the tenant as part of the tenancy. A utility or service charge that shall be assessed to a tenant for a common area must be described in the written rental agreement separately and distinctly from such a charge for the tenant's dwelling unit. Unless the method of allocating the charges to the tenant is described in the tenant's written rental agreement, the tenant may require that the landlord give the tenant a copy of the provider's bill as a condition of paying the charges. (Or. Rev. Stat. Ann. § 90.315)

Recycling: In a city or the county within the urban growth boundary of a city that has implemented multifamily recycling service, a landlord who has five or more residential dwelling units on a single premises must notify new tenants at the time of entering into a rental agreement of the opportunity to recycle. (Or. Rev. Stat. Ann. § 90.318)

Smoking policy: Landlord must disclose the smoking policy for the premises, by stating whether smoking is prohibited on the premises, allowed on the entire premises, or allowed in limited areas. If landlord allows smoking in limited areas, the disclosure must identify those areas. (Or. Rev. Stat. Ann. § 90.220)

Carbon monoxide alarm instructions: If rental contains a CO source (a heater, fireplace, appliance, or cooking source that uses coal, kerosene, petroleum products, wood, or other fuels that emit carbon monoxide as a by product of combustion; or an attached garage with an opening that communicates

Required Landlord Disclosures (continued)

directly with a living space), landlord must install one or more CO monitors and give tenant written instructions for testing the alarm(s), before tenant takes possession. (Or. Rev. Stat. Ann. §§ 90.316, 90.317)

Smoke alarm or smoke detector: When tenant moves in, landlord must give tenant written instructions for testing smoke alarms and smoke detectors. (Or. Rev. Stat. Ann. § 479.270)

Floodplain: If a dwelling unit is located in a 100-year floodplain, the landlord must provide notice in the dwelling unit rental agreement that the dwelling unit is located within the floodplain. If a landlord fails to provide a notice as required under this section, and the tenant of the dwelling unit suffers an uninsured loss due to flooding, the tenant may recover from the landlord the lesser of the actual damages for the uninsured loss or two months' rent. (Or. Rev. Stat. Ann. § 90.228)

Renters' insurance: Landlord may require tenants to maintain liability insurance (certain low-income and subsidized tenancies excepted), but only if the landlord obtains and maintains comparable liability insurance and provides documentation to any tenant who requests the documentation, orally or in writing. The landlord may provide documentation to a tenant in person, by mail, or by posting in a common area or office. The documentation may consist of a current certificate of coverage. Any landlord who requires tenants to obtain renters' insurance must disclose the requirement and amount in writing prior to entering into a new tenancy, and may require the tenant to provide documentation before the tenancy begins. (Or. Rev. Stat. Ann. § 90.222)

Homeowner assessments: If landlord wants to pass on homeowners' association assessments that are imposed on anyone moving into or out of the unit, the written rental agreement must include this requirement. Landlord must give tenants a copy of each assessment before charging the tenant. (Or. Rev. Stat. Ann. § 90.302)

Applicant screening fees: Before accepting application fees, landlords must: Know that a rental unit is or soon will be available, adopt and disclose their screening criteria, explain the screening process and applicants rights to dispute the accuracy of any information from a screening company or credit reporting agency, disclose how many comparable units are (or will soon be) available, disclose in writing the rent and any deposits, and disclose in writing whether tenants must obtain renters insurance (including policy minimums). Applicants whose rejection is based in whole or in part on information supplied by a screening company or credit reporting agency must be told at the time of denial, and given written notice of the name and address of the company or agency (unless previously supplied). (Or. Rev. Stat. Ann. § 90.295)

Pennsylvania

No disclosure statutes.

Rhode Island

R.I. Gen. Laws §§ 34-18-20, 34-18-22.1

Owner disclosure: Landlord must disclose to the tenant in writing at or before the commencement of the tenancy the name and address of the person authorized to manage the premises, and an owner of the premises or a person authorized to act for and on behalf of the owner for the purpose of service of process and for the purpose of receiving notices and demands. (R.I. Gen. Laws § 34-18-20)

Code violations: Before entering into any residential rental agreement, landlord must inform a prospective tenant of any outstanding minimum housing code violations that exist on the building that is the subject of the rental agreement. (R.I. Gen. Laws § 34-18-22.1)

Notice of foreclosure: A landlord who becomes delinquent on a mortgage securing real estate upon which the rental is located for a period of 120 days must notify the tenant that the property may be subject to foreclosure; and until the foreclosure occurs, the tenant must continue to pay rent to the landlord as provided under the rental agreement. (R.I. Gen. Laws § 34-18-20)

Required Landlord Disclosures (continued)

South Carolina

S.C. Code Ann. §§ 5-25-1330, 27-40-410, 27-40-420

Owner or agent identity: Landlord must disclose to the tenant in writing at or before the commencement of the tenancy the name and address of the person authorized to manage the premises, and an owner of the premises or a person authorized to act for and on behalf of the owner for the purpose of service of process and for the purpose of receiving notices and demands. (S.C. Code Ann. § 27-40-420)

Unequal security deposits: If landlord rents five or more adjoining units on the premises, and imposes different standards for calculating deposits required of tenants, landlord must, before a tenancy begins, post in a conspicuous place a statement explaining the standards by which the various deposits are calculated (or, landlord may give the tenant the written statement). (S.C. Code Ann. § 27-40-410)

Smoke detectors: When tenant moves in, owner must give tenant written or verbal instructions, or both, for testing the detectors and replacing batteries in battery-powered detectors. (S.C. Code Ann. § 5-25-1330)

South Dakota

S.D. Codified Laws Ann. § 43-32-30

Methamphetamine contamination: Landlord who has actual knowledge of the existence of any prior manufacturing of methamphetamines on the premises must disclose that information to any lessee or any person who may become a lessee. If the residential premises consists of two or more housing units, the disclosure requirements apply only to the unit where there is knowledge of the existence of any prior manufacturing of methamphetamines. (S.D. Codified Laws Ann. § 43-32-30)

Tennessee

Tenn. Code Ann. § 66-28-302, 66-28-403

Owner or agent identity: The landlord or any person authorized to enter into a rental agreement on the landlord's behalf must disclose to the tenant in writing at or before the commencement of the tenancy the name and address of the agent authorized to manage the premises, and an owner of the premises or a person or agent authorized to act for and on behalf of the owner for the acceptance of service of process and for receipt of notices and demands. (Tenn. Code Ann. § 66-28-302)

Showing rental to prospective tenants: Landlord may enter to show the premises to prospective renters during the final 30 days of a tenancy (with 24 hours' notice), but only if this right of access is set forth in the rental agreement or lease. (Tenn. Code Ann. § 66-28-403)

Texas

Tex. Prop. Code Ann. §§ 92.008, 92.016, 92.019, 92.020, 92.056, 92.103, 92.159, 92.201, 92.0131, 92.3515; Holmes v. Canlen Management Corp., 542 S.W. 2d 199 (1976)

Nonrefundable fees permitted? Yes. Landlords cannot collect late fees unless notice of the fee is included in a written lease. *(Tex. Prop. Code Ann. § 92.019; Holmes v. Canlen Management Corp., 542 S.W.2d 199 (1976))*

Owner or agent identity: In the lease, other writing, or posted on the property, landlord must disclose the name and address of the property's owner and, if an entity located off-site from the dwelling is primarily responsible for managing the dwelling, the name and street address of the management company. (Tex. Prop. Code Ann. § 92.201)

Emergency contact information: Landlords must provide tenants with an emergency phone number to call when there is a condition affecting physical health or safety of tenant. (Tex. Prop. Code Ann. § 92.020)

Security device requests: If landlord wants tenant requests concerning security devices to be in writing, this requirement must be in the lease in boldface type or underlined. (Tex. Prop. Code Ann. § 92.159)

Return of security deposit: A requirement that a tenant give advance notice of moving out as a condition for refunding the security deposit is effective only if the requirement is in the lease, underlined or printed in conspicuous bold print. (Tex. Prop. Code Ann. § 92.103)

Required Landlord Disclosures (continued)

Domestic violence victims' rights: Victims of sexual abuse or assault on the premises may break a lease, after complying with specified procedures, without responsibility for future rent. Tenants will be responsible for any unpaid back rent, but only if the lease includes the following statement, or one substantially like it: "Tenants may have special statutory rights to terminate the lease early in certain situations involving family violence or a military deployment or transfer." (Tex. Prop. Code Ann. § 92.016)

Tenant's rights when landlord fails to repair: A lease must contain language in underlined or bold print that informs the tenant of the remedies available when the landlord fails to repair a problem that materially affects the physical health or safety of an ordinary tenant. These rights include the right to: repair and deduct; terminate the lease; and obtain a judicial order that the landlord make the repair, reduce the rent, pay the tenant damages (including a civil penalty), and pay the tenant's court and attorneys' fees. (Tex. Prop. Code Ann. § 92.056)

Landlord's towing or parking rules and policies: For tenants in multiunit properties, if the landlord has vehicle towing or parking rules or policies that apply to the tenant, the landlord must give the tenant a copy of the rules or policies before the lease agreement is signed. The copy must be signed by the tenant, included in the lease or rental agreement, or be made an attachment to either. If included, the clause must be titled "Parking" or "Parking Rules" and be capitalized, underlined, or printed in bold print.) (Tex. Prop. Code Ann. § 92.0131)

Electric service interruption: Landlord who submeters electric service, or who allocates master metered electricity according to a prorated system, may interrupt tenant's electricity service if tenant fails to pay the bill, but only after specific notice and according to a complex procedure. Exceptions for ill tenants and during extreme weather. (Tex. Prop. Code Ann. § 92.008(h))

Selection criteria for applicants: At the time landlords provide prospective tenants with applications, they must also provide printed notice of their tenant selection criteria, including reasons why applications may be denied. The notice must contain certain acknowledgement language that the applicant must sign. (Tex. Prop. Code Ann. § 92.3515)

Utah

Utah Code Ann. §§ 57-22-4, 57-27-201, 57-17-2

Move-in checklists required? Yes. Landlords must give prospective renters a written inventory of the condition of the residential rental unit, excluding ordinary wear and tear; give the renter a form to document the condition of the residential rental and allow the resident a reasonable time after the renter's occupancy of the unit to complete and return the form; or provide the prospective renter an opportunity to conduct a walkthrough inspection of the rental. (Utah Code Ann. § 57-22-4)

Nonrefundable fees permitted? Yes. If there is a written agreement and if any part of the deposit is to be made non-refundable, it must be so stated in writing to the renter at the time the deposit is taken. (Utah Code Ann. § 57-17-2)

Applicant disclosures: Before accepting an application or collecting an application fee, landlord must disclose whether the rental unit is expected to be available, and the criteria landlord will use in evaluating potential renter's application. Failure to comply will not invalidate the lease or provide tenant with a legal cause of action. (Utah Code Ann. § 57-22-4)

Methamphetamine contamination: If landlord has actual knowledge that the property is currently contaminated from the use, storage, or manufacture of methamphetamine, the landlord must disclose that the property is contaminated in the lease. (Utah Code Ann. § 57-27-201)

Required Landlord Disclosures (continued)

Vermont

No disclosure statutes.

Virginia

Va. Code Ann. §§ 55.1-1212, 55.1-1214 to 1219, 55.1-1223

Move-in checklist required? Yes. Within five days of move-in, landlord or tenant or both together must prepare a written report detailing the condition of the premises. Landlord must disclose within this report the known presence of mold. (Va. Code Ann. § 55.1-1214)

Owner or agent identity: Landlord must disclose to the tenant in writing at or before the commencement of the tenancy the name and address of the person authorized to manage the premises, and an owner of the premises or a person authorized to act for and on behalf of the owner for the purpose of service of process and for the purpose of receiving notices and demands. (Va. Code Ann. § 55.1-1216)

Sale plans: In the event of the sale of the premises, the landlord must notify tenants of the sale and disclose to tenants the name and address of the purchaser and a telephone number for contacting the purchaser. (Va. Code Ann. § 55.1-1216)

Miltary zone: The landlord of property in any locality in which a military air installation is located, or any person authorized to enter into a rental agreement on landlord's behalf, must provide to a prospective tenant a written disclosure that the property is located in a noise zone or accident potential zone, or both, as designated by the locality on its official zoning map. (Va. Code Ann. § 55.1-1217)

Mold: Move-in inspection report must include whether there is any visible evidence of mold (deemed correct unless tenant objects within five days); if evidence is present, tenant may terminate or not move in. If tenant stays, landlord must remediate the mold condition within five business days, reinspect, and issue a new report indicating that there is no evidence of mold. (Va. Code Ann. § 55.1-1215)

Ratio utility billing: Landlords who use a ratio utility billing service or who intend to collect monthly billing and other administrative and late fees, must disclose these fees in a written rental agreement. (Va. Code Ann. § 55.1-1212)

Condominium plans: If an application for registration as a condominium or cooperative has been filed with the Real Estate Board, or if there is within six months an existing plan for tenant displacement resulting from demolition or substantial rehabilitation of the property, or conversion of the rental property to office, hotel, or motel use or planned unit development, the landlord or any person authorized to enter into a rental agreement on his behalf must disclose that information in writing to any prospective tenant. (Va. Code Ann. § 55.1-1216)

Defective drywall: Landlords who know of the presence of unrepaired defective drywall in the rental must disclose this before the tenant signs a lease or rental agreement. (Va. Code Ann. § 55.1-1218)

Methamphetamine disclosure: When the landlord knows that the unit was used to manufacture methamphetamine, landlord must give the tenant a written disclosure of this use before the tenant signs a lease, if the unit hasn't been mitigated as required by law. (Va. Code Ann. § 55.1-1219)

Insecticide/pesticide application: Landlords must give tenants written notice no less than 48 hours prior to applying an insecticide or pesticide in the tenant's dwelling unit unless the tenant agrees to a shorter notification period. If a tenant requests the application of the insecticide or pesticide, the 48-hour notice is not required. Tenants who have concerns about specific insecticides or pesticides must notify the landlord in writing no less than 24 hours before the scheduled insecticide or pesticide application. The tenant shall prepare the dwelling unit for the application of insecticides or pesticides in accordance with any written instructions of the landlord and, if insects or pests are found to be present, follow any

Required Landlord Disclosures (continued)

written instructions of the landlord to eliminate the insects or pests following the application of insecticides or pesticides. In addition, landlords must post notice of all insecticide or pesticide applications in areas of the rental other than the dwelling units. Such notice shall consist of conspicuous signs placed in or upon the rental where the insecticide or pesticide will be applied at least 48 hours prior to the application. (Va. Code Ann. § 55.1-1223)

Washington

Wash. Rev. Code Ann. §§ 59.18.060, 59.18.253, 59.18.257, 59.18.260, 59.18.285

Move-in checklists required? Checklists are required when landlords collect a security deposit. If landlord fails to provide checklist, landlord is liable to the tenant for the amount of the deposit. (Wash. Rev. Code Ann. § 59.18.260)

Nonrefundable fees permitted? Yes. If landlord collects a nonrefundable fee, the rental document must clearly specify that it is nonrefundable. Landlords cannot collect fees to put a prospective tenant on a wait list for a rental. (Wash. Rev. Code Ann. § 59.18.285)

Fire protection: At the time the lease is signed, landlord must provide fire protection and safety information, including whether the building has a smoking policy, an emergency notification plan, or an evacuation plan. (Wash. Rev. Code Ann. § 59.18.060)

Owner or agent identity: In the rental document or posted conspicuously on the premises, landlord must designate to the tenant the name and address of the person who is the landlord by a statement on the rental agreement or by a notice conspicuously posted on the premises. If the person designated does not reside in Washington, landlord must also designate a person who resides in the county to act as an agent for the purposes of service of notices and process. (Wash. Rev. Code Ann. § 59.18.060)

Mold: At the time the lease is signed, landlord must provide tenant with information provided or approved by the department of health about the health hazards associated with exposure to indoor mold. (Wash. Rev. Code Ann. § 59.18.060)

Screening criteria: Before obtaining any information about an applicant, landlord must provide (in writing or by posting) the type of information to be accessed, criteria to be used to evaluate the application, and (for consumer reports) the name and address of the consumer reporting agency to be used, including the applicant's rights to obtain a free copy of the report and dispute its accuracy. Landlord must advise tenants whether landlord will accept a comprehensive reusable tenant screening report done by a consumer reporting agency (in which case the landlord may not charge the tenant a fee for a screening report). If landlord maintains a website that advertises residential rentals, the home page must include this information. (Wash. Rev. Code Ann. § 59.18.257)

Tenant screening fee: Landlords who do their own screening may charge a fee for time and costs to obtain background information, but only if they provide the information explained in "Screening criteria," above. (Wash. Rev. Code Ann. § 59.18.257)

Holding deposits: Fees or deposits to hold a rental cannot exceed 25% of the first month's rent. Upon receipt of the fee or deposit, landlords must issue a receipt and a written statement of the conditions, if any, under which the fee or deposit may be retained. (Wash. Rev. Code Ann. § 59.18.253)

West Virginia

W.Va. Code §§ 15A-10-12; W.Va. Code R. § 64-92-6, 37-6A-1(14)

Nonrefundable fees permitted? Nonrefundable fee must be expressly agreed to in writing. (W.Va. Code § 37-6A-1(14))

Carbon monoxide (CO): Anyone who installs a CO detector in a rental unit must inform either the owner, landlord, or resident of the dangers of CO poisoning, and must supply instructions on how to operate the detector. When landlords work on fuel-burning heating or cooking equipment or a units venting system, they must inform tenants of the dangers of CO poisoning and recommend the purchase of a CO detector.

Required Landlord Disclosures (continued)

Any landlord who performs repair or maintenance work on a fuel-burning heating or cooking source or a venting system in a rental unit must inform the tenant of the dangers of carbon monoxide poisoning and recommend the installation of a carbon monoxide detector. (W.Va. Code § 15A-10-12)

Methamphetamine contamination: Landlord who has successfully cleaned up a meth lab must give potential tenants the certificate of remediation that was issued by the West Virginia Department of Health and Human Resources. (W.Va. Code R. § 64-92-6)

Wisconsin

Wis. Admin. Code §§ 134.04-.06, 134.09, Wis. Stat. Ann. §§ 704.05, 704.07, 704.14, 704.08 ;. § 704.07(2) (bm); § 704.05(5))

Move-in checklist required? Yes. Tenant has a right to inspect the rental and give landlord a list of defects, and to receive a list of damages charged to the prior tenant. Tenant has seven days after start of the tenancy to return the list to the landlord. (Wis. Admin. Code § 134.06; Wis. Stat. Ann. § 704.08)

Owner or agent identity: Landlord must disclose to the tenant in writing, at or before the time a rental agreement is signed, the name and address of: the person or persons authorized to collect or receive rent and manage and maintain the premises, and who can readily be contacted by the tenant; and the owner of the premises or other person authorized to accept service of legal process and other notices and demands on behalf of the owner. The address must be an address within the state at which service of process can be made in person. (Wis. Admin. Code § 134.04)

Nonstandard rental provisions: If landlord wants to enter premises for reasons not specified by law, landlord must disclose the provision in a separate written document entitled "NONSTANDARD RENTAL PROVISIONS" before the rental agreement is signed. (Wis. Admin. Code § 134.09)

Habitability deficiencies: Landlord must disclose serious problems that affect the rental unit's habitability. (Wis. Admin. Code § 134.04)

Utility charges: If charges for water, heat, or electricity are not included in the rent, the landlord must disclose this fact to the tenant before entering into a rental agreement or accepting any earnest money or security deposit from the prospective tenant. If individual dwelling units and common areas are not separately metered, and if the charges are not included in the rent, the landlord must disclose the basis on which charges for utility services will be allocated among individual dwelling units. (Wis. Admin. Code § 134.04)

Disposing of abandoned property: If landlord intends to immediately dispose of any tenant property left behind after move-out, landlord must notify tenant at the time lease is signed. (But landlord must hold prescription medications and medical equipment for seven days, and must give notice before disposing of vehicles or manufactured homes to owner and any known secured party.) (Wis. Stat. Ann. § 704.05(5))

Notice of domestic abuse protections: Landlords must include the following notice in the rental agreement or in an addendum to the agreement: "NOTICE OF DOMESTIC ABUSE PROTECTIONS"

(1) As provided in section 106.50(5m)(dm) of the Wisconsin statutes, a tenant has a defense to an eviction action if the tenant can prove that the landlord knew, or should have known, the tenant is a victim of domestic abuse, sexual assault, or stalking and that the eviction action is based on conduct related to domestic abuse, sexual assault, or stalking committed by either of the following:

(a) A person who was not the tenant's invited guest.

(b) A person who was the tenant's invited guest, but the tenant has done either of the following:

1. Sought an injunction barring the person from the premises.

2. Provided a written statement to the landlord stating that the person will no longer be an invited guest of the tenant and the tenant has not subsequently invited the person to be the tenant's guest.

Required Landlord Disclosures (continued)

(2) A tenant who is a victim of domestic abuse, sexual assault, or stalking may have the right to terminate the rental agreement in certain limited situations, as provided in section 704.16 of the Wisconsin statutes. If the tenant has safety concerns, the tenant should contact a local victim service provider or law enforcement agency.

(3) A tenant is advised that this notice is only a summary of the tenant's rights and the specific language of the statutes governs in all instances." (Wis. Stat. Ann. § 704.14)

Wyoming

Wyo. Stat. Ann. § 1-21-1207

Nonrefundable fees permitted? Yes. If any portion of the deposit is not refundable, rental agreement must include this information and tenant must be told before paying a deposit.

State Laws on Landlord's Access to Rental Property

This is a synopsis of state laws that specify circumstances when a landlord may enter rental premises and the amount of notice required for such entry.

State	State Law Citation	Amount of Notice Required in Nonemergency Situations	Form of Notice	Reasons Landlord May Enter					
				To Deal With an Emergency	To Inspect the Premises	To Make Repairs, Alterations, or Improvements	To Show Property to Prospective Tenants or Purchasers	During Tenant's Extended Absence	When tenant has abandoned the property
Alabama	Ala. Code §§ 35-9A-303, 35-9A-423	Two days	Not specified	✓	✓	✓	✓	✓	✓
Alaska	Alaska Stat. §§ 34.03.140, 34.03.230	24 hours	Not specified	✓	✓	✓	✓	✓	✓
Arizona	Ariz. Rev. Stat. Ann. § 33-1343	Two days; notice period does not apply, and tenant's consent is assumed, if entry is pursuant to tenant's request for maintenance as prescribed in Ariz. Rev. Stat. § 33-1341, paragraph 8.	Not specified	✓	✓	✓	✓		✓
Arkansas	Ark. Code Ann. § 18-17-602	No notice specified	Not specified		✓	✓	✓		
California	Cal. Civ. Code §§ 1950.5, 1954	Reasonable notice; 24 hours is presumed reasonable (48 hours for initial move-out inspection).	Written notice required, but oral notice is sufficient if the entry is to show the property to prospective or actual purchasers, but only if the landlord has given written notice within the previous 120 days, telling the tenant that the property is for sale and such oral notice might be given (24 hours' notice is presumed reasonable; landlord must leave a note when leaving).	✓	✓	✓	✓		✓

State Laws on Landlord's Access to Rental Property (continued)

State	State Law Citation	Amount of Notice Required in Nonemergency Situations	Form of Notice	Reasons Landlord May Enter					
				To Deal With an Emergency	To Inspect the Premises	To Make Repairs, Alterations, or Improvements	To Show Property to Prospective Tenants or Purchasers	During Tenant's Extended Absence	When tenant has abandoned the property
Colorado	Colo. Rev. Stat. Ann. § 38-12-1004	Notice statute relates only to access for inspecting for or treating a bed bug infestation. 48 hours' notice required unless lease says otherwise.	Not specified, unless the access is related to a possible or actual bed bug infestation, in which case notice must be electronic or written.						
Connecticut	Conn. Gen. Stat. Ann. §§ 47a-16 to 47a-16a	Reasonable notice	Written or oral	✓	✓	✓	✓	✓	✓
Delaware	Del. Code Ann. tit. 25, §§ 5113, 5507, 5509, 5510	48 hours	Written, by giving a copy to an adult who resides at the rental unit or at the tenant's usual residence (if it's not the rental) or by mailing via registered or certified mail or first class mail as evidenced by a certificate of mailing postage-prepaid, addressed to the tenant at the rental. The notice can also be posted at the rental unit when it's combined with a return receipt of a certificate of mailing.	✓	✓	✓	✓	✓	
District of Columbia	D.C. Code Ann. § 42-3505.51	48 hours	Written and electronic (including email and mobile text messaging), but if the tenant doesn't provide an acknowlegment of the electronic notice in writing, the landlord must provide a paper notice.	✓	✓	✓	✓		
Florida	Fla. Stat. Ann. § 83.53	12 hours	Not specified	✓	✓	✓	✓	✓	

				Reasons Landlord May Enter					
State	**State Law Citation**	**Amount of Notice Required in Nonemergency Situations**	**Form of Notice**	**To Deal With an Emergency**	**To Inspect the Premises**	**To Make Repairs, Alterations, or Improvements**	**To Show Property to Prospective Tenants or Purchasers**	**During Tenant's Extended Absence**	**When tenant has abandoned the property**
Georgia	No statute								
Hawaii	Haw. Rev. Stat. §§ 521-53, 521-70(b)	Two days	Not specified	✓	✓	✓	✓	✓	✓
Idaho	No statute								
Illinois	No statute								
Indiana	Ind. Code Ann. § 32-31-5-6	Reasonable notice	Written or oral	✓	✓	✓	✓		✓
Iowa	Iowa Code Ann. §§ 562A.19, 562A.28, 562A.29	24 hours	Not specified	✓	✓	✓	✓	✓	✓
Kansas	Kan. Stat. Ann. §§ 58-2557, 58-2565	Reasonable notice	Not specified	✓	✓	✓	✓	✓	✓
Kentucky	Ky. Rev. Stat. Ann. §§ 383.615, 383.670	Two days	Not specified	✓	✓	✓	✓	✓	✓
Louisiana	La. Civ. Code art. 2693	No notice specified	Not specified			✓			
Maine	Me. Rev. Stat. Ann. tit. 14, § 6025	24 hours	Not specified	✓	✓	✓	✓		
Maryland	No statute								
Massachusetts	Mass. Gen. Laws Ann. ch. 186, § 15B(1)(a)	No notice specified	Not specified		✓	✓	✓		✓
Michigan	No statute								
Minnesota	Minn. Stat. Ann. § 504B.211	Reasonable notice	Not specified	✓	✓	✓	✓		
Mississippi	Miss. Code Ann. § 89-7-49	When a landlord believes tenant has abandoned property, and the tenant owes rent, the landlord may request the constable of the county to go onto the premises to ascertain abandonment and leave a notice.	Written notice						✓

					Reasons Landlord May Enter					
State	State Law Citation	Amount of Notice Required in Nonemergency Situations	Form of Notice	To Deal With an Emergency	To Inspect the Premises	To Make Repairs, Alterations, or Improvements	To Show Property to Prospective Tenants or Purchasers	During Tenant's Extended Absence	When tenant has abandoned the property
Missouri	No statute								
Montana	Mont. Code Ann. §§ 70-24-312, 70-24-426	24 hours	Not specified	✓	✓	✓	✓	✓	✓
Nebraska	Neb. Rev. Stat. §§ 76-1423, 76-1432	One day	Not specified	✓	✓	✓	✓	✓	✓
Nevada	Nev. Rev. Stat. Ann. § 118A.330	24 hours	Not specified	✓	✓	✓	✓		✓
New Hampshire	N.H. Rev. Stat. Ann. § 540-A:3	Notice that is adequate under the circumstances; however, 48 hours' notice when entering after receiving notice of a bed bug infestation in an adjacent unit.	Not specified, but 48 hours when entering to evaluate a possible or actual bed bug infestation.	✓	✓	✓	✓		
New Jersey	N.J. Stat. Ann. § 2A:39-1; N.J.A.C. 5:10-5.1 (for buildings with more than one unit)	In buildings with fewer than three units: Landlords can enter only when they have the tenant's permission or a court order. In buildings with three or more units: Landlords have a right to access the unit to inspect it, make repairs or perform maintenance, and deal with emergencies, but must give reasonable notice (one day under ordinary circumstances) before entering.	Not specified						
New Mexico	N.M. Stat. Ann. §§ 47-8-24, 47-8-34	24 hours	Written notice	✓	✓	✓	✓	✓	✓

State Laws on Landlord's Access to Rental Property (continued)

				Reasons Landlord May Enter					
State	State Law Citation	Amount of Notice Required in Nonemergency Situations	Form of Notice	To Deal With an Emergency	To Inspect the Premises	To Make Repairs, Alterations, or Improvements	To Show Property to Prospective Tenants or Purchasers	During Tenant's Extended Absence	When tenant has abandoned the property
New York	No statute								
North Carolina	No statute								
North Dakota	N.D. Cent. Code § 47-16-07.3	Reasonable notice	Not specified	✓	✓	✓	✓		✓
Ohio	Ohio Rev. Code Ann. §§ 5321.04(A)(8), 5321.05(B)	24 hours	Not specified	✓	✓	✓	✓		
Oklahoma	Okla. Stat. Ann. tit. 41, § 128	One day	Not specified	✓	✓	✓	✓		✓
Oregon	Or. Rev. Stat. §§ 90.322, 90.410	24 hours	Not specified	✓	✓	✓	✓	✓	✓
Pennsylvania	No statute								
Rhode Island	R.I. Gen. Laws § 34-18-26	Two days	Not specified	✓	✓	✓	✓	✓	✓
South Carolina	S.C. Code Ann. §§ 27-40-530, 27-40-730	24 hours	Not specified	✓	✓	✓	✓		✓
South Dakota	No statute								
Tennessee	Tenn. Code Ann. §§ 66-28-403, 66-28-507	24 hours (applies only within the final 30 days of the rental agreement term, when landlord intends to show the premises to prospective renters and this right of access is set forth in the rental agreement).	Not specified	✓	✓	✓	✓	✓	✓
Texas	No statute								
Utah	Utah Code Ann. §§ 57-22-4, 57-22-5(2)(c)	24 hours, unless rental agreement specifies otherwise.	Not specified			✓			

State Laws on Landlord's Access to Rental Property (continued)									
				Reasons Landlord May Enter					
State	**State Law Citation**	**Amount of Notice Required in Nonemergency Situations**	**Form of Notice**	**To Deal With an Emergency**	**To Inspect the Premises**	**To Make Repairs, Alterations, or Improvements**	**To Show Property to Prospective Tenants or Purchasers**	**During Tenant's Extended Absence**	**When tenant has abandoned the property**
Vermont	Vt. Stat. Ann. tit. 9, § 4460	48 hours	Not specified	✓	✓	✓	✓		
Virginia	Va. Code Ann. §§ 55.1-1229, 55.1-1249	For routine maintenance only: 24 hours, but no notice needed if entry follows tenant's request for maintenance.	Not specified	✓	✓	✓	✓	✓	✓
Washington	Wash. Rev. Code Ann. § 59.18.150	Two days; one day to show property to actual or prospective tenants or buyers	Written notice, unless it is impracticable to do so.	✓	✓	✓	✓		✓
West Virginia	No statute								
Wisconsin	Wis. Stat. Ann. § 704.05(2); Wis. Adm. Code § ATCP 134.09(2)	With 12 hours' advance notice, landlords may enter at reasonable times. Landlords and tenants may sign a separate "Nonstandard Rental Provision" agreement, in which they provide for entry for reasons not enumerated in this chart.	Not specified	✓	✓	✓	✓	✓	✓
Wyoming	No statute								

State Landlord-Tenant Exemption Statutes

Your state's general landlord-tenant statutes (listed in the "State Landlord-Tenant Statutes" chart above) might not apply to all types of rentals and landlord-tenant relationships: Most states define what a rental is for purposes of the statutes. Other states might not define what a rental is, but instead exempt certain types of occupancies from the general landlord-tenant statutes. Some states do both. To check whether your state's general landlord-tenant statutes apply to your situation, review the statutes listed in the "State Landlord-Tenant Statutes" chart for any definition of what your state considers a rental. Next, you'll need to find out whether your situation falls within any exemptions from the general landlord-tenant statutes. This chart provides information about the exemptions that are most relevant to readers of this book. If your state does not have an exemption statute, you'll see "No statute" written in the Exemptions column.

Alabama

Ala. Code §§ 35-9A-122, 35-9A-601

1. Occupancy under a contract of sale of a dwelling unit or the property of which it is a part, if the occupant is the purchaser or a person who succeeds to the interest of the purchaser

2. Occupancy by a member of a social organization in the portion of a structure operated for the benefit of the organization

3. Transient occupancy in a hotel, motel, or lodgings

4. Occupancy by an employee of a landlord whose right to occupancy is conditional upon employment at the premises

5. Occupancy under a rental agreement covering premises rented by the occupant primarily for agricultural purposes

6. Continuation of occupancy by the seller or a member of the seller's family for a period of not more than 36 months after the sale of a dwelling unit or the property of which it is a part; and

7. Rental agreements most recently entered into, extended, or renewed before January 1, 2007.

Alaska

Alaska Stat. §§ 34.03.330, 34.03.370

1. Occupancy under a contract of sale of a dwelling unit or the property of which it is a part if the occupant is the purchaser or a person who succeeds to the interest of a purchaser

2. Occupancy by a member of a social organization in the portion of a structure operated for the benefit of the organization

3. Transient occupancy in a hotel, motel, lodgings, or other transient facility

4. Occupancy by an employee of a landlord whose right to occupancy is conditioned upon employment substantially for services, maintenance, or repair to the premises

5. Occupancy under a rental agreement covering premises used by the occupant primarily for agricultural purposes

6. Occupancy under a rental agreement covering premises used as part of a transitional or supportive housing program that is sponsored or operated by a public corporation or by a nonprofit corporation and that provides shelter and related support services; and

7. Any rental agreement, lease, or tenancy most recently entered into, extended, or renewed before March 19, 1974.

Arizona

Ariz. Rev. Stat. Ann. § 33-1308

1. Occupancy under a contract of sale of a dwelling unit or the property of which it is a part, if the occupant is the purchaser or a person who succeeds to the purchaser's interest

2. Occupancy by a member of a social organization in the portion of a structure operated for the benefit of the organization

3. Transient occupancy in a hotel, motel or recreational lodging

State Landlord-Tenant Exemption Statutes (continued)

4. Occupancy by an employee of a landlord as a manager or custodian whose right to occupancy is conditional upon employment at the premises; and

5. Occupancy in or operation of public housing as authorized, provided or conducted under or pursuant to any federal law or regulation.

Arkansas

Ark. Code Ann. § 18-17-202

1. Occupancy under a contract of sale of a dwelling unit or the property of which it is a part, if the occupant is the purchaser or a person who succeeds to the purchaser's interest

2. Occupancy by a member of a social organization in the portion of a structure operated for the benefit of the organization

3. Transient occupancy in a hotel, motel, or other accommodations subject to any sales tax on lodging

4. Occupancy by an employee of a landlord whose right to occupancy is conditional upon employment in and about the premises

5. Occupancy under a rental agreement covering the premises used by the occupant primarily for agricultural purposes; and

6. Residence, whether temporary or not, at a public or private charitable or emergency protective shelter.

California

Cal. Civ. Code § 1940

1. Transient occupancy in a hotel, motel, residence club, or other facility; and

2. Occupancy at a hotel or motel where the innkeeper retains a right of access to and control of the dwelling unit and the hotel or motel provides or offers certain services.

Colorado

Colo. Rev. Stat. Ann. § 38-12-511

1. Occupancy under a contract of sale of a dwelling unit or the property of which it is a part, if the occupant is the purchaser, seller, or a person who succeeds to the purchaser's or seller's interest

2. Occupancy by a member of a social organization in the portion of a structure operated for the benefit of the organization

3. Transient occupancy in a hotel or motel that lasts less than 30 days

4. Occupancy by an employee or independent contractor whose right to occupancy is conditional upon performance of services for an employer or contractor

5. Occupancy in a structure that is located within an unincorporated area of a county, does not receive water, heat, and sewer services from a public entity, and is rented for recreational purposes, such as a hunting cabin, yurt, hut, or other similar structure

6. Occupancy under rental agreement covering a residential premises used by the occupant primarily for agricultural purposes; and

7. Any relationship between the owner of a mobile home park and the owner of a mobile home situated in the park.

Connecticut

Conn. Gen. Stat. Ann. § 47a-2

1. Occupancy under a contract of sale of a dwelling unit or the property of which such unit is a part, if the occupant is the purchaser or a person who succeeds to the purchaser's interest

2. Occupancy by a member of a social organization in the portion of a structure operated for the benefit of such organization

3. Transient occupancy in a hotel, motel, or similar lodging; and

4. Occupancy by a personal care assistant or other person who is employed by a person with a disability to assist and support such disabled person with daily living activities or housekeeping chores and is provided dwelling space in the personal residence of such disabled person as a benefit or condition of such employment.

State Landlord-Tenant Exemption Statutes (continued)

Delaware

Del. Code Ann. tit. 25, §§ 5101, 5102

1. Residence at an institution where such residence is merely incidental to detention or to the provision of medical, geriatric, educational, counseling, religious, or similar services

2. Residence by a member of a fraternal organization in a structure operated for the benefit of the organization

3. Residence in a hotel, motel, cubicle hotel or other similar lodgings

4. Nonrenewable rental agreements of 120 days or less for any calendar year for a dwelling located within the boundaries of Broadkill Hundred, Lewes-Rehoboth Hundred, Indian River Hundred, Baltimore Hundred and Cedar Creek Hundred; and

5. Rental agreements for ground upon which improvements were constructed or installed by the tenant and used as a dwelling, where the tenant retains ownership or title thereto, or obtains title to existing improvement on the property.

District of Columbia

D.C. Code Ann. § 42-3502.05

1. Rental units operated by a foreign government as a residence for diplomatic personnel

2. Rental units in an establishment which has as its primary purpose providing diagnostic care and treatment of diseases; and

3. Dormitories.

Also: Following a determination by the Rent Administrator, any rental intended for use as long-term temporary housing by families with 1 or more members that satisfies each of the following requirements:

A. The rental is occupied by families that, at the time of their initial occupancy, have had incomes at or below 50% of the District median income for families of the size in question for the immediately preceding 12 months;

B. The provider of the rental is a nonprofit charitable organization that operates the rental on a strictly not-for-profit basis; and

C. The housing provider offers a comprehensive social services program to resident families.

Florida

Fla. Stat. Ann. § 83.42

1. Occupancy under a contract of sale of a dwelling unit or the property of which it is a part in which the buyer has paid at least 12 months' rent or in which the buyer has paid at least 1 month's rent and a deposit of at least 5% of the purchase price of the property; and

2. Transient occupancy in a hotel, condominium, motel, roominghouse, or similar public lodging, or transient occupancy in a mobile home park.

Georgia

No statute

Hawaii

Haw. Rev. Stat. § 521-7

1. Residence in a structure directly controlled and managed by:

A. The University of Hawaii or any other university or college in the State for housing its own students or faculty or residence in a structure erected on land leased from the university or college by a nonprofit corporation for the exclusive purpose of housing students or faculty of the college or university; or

B. A private dorm management company that offers a minimum of 50 beds to students of any college, university, or other institution of higher education in the State

2. Occupancy under a bona fide contract of sale of the dwelling unit or the property of which it is a part where the tenant is, or succeeds to the interest of, the purchaser

3. Residence by a member of a fraternal organization in a structure operated without profit for the benefit of the organization

State Landlord-Tenant Exemption Statutes (continued)

4. Transient occupancy on a day-to-day basis in a hotel or motel

5. Occupancy by an employee of the owner or landlord whose right to occupancy is conditional upon that employment for a period of up to four years, pursuant to a plan for the transfer of the dwelling unit or the property of which it is a part to the occupant

6. A lease of improved residential land for a term of 15 years or more

7. Occupancy by the prospective purchaser after an accepted offer to purchase and prior to the actual transfer of the owner's rights; and

8. Occupancy by the seller of residential real property after the transfer of the seller's ownership rights.

Idaho

No statute

Illinois

No statute

Indiana

Ind. Code Ann. § 32-31-2.9-4

1. Occupancy under a contract of sale of a rental unit or the property of which the rental unit is a part if the occupant is the purchaser or a person who succeeds to the purchaser's interest

2. Occupancy by a member of a social organization in the part of a structure operated for the benefit of the organization

3. Transient occupancy in a hotel, motel, or other lodging

4. Occupancy by an employee of a landlord whose right to occupancy is conditional upon employment at the premises; and

5. Rental agreements covering property used by the occupant primarily for agricultural purposes.

Iowa

Iowa Code Ann. §§ 562A.5, 562A.37

1. Occupancy under a contract of sale of a dwelling unit or the property of which it is a part, if the occupant is the purchaser or a person who succeeds to the purchaser's interest

2. Occupancy by a member of a social organization in the portion of a structure operated for the benefit of the organization

3. Transient occupancy in a hotel, motel, or other similar lodgings

4. Occupancy by an employee of a landlord whose right to occupancy is conditional upon employment at the premises

5. Rental agreements covering premises used by the occupant primarily for agricultural purposes; and

6. Rental agreements most recently entered into, extended, or renewed on or before January 1, 1979.

Kansas

Kan. Stat. Ann. §§ 58-2541, 58-2573

1. Occupancy under a contract of sale of a dwelling unit or the property of which it is a part, if the occupant is the purchaser or a person who succeeds to the purchaser's interest

2. Occupancy by a member of a social organization in the portion of a structure operated for the benefit of the organization

3. Transient occupancy in a hotel, motel, or rooming house

4. Occupancy by an employee of a landlord whose right to occupancy is conditional upon employment at the premises

5. Occupancy under a rental agreement covering premises used by the occupant primarily for agricultural purposes; and

6. Any rental agreement most recently entered into, extended, or modified before July 1, 1975.

Kentucky

Ky. Rev. Stat. Ann. §383.535

1. Occupancy under a contract of sale of a dwelling unit or the property of which it is a part, if the occupant is the purchaser or a person who succeeds to the purchaser's interest

State Landlord-Tenant Exemption Statutes (continued)

2. Occupancy by a member of a social organization in the portion of a structure operated for the benefit of the organization

3. Transient occupancy in a hotel, or motel, or lodgings subject to state transient lodgings or room occupancy excise tax act

4. Occupancy by an employee of a landlord whose right to occupancy is conditional upon employment at the premises; and

5. Occupancy of a dwelling located on land devoted to the production of livestock, livestock products, poultry, poultry products, or the growing of tobacco or other crops.

Louisiana

No statute

Maine

No statute

Maryland

Md. Code Ann. [Real Prop.] § 8-201

Tenancies arising after the sale of owner-occupied residential property where the seller and purchaser agree that the seller may remain in possession of the property for a period of not more than 60 days after the settlement.

Massachusetts

No statute

Michigan

Mich. Comp. Laws § 554.601 // Mich. Comp. Laws § 554.632

1. Occupancy in a motel, motor home, or other tourist accommodation, when used as a temporary accommodation for guests or tourists; and

2. Premises used as the principal place of residence of the owner and rented occasionally during temporary absences.

Minnesota

No statute

Mississippi

Miss. Code Ann. § 89-8-3

1. Occupancy under a contract of sale of a dwelling unit or the property of which it is a part, if the occupant is the purchaser or a person who succeeds to the purchaser's interest

2. Occupancy by a member of a social organization in the portion of a structure operated for the benefit of the organization

3. Transient occupancy in a hotel, motel, or lodgings

4. Occupancy under a rental agreement covering premises used by the occupant primarily for agricultural purposes

5. Occupancy when the occupant is performing agricultural labor for the owner and such premises are rented for less than fair rental value; and

6. Any rental agreement entered into before July 1, 1991.

Missouri

No statute

Montana

Mont. Code Ann. § 70-24-104

1. Occupancy under a contract of sale of a dwelling unit or the property of which it is a part if the occupant is the purchaser or a person who succeeds to the purchaser's interest

2. Occupancy by a member of a social organization in the portion of a structure operated for the benefit of the organization

3. Transient occupancy in a hotel or motel

4. Occupancy under a rental agreement covering premises used by the occupant primarily for commercial or agricultural purposes

5. Occupancy by an employee of a landlord whose right to occupancy is conditional upon employment at the premises; and

6. Occupancy outside a municipality under a rental agreement that includes hunting, fishing, or agricultural privileges, along with the use of the dwelling unit.

State Landlord-Tenant Exemption Statutes (continued)

Nebraska

Neb. Rev. Stat. §§ 76-1408, 76-1448

1. Occupancy under a contract of sale of a dwelling unit or the property of which it is a part, if the occupant is the purchaser or a person who succeeds to the purchaser's interest

2. Occupancy by a member of a social organization in the portion of a structure operated for the benefit of the organization

3. Transient occupancy in a hotel or motel

4. Occupancy by an employee of a landlord whose right to occupancy is conditional upon employment at the premises

5. Occupancy under a rental agreement covering premises used by the occupant primarily for agricultural purposes

6. A lease of improved or unimproved residential land for a term of five years or more; and

7. Rental agreements most recently entered into, extended, or renewed on or before July 1, 1975.

Nevada

Nev. Rev. Stat. Ann. §§ 118A.180, 118A.530

1. Rental agreements for manufactured homes

2. Occupancy under a contract of sale of a dwelling unit or the property of which it is a part, if the occupant is the purchaser or successor to the purchaser's interest

3. Occupancy by a member of a social organization in the portion of a structure operated for the benefit of the organization

4. Occupancy in a hotel or motel for less than 30 consecutive days unless the occupant clearly manifests an intent to remain for a longer continuous period

5. Occupancy by an employee of a landlord whose right to occupancy is solely conditional upon employment at the premises

6. Occupancy under a rental agreement covering premises used by the occupant primarily for agricultural purposes

7. Occupancy by a person who is guilty of a forcible entry or forcible detainer; and

8. Rental agreements most recently entered into, extended, or renewed before July 1, 1977.

New Hampshire

N.H. Rev. Stat. Ann. § 540:1-a

1. Rooms in rooming or boarding houses which are rented to transient guests for fewer than 90 consecutive days

2. Rooms in hotels, motels, inns, tourist homes, and other dwellings rented for recreational or vacation use

3. Single-family homes in which the occupant has no lease, which is the primary and usual residence of the owner

4. Shared residential facilities (properties with separate sleeping areas for each occupant and in which each occupant has access to and shares with the owner one or more areas of the property)

5. Vacation or recreational rentals

6. Residential units leased by a member of a social organization that provides student housing for a postsecondary institution in a structure owned and operated by the social organization; and

7. Occupancies in which the occupant is hired to provide care or assistance for a person with disabilities.

New Jersey

N.J. Stat. Ann. § 46:8-9.12 // N.J. Stat. Ann. § 46:8-44

1. Seasonal rentals (does not include use or rental of living quarters for seasonal, temporary or migrant farm workers in connection with any work or place where work is being performed)

2. Dwelling units in rentals containing not more than two such units

3. Owner-occupied premises of not more than three dwelling units; and

4. Hotels, motels, or other guest houses serving transient or seasonal guests.

State Landlord-Tenant Exemption Statutes (continued)

New Mexico

N.M. Stat. Ann. §§ 47-8-9, 47-8-51

1. Occupancy under a contract of sale of a dwelling unit or the property of which it is part, if the occupant is the purchaser or a person who succeeds to the purchaser's interest

2. Occupancy by a member of a social organization in the portion of a structure operated for the benefit of the organization

3. Transient occupancy in a hotel or motel

4. Occupancy by an employee of an owner pursuant to a written rental or employment agreement that specifies that the employee's right to occupancy is conditional upon employment at the premises

5. Occupancy under a rental agreement covering premises used by the occupant primarily for agricultural purposes; and

6. Rental agreements most recently entered into, extended, or renewed on or before July 1, 1975.

New York

N.Y. Mult. Dwell. Law §§ 3, 4, 8, 9, 13, 14

1. Rentals in cities with a population of less than 325,000; and

2. Rentals occupied by fewer than three families living independently of each other.

N.Y. Mult. Resid. Law §§ 3, 4, 9

1. Rentals in cities with a population equal to or greater than 325,000; and

2. Rentals occupied by fewer than three families living independently of each other.

North Carolina

N.C. Gen. Stat. Ann. § 42-39

1. Transient occupancy in a hotel, motel, or similar lodging

2. Vacation rentals; and

3. Dwellings provided without charge or rent.

North Dakota

No statute

Ohio

Ohio Rev. Code Ann. § 5321.01

1. Tourist homes, hotels, motels, recreational vehicle parks, recreation camps, combined park-camps, temporary park-camps, and other similar facilities where circumstances indicate a transient occupancy

2. Farm residences furnished in connection with the rental of land of a minimum of two acres for production of agricultural products by one or more of the occupants

3. Manufactured home parks, marinas, and agricultural labor camps; and

4. Occupancy in hotels and single room occupancy facilities.

Oklahoma

Okla. Stat. Ann. tit. 41, § 104

1. Occupancy under a contract of sale or contract for deed of a dwelling unit or of the property of which it is a part, if the occupant is the purchaser or a person who succeeds to the purchaser's interest

2. Occupancy by a member of a social organization in a structure operated for the benefit of the organization

3. Transient occupancy in a hotel, motel, or other similar lodging; and

4. Occupancy under a rental agreement covering premises used by the occupant primarily for agricultural purposes.

Oregon

Or. Rev. Stat. §§ 90.110, 90.113, 90.120

1. Occupancy of a dwelling unit for no more than 90 days by a purchaser prior to the scheduled closing of a real estate sale or by a seller following the closing of a sale, in either case as permitted under the terms of an agreement for sale of the property

State Landlord-Tenant Exemption Statutes (continued)

2. Occupancy by a member of a social organization in the portion of a structure operated for the benefit of the organization

3. Transient occupancy in a hotel or motel

4. Occupancy by a squatter

5. Vacation occupancy

6. Occupancy by an employee of a landlord whose right to occupancy is conditional upon employment at the premises; and

7. Occupancy under a rental agreement covering premises used by the occupant primarily for agricultural purposes.

Note that different rules might apply to occupancy of manufactured dwellings, floating homes, and recreational vehicles.

Pennsylvania

No statute

Rhode Island

R.I. Gen. Laws § 34-18-8

Unless the parties expressly agree to be governed by them, the following occupancies are exempted from the residential landlord-tenant statutes:

1. Occupancy under a contract of sale of a dwelling unit or the property of which it is a part, if the occupant is the purchaser or a person who succeeds to the purchaser's interest

2. Occupancy by a member of a social organization in the portion of a structure operated for the benefit of the organization

3. Transient occupancy in a hotel, motel, or other lodging

4. Occupancy by a paid employee of a landlord, whose right to occupancy is conditional upon employment substantially for services, maintenance, or repair of premises containing more than eleven units; and

5. Residence at a transitional housing facility.

South Carolina

S.C. Code Ann. § 27-40-120

1. Occupancy under a contract of sale of a dwelling unit or the property of which it is a part, if the occupant is the purchaser or a person who succeeds to the purchaser's interest

2. Occupancy by a member of a social organization in the portion of a structure operated for the benefit of the organization

3. Transient occupancy in a hotel, motel, or other accommodations subject to the sales tax on accommodations

4. Occupancy by an employee of a landlord whose right to occupancy is conditional upon employment at the premises

5. Occupancy under a rental agreement covering the premises used by the occupant primarily for agricultural purposes; and

6. Occupancy under a rental agreement for a vacation time share.

South Dakota

No statute

Tennessee

Tenn. Code Ann. § 66-28-102

1. Rentals in counties with a population of less than 75,000, according to the 2010 federal census or any subsequent federal census

2. Rental agreements most recently entered into, extended, or renewed before July 1, 1975

3. Occupancy under a contract of sale of a dwelling unit or the property of which it is a part, if the occupant is the purchaser or a person who succeeds to the purchaser's interest

4. Transient occupancy in a hotel, motel, or lodgings subject to city, state, or transient lodgings laws; and

5. Occupancy under a rental agreement covering premises used by the occupant primarily for agricultural purposes.

State Landlord-Tenant Exemption Statutes (continued)

Texas

No statute

Utah

Utah Code Ann. § 57-22-2

1. Boarding houses or similar facilities

2. Mobile home lots; and

3. Recreational properties rented on an occasional basis.

Vermont

Vt. Stat. Ann. tit. 9, § 4452

1. Occupancy under a contract of sale of a dwelling unit or the property of which it is a part, if the occupant is the purchaser or a person who succeeds to the purchaser's interest

2. Occupancy by a member of a social or religious organization in the portion of a building operated for the benefit of the organization

3. Transient occupancy in a hotel or motel

4. Rental of a mobile home lot

5. Transient residence in seasonal or short-term vacation or recreational properties; and

6. Occupancy of a dwelling unit without right or permission by a person who is not a tenant.

Virginia

Va. Code Ann. § 55.1-1201

1. Occupancy by a member of a social organization in the portion of a structure operated for the benefit of the organization

2. Occupancy in a campground

3. Occupancy by a tenant who pays no rent pursuant to a rental agreement

4. Occupancy by an employee of a landlord whose right to occupancy in a multifamily dwelling unit is conditioned upon employment at the premises or a former employee whose occupancy continues less than 60 days

5. Occupancy under a contract of sale of a dwelling unit or the property of which it is a part, if the occupant is the purchaser or a person who succeeds to the purchaser's interest; and

6. Occupancy in a hotel, motel, extended stay facility, vacation residential facility, timeshare, boardinghouse, or similar transient lodging when the occupancy is not the resident's primary residence, or when the resident uses it as a primary residence for less than 90 days.

Washington

Wash. Rev. Code Ann. §§ 59.18.040, 59.18.415, 59.18.430, 59.18.435

1. Occupancy under a bona fide earnest money agreement to purchase or contract of sale of the dwelling unit or the property of which it is a part, where the tenant is, or stands in the place of, the purchaser

2. Residence in a hotel, motel, or other transient lodging

3. Rental agreements for the use of any single-family residence which are incidental to leases or rentals entered into in connection with a lease of land to be used primarily for agricultural purposes

4. Rental agreements providing housing for seasonal agricultural employees while provided in conjunction with such employment

5. Rental agreements with the state of Washington, department of natural resources, on public lands

6. Occupancy by an employee of a landlord whose right to occupy is conditioned upon employment at the premises

7. Leases of single-family dwellings for a period of a year or more or leases of a single-family dwelling containing a bona fide option to purchase by the tenant (but an attorney for the tenant must approve on the face of the agreement any lease exempted from these laws); and

8. Leases entered into before July 16, 1973.

Required Landlord Disclosures (continued)

West Virginia

No statute

Wisconsin

Wis. Admin. Code ATCP 134.01

1. Occupancy by a member of a fraternal or social organization which operates that dwelling unit

2. Occupancy under a contract of sale, by the purchaser of the dwelling unit or the purchaser's successor in interest

3. Occupancy by tourist or transient occupants

4. Occupancy that the landlord provides free of charge to any person, or that the landlord provides as consideration to a person whom the landlord currently employs to operate or maintain the premises; and

5. Occupancy by a tenant who is engaged in commercial agricultural operations on the premises.

Wyoming

No statute

How to Use the Downloadable Forms on the Nolo Website

This book comes with forms that you can download online at:

www.nolo.com/back-of-book/LEAR.html

To use the files, your computer must have specific software programs installed. Here is a list of types of files provided by this book, as well as the software programs you'll need to access them.

- **RTF.** You can open, edit, save, and print these form files with most word processing programs such as Microsoft *Word*, Windows *WordPad*, and recent versions of *WordPerfect*.
- **PDF.** You can view these files with Adobe *Reader*, free software from www.adobe.com. Unless you have a pdf editing tool or software, you must print out our PDFs and complete them by hand.

Editing RTFs

Here are some general instructions about editing RTF forms in your word processing program. Refer to the book's instructions and sample agreements for help about what should go in each blank.

- **Underlines.** Underlines indicate where to enter information. After filling in the needed text, delete the underline. In most word processing programs you can do this by highlighting the underlined portion and typing CTRL-U.

- **Bracketed and italicized text.** Bracketed and italicized text indicates instructions. Be sure to remove all instructional text before you finalize your document.
- **Optional text.** Optional text gives you the choice to include or exclude it. Delete any optional text you don't want to use. Renumber numbered items, if necessary.
- **Alternative text.** Alternative text gives you the choice between two or more text options. Delete those options you don't want to use. Renumber numbered items, if necessary.
- **Signature lines.** Signature lines should appear on a page with at least some text from the document itself.

Every word processing program uses its own commands to open, format, save, and print documents, so refer to your software's help documents for help using your program. Nolo cannot provide technical support for questions about how to use your computer or your software.

CAUTION

In accordance with U.S. copyright laws, the forms provided by this book are for your personal use only.

List of Forms Available on the Nolo Website

Use the tables below to find the file name for each form. All forms listed are available for download at: **www.nolo.com/back-of-book/LEAR.html**

Forms in RTF Format	
Form Title	**File Name**
Notice of Conditional Acceptance Based on Credit Report or Other Information	Acceptance.rtf
Rental Application	Application.rtf
Consent to Contact References and Perform Credit Check	CheckConsent.rtf
Landlord-Tenant Checklist	Checklist.rtf
Notice of Denial Based on Credit Report or Other Information	Denial.rtf
Fixed-Term Residential Lease	FixedLease.rtf
Fixed-Term Residential Lease (Spanish Version)	PlazoFijo.rtf
Month-to-Month Residential Rental Agreement	MonthToMonth.rtf
Month-to-Month Residential Rental Agreement (Spanish Version)	Mensual.rtf
Move-In Letter	MoveIn.rtf
Move-Out Letter	MoveOut.rtf
Tenant's Notice of Intent to Move Out	MoveNotice.rtf
Tenant References	References.rtf

Forms in PDF Format	
Form Title	**File Name**
Rental Application	Application.pdf
Tenant's Notice of Intent to Move Out	MoveNotice.pdf
Protect Your Family From Lead in Your Home Pamphlet	leadpdfe.pdf
Protect Your Family From Lead in Your Home Pamphlet (Spanish Version)	leadpdfs.pdf
Disclosure of Information on Lead-Based Paint or Lead-Based Paint Hazards	lesr_eng.pdf
Disclosure of Information on Lead-Based Paint or Lead-Based Paint Hazards (Spanish Version)	spanless.pdf

Forms

Month-to-Month Residential Rental Agreement

Clause 1. Identification of Landlord and Tenant

This Agreement is between _____ ("Tenant") and

_____ ("Landlord").

Each Tenant is jointly and severally liable for the payment of rent and performance of all other terms of this Agreement.

Clause 2. Identification of Premises

Subject to the terms and conditions in this Agreement, Landlord rents to Tenant, and Tenant rents from Landlord, for residential purposes only, the premises located at _____

_____ ("the Premises").

Rental of the Premises also includes: _____

_____ .

Rental of the Premises excludes: _____

_____ .

Clause 3. Limits on Use and Occupancy

The Premises are to be used only as a private residence for Tenant(s) listed in Clause 1 of this Agreement, and their minor children: _____ . Occupancy by guests for more than _____ is prohibited without Landlord's written consent and will be considered a breach of this Agreement.

Clause 4. Term of the Tenancy

The rental will begin on _____ , and continue on a month-to-month basis. Landlord may terminate the tenancy or modify the terms of this Agreement by giving the Tenant _____ days' written notice. Tenant may terminate the tenancy by giving the Landlord _____ days' written notice.

Clause 5. Payment of Rent

Regular monthly rent

Tenant will pay to Landlord a monthly rent of $_____ , payable in advance on the first day of each month, except when that day falls on a weekend or legal holiday, in which case rent is due on the next business day. Rent will be paid as follows, or in another manner as Landlord designates from time to time:

Delivery of payment

Rent will be paid:

☐ by mail, to _____

☐ in person, at _____

☐ electronically, to _____

Form of payment

Landlord will accept payment in these forms:

☐ cash

☐ personal check made payable to _____

☐ certified funds or money order payable to _____

☐ credit card or debit card

☐ other electronic funds transfer: _____

Prorated first month's rent

☐ On signing this Agreement, Tenant will pay to Landlord for the period of _____

through _____ the sum of $_____ as rent, payable in advance of the start

of the tenancy.

☐ Upon move-in, Tenant will owe as rent the prorated rent specified above, plus one full month's rent in the

amount designated above, for a total of $_____.

Clause 6. Late Charges

Because Landlord and Tenant agree that actual damages for late rent payments are very difficult or impossible

to determine, Landlord and Tenant agree to the following:

- Tenant will pay Landlord a late charge if Tenant fails to pay the rent in full within _____ days after

  the date it is due.

- The late charge will be $_____, plus $_____ for each individual day that the rent continues

  to be unpaid. The total late charge for any one month will not exceed $_____.

Landlord does not waive the right to insist on payment of the rent in full on the date it is due.

Clause 7. Returned Check and Other Bank Charges

If any check offered by Tenant to Landlord in payment of rent or any other amount due under this Agreement

is returned for lack of sufficient funds, a "stop payment," or any other reason, Landlord will make a demand for

payment and otherwise pursue remedies as allowed by law.

Clause 8. Security Deposit

On signing this Agreement, Tenant will pay to Landlord the sum of $_____ as a security deposit. Tenant may not, without Landlord's prior written consent, apply this security deposit to the last month's rent or to any other sum due under this Agreement. Within _____ after Tenant has vacated the Premises, returned keys, and provided Landlord with a forwarding address, Landlord will return the deposit in full or give Tenant an itemized written statement of the reasons for, and the dollar amount of, any of the security deposit retained by Landlord, along with a check for any deposit balance.

Optional clauses here, if any: _____

Clause 9. Utilities

Tenant will pay all utility charges, except for the following, which will be paid by Landlord:

_____

_____.

Clause 10. Prohibition of Assignment and Subletting

Tenant will not sublet any part of the Premises or assign this Agreement without the prior written consent of Landlord. Violating this clause is grounds for terminating the tenancy.

☐ a. Tenant will not sublet or rent any part of the Premises for short-term stays of any duration, including but not limited to vacation rentals.

☐ b. Short-stay rentals are prohibited except as authorized by law. Any short-stay rental is expressly conditioned upon the Tenant's following all regulations, laws, and other requirements as a condition to offering a short-stay rental. Failure to follow all laws, ordinances, regulations, and other requirements, including any registration requirement, will be deemed a material, noncurable breach of this Agreement and will furnish cause for termination.

Clause 11. Tenant's Maintenance Responsibilities

Tenant agrees to: (1) keep the Premises clean, sanitary, and in good condition and, upon termination of the tenancy, return the Premises to Landlord in a condition identical to that which existed when Tenant took occupancy, except for ordinary wear and tear; (2) immediately notify Landlord of any defects or dangerous conditions in and about the Premises of which Tenant becomes aware; and (3) reimburse Landlord, on demand by Landlord, for the cost of any repairs to the Premises, including Landlord's personal property therein, damaged by Tenant or Tenant's guests or business invitees through misuse or neglect.

Tenant has examined the Premises, including appliances, fixtures, carpets, drapes, and paint, and has found them to be in good, safe, and clean condition and repair, except as noted in the Landlord-Tenant Checklist.

Clause 12. Repairs and Alterations by Tenant

    a. Except as provided by law, or as authorized by the prior written consent of Landlord, Tenant will not make any repairs or alterations to the Premises, including nailing holes in the walls or painting the rental unit.

    b. Tenant will not, without Landlord's prior written consent, alter, rekey, or install any locks to the Premises or install or alter any security alarm system. Tenant will provide Landlord with a key or keys capable of unlocking all such rekeyed or new locks as well as instructions on how to disarm any altered or new security alarm system.

Clause 13. Violating Laws and Causing Disturbances

Tenant is entitled to quiet enjoyment of the Premises. Tenant and guests or invitees will not use the Premises or adjacent areas in such a way as to: (1) violate any law or ordinance, including laws prohibiting the use, possession, or sale of illegal drugs; (2) commit waste (severe property damage) or cause or tolerate a nuisance; or (3) annoy, disturb, inconvenience, or interfere with the quiet enjoyment and peace and quiet of any other tenant or nearby resident.

Clause 14. Damage to the Premises

In the event the Premises are partially or totally damaged or destroyed by fire or other cause, the following will apply:

    ☐ a. Premises totally damaged and destroyed. Landlord will have the option to: (1) repair such damage and restore the Premises, with this Agreement continuing in full force and effect, except that Tenant's rent will be abated while repairs are being made; or (2) give written notice to Tenant terminating this Agreement at any time within thirty (30) days after such damage, and specifying the termination date; in the event that Landlord gives such notice, this Agreement will expire and all of Tenant's rights pursuant to this Agreement will cease.

    ☐ b. Premises partially damaged by fire or other cause. Landlord will attempt to repair such damage and restore the Premises within thirty (30) days after such damage. If only part of the Premises cannot be used, Tenant must pay rent only for the usable part, to be determined by Landlord. If Landlord is unable to complete repairs within thirty (30) days, this Agreement will expire and all of Tenant's rights pursuant to this Agreement will terminate at the option of either party. Whether the Premises are totally or partially destroyed will be decided by Landlord, in the exercise of its sole discretion.

    ☐ c. In the event that Tenant, or Tenant's guests or invitees, in any way caused or contributed to the damage of the Premises, Landlord will have the right to terminate this Agreement at any time, and Tenant will be responsible for all losses, including, but not limited to, damage and repair costs as well as loss of rental income.

    ☐ d. Landlord will not be required to repair or replace any property brought onto the Premises by Tenant.

Clause 15. Renters' Insurance

Tenant acknowledges that Landlord's property insurance policy will not cover damage to or loss of Tenant's personal property. Tenant will obtain a renters' insurance policy that will:

- reimburse Landlord for cost of fire or water damage caused by Tenant or Tenant's guests, and vandalism to the Premises
- indemnify Landlord against liability to third parties for any negligence on the part of Tenant, Tenant's guests, or invitees; and
- cover damage to Tenant's personal possessions to a minimum of $100,000.

Tenant will provide Landlord with proof of such policy by giving Landlord a certificate of insurance issued by the insurance company within fifteen (15) days of _____. The policy will include Landlord as an "additional insured." Tenant will provide Landlord with a certificate of insurance upon every renewal. Tenant will not allow such policy to expire during the rental term. Failure to obtain and maintain a renters' insurance policy will be treated as a material breach of this Agreement.

Clause 16. Pets

No animal may be kept on the Premises without Landlord's prior written consent, except animals needed by tenants who have a disability, as that term is understood by law, and _____, under the following conditions: _____
_____.

Clause 17. Landlord's Right to Access

Landlord or Landlord's agents may enter the Premises in the event of an emergency, to make repairs or improvements, or to show the Premises to prospective buyers or tenants. Landlord may also enter the Premises to conduct an annual inspection to check for safety or maintenance problems. Except in cases of emergency, Tenant's abandonment of the Premises, court order, or where it is impractical to do so, Landlord will give Tenant _____ notice before entering.

Clause 18. Extended Absences by Tenant

Tenant will notify Landlord in advance if Tenant will be away from the Premises for _____ or more consecutive days. During such absence, Landlord may enter the Premises at times reasonably necessary to maintain the property and inspect for damage and needed repairs.

Clause 19. Possession of the Premises

a. Tenant's failure to take possession.

If, after signing this Agreement, Tenant fails to take possession of the Premises, Tenant will still be responsible for paying rent and complying with all other terms of this Agreement.

b. *Landlord's failure to deliver possession.*

If Landlord is unable to deliver possession of the Premises to Tenant for any reason not within Landlord's control, including, but not limited to, failure of prior occupants to vacate or partial or complete destruction of the Premises, Tenant will have the right to terminate this Agreement upon proper notice as required by law. In such event, Landlord's liability to Tenant will be limited to the return of all sums previously paid by Tenant to Landlord.

Clause 20. Tenant Rules and Regulations

☐ Tenant acknowledges receipt of, and has read a copy of, the Tenant Rules and Regulations, which are labeled Attachment _____ and attached to and incorporated into this Agreement by this reference. Tenant understands that serious or repeated violations of the rules may be grounds for termination.

Clause 21. Payment of Court Costs and Attorneys' Fees in a Lawsuit

In any action or legal proceeding to enforce any part of this Agreement, the prevailing party (*choose one:* will not/will) recover reasonable attorneys' fees and court costs.

Clause 22. Disclosures

Tenant acknowledges that Landlord has made the following disclosures regarding the Premises:

☐ *Disclosure of Information on Lead-Based Paint and/or Lead-Based Paint Hazards* and the pamphlet *Protect Your Family From Lead in Your Home*

☐ Other disclosures: _____

_____

_____

_____ .

Clause 23. Authority to Receive Legal Papers

The Landlord, any person managing the Premises, and anyone designated by the Landlord are authorized to accept service of process and receive other notices and demands, which may be delivered to:

☐ The Landlord, at the following address: _____

_____ .

☐ The manager, at the following address: _____

_____ .

☐ The following person, at the following address: _____

_____ .

Clause 24. Additional Provisions

Additional provisions are as follows: _____

_____

_____

_____

_____ .

Clause 25. Validity of Each Part

If a court holds any portion of this Agreement to be invalid, its invalidity will not affect the validity or enforceability of any other provision of this Agreement.

Clause 26. Grounds for Termination of Tenancy

The failure of Tenant or Tenant's guests or invitees to comply with any term of this Agreement, or the misrepresentation of any material fact on Tenant's Rental Application, is grounds for termination of the tenancy, with appropriate notice to Tenant and procedures as required by law.

Clause 27. Entire Agreement

This document constitutes the entire Agreement between the parties, and no promises or representations, other than those contained here and those implied by law, have been made by Landlord or Tenant. Any modifications to this Agreement must be in writing, signed by Landlord and Tenant.

_____   _____   _____
Date   Landlord or Landlord's Agent   Title

_____
Street Address

_____   _____   _____   _____
City   State   Zip   Phone

_____
Email

_____   _____   _____   _____
Date   Tenant   email   Phone

_____   _____   _____   _____
Date   Tenant   email   Phone

_____   _____   _____   _____
Date   Tenant   email   Phone

Contrato Mensual de Arrendamiento

Cláusula 1. Identificación del Arrendador y del Inquilino.

Este Contrato es entre _____

_____ ("Inquilino") y

_____ ("Arrendador"). Cada

Inquilino es conjuntamente e individualmente responsable del pago de renta y del cumplimiento de todos los

demás términos de este Contrato.

Cláusula 2. Identificación de la Propiedad.

De acuerdo con los términos y condiciones establecidos en este Contrato, el Arrendador alquila al Inquilino, y el

inquilino alquila al la Propiedad del Arrendador, sólamente para residir, la propiedad ubicada en, _____

_____ , ("la Propiedad"). Alquiler de la Propiedad tambien incluye:

Alquiler de la Propiedad excluye: _____

_____ .

Cláusula 3. Límitaciones en el Uso y Ocupación.

La Propiedad se utilizará sólo como residencia privada por el Inquilino designado en la Cláusula 1 de este

Contrato y sus hijos menores: _____

_____ , Está prohibido que invitados habiten la Propiedad

por más de _____ excepto con previo consentimiento por escrito del Arrendador. De lo

contrario, será considerado como una violación a este Contrato.

Cláusula 4. Período de Arrendamiento.

El alquiler comenzará el día _____ de _____ de _____ , y continuará

mes a mes. El Arrendador puede rescindir esta tenencia o modificar los términos de este Contrato mediante

notificación por escrito al Inquilino con _____ días de antelación. El Inquilino puede terminar el

arrendamiento dando al Arrendador _____ días de aviso por escrito.

Cláusula 5. Renta y Fechas de Pago.

Renta Regular Mensual.

El Inquilino pagará por adelantado, una renta mensual de $ _____ , el primer día del mes; excepto cuando

éste día sea en un fin de semana o en un día feriado oficial, en cuyo caso debe ser pagada el próximo día laboral.

La renta se pagará de la siguiente manera, o de otra manera como el Arrendador designe de vez en cuando:

Entrega de pago.

La renta será pagado:

☐ Por correo, dirigido a _____

☐ Personalmente, en _____

☐ electrónicamente, a _____

Forma de Pago.

El Arrendador recibirá los pagos en:

☐ efectivo

☐ cheque personal escrito en favor de _____

☐ fondos certificados o giro postal escrito en favor de _____

☐ tarjeta de crédito o de débito

☐ otra transferencia electrónica de fondos: _____

Prorrateo del primer mes de renta

☐ Al firmar este Contrato, el Inquilino pagará al Arrendador por el período de _____ a través de _____ la suma de $ _____ como renta, pagadero antes del inicio del arrendamiento.

☐ Al mudarse, el Inquilino debe como alquiler la renta prorrateado especificado anteriormente, más un mes completo de alquiler en la cantidad designada anteriormente, para un total de $ _____ .

Cláusula 6. Cobros por Mora.

Como Arrendador y Inquilino están de acuerdo que los daños actuales para pagos de renta tarde son muy difíciles o imposibles de determinar, Arrendador y Inquilino están de acuerdo con lo siguiente:

- El Inquilino pagará al Arrendador un cargo por retraso si el Inquilino no paga el alquiler en su totalidad dentro de _____ días después de la fecha en que se debe.
- El cargo por retraso será $ _____ más $ _____ por cada día individual que el alquiler continúa sin pagar. El cargo total por retraso para cualquier mes no excederá $ _____ .

El Arrendador no descartará el derecho de insistir en el pago total de la renta en la fecha debida.

Cláusula 7. Pagos por Cheques Sin Fondo y Recargos Bancarios.

En el caso de cualquier cheque, ofrecido por el Inquilino al Arrendador como pago de renta o cualquier otra suma debida bajo este Contrato, sea regresado por insuficiencia de fondos, un "paro de pago," o cualquier otra razón, el Arrendador hará una demanda de pago y buscar otro tipo de recursos como permitido por la ley.

Cláusula 8. Depósito de Garantía.

Al firmar el presente Contrato, el Inquilino pagará al Arrendador, la cantidad de $ _____ como depósito de seguridad. Este depósito no puede aplicarse al último mes de renta o a cualquier cantidad debida bajo este Contrato; excepto con previo consentimiento por escrito del Arrendador. Dentro de _____, después de que el Inquilino haya desocupado la Propiedad, haya entregado las llaves y proveído la dirección donde contactarse, el Arrendador le entregará el depósito en su totalidad o le detallará de manera escrita las razones y la cantidad que es retenido por él Arrendador, junto con un cheque por la cantidad de su diferencia.

[Si quiere incluir alguna claúsula opcional, escríbalo aquí]

Cláusula 9. Servicios Públicos.

El Inquilino pagará todos los servicios públicos, exceptuando los siguientes, los cuales serán pagados por el Arrendador: _____

_____ .

Cláusula 10. Prohibición de Traspaso o Subarrendamiento.

El Inquilino no puede subarrendar cualquier parte de la Propiedad o traspasar este Contrato, sin previo consentimiento por escrito del Arrendador. Violación de esta cláusula es un violación material y incurable de este Contrato y puede ser motivo de su terminación.

☐ a. El Inquilino no puede subarrendar o alquilar de cualquier parte de la Propiedad para estancias cortas de cualquier duración, incluyendo pero no limitado a alquileres de vacaciones.

☐ b. Alquileres a corto plazo son prohibidos, excepto los que son autorizado por ley. El Inquilino debe seguir todas las regulaciones, leyes, y otros requistos como condición para poder ofrecer un alquiler a corto plazo. El incumplimiento de las leyes, ordenanzas, regulaciones, y otros requerimientos, incluso cualquier requisito de registro, se considerará un violación material y incurable de este Contrato y puede ser motivo de su terminación.

Cláusula 11. Responsabilidad del Inquilino de Mantenimiento de la Propiedad.

El Inquilino acepta: (1) mantener la Propiedad limpia e higiénica, en buena condición, y cuando el arrendamiento termine, regresar la Propiedad al Arrendador en idéntica condición a la que existía cuando la habitaron, exceptuando el deterioro causado por el uso; (2) notificar de inmediato al Arrendador, sobre cualquier defecto o condición peligrosa que note en o alrededor de la Propiedad; y (3) reembolsar al Arrendador, bajo demanda de Arrendador, los costos de cualquier reparación de daños a la Propiedad, ocasionados por uso indebido o negligencia del Inquilino o sus invitados.

El Inquilino ha revisado la Propiedad, incluyendo los aparatos electrodomésticos, accesorios, alfombras, cortinas, y pintura, y los ha encontrado en buenas condiciones, seguras, y limpias, exceptuando las que están en la Lista Arrendador-Inquilino.

Cláusula 12. Reparaciones y Modificaciones Hechas por el Inquilino.

a. Exceptuando lo provisto por la ley o con la autorización previa y por escrito del Arrendador, el Inquilino no debe hacer modificaciones o reparaciones en la Propiedad, incluído el hacer hoyos en las paredes o pintar el unidad de alquiler.

b. El Inquilino no debe alterar las cerraduras, ni cambiarlas, ni instalar o modificar el sistema de alarma; excepto que haya recibido del Arrendador, una autorización previa y por escrito. El Inquilino deberá proveer al Arrendador una copia de llave o llaves para abrir cada cerradura modificada o nueva, y instrucciones de cómo desarmar un sistema de alarma de seguridad modificado o nuevo.

Cláusula 13. Disturbios y Violaciones de Leyes.

El Inquilino tiene derecho a un disfrute tranquilo de la Propiedad. El Inquilino y sus invitados no deben usar la Propiedad o áreas aledañas, de manera que: (1) viole cualquier ley o reglamento, incluyendo leyes que prohiben el uso, posesión o venta ilegal de drogas; (2) permite el uso abusivo de la Propiedad (daño serio a la Propiedad) o crear o tolerar una molestia; o (3) provocar disturbios, provocar inconvenientes, o interferir en el disfrute de paz y tranquilidad de otros inquilinos o vecinos.

Cláusula 14. Daños a la Propiedad.

En el caso de que la Propiedad esté parcial o totalmente dañada o destruida por un incendio u otra causa, se aplicará lo siguiente:

a. La Propiedad totalmente dañada o destruida. El Arrendador tendrá la opción de: (1) reparar dichos daños y restaurar la Propiedad, con este Contrato continuando en pleno vigor y efecto, excepto que la renta del Inquilino será reducida o disminuida mientras se realizan las reparaciones; o (2) dar aviso por escrito al Inquilino terminando este Contrato en cualquier momento dentro de los treinta (30) días después de dicho daño, y especificando la fecha de terminación; en caso de que el Arrendador dé dicha notificación, este Contrato expirará y todos los derechos del Inquilino de conformidad con este Contrato cesarán.

b. La Propiedad parcialmente dañada por incendio u otra causa. El Arrendador intentará reparar dichos daños y restaurar la Propiedad dentro de los treinta (30) días posteriores a dicho daño. Si sólo una parte de la Propiedad no se puede utilizar, el Inquilino debe pagar la renta sólo por la parte utilizable, que será determinado por el Arrendador. Si el Arrendador no puede completar las reparaciones en un plazo de treinta (30) días, este Contrato expirará y todos los derechos del Inquilino de conformidad con este Contrato terminarán a elección de cualquiera de las partes. Si la Propiedad son total o parcialmente destruidas será decidida por el Arrendador, en el ejercicio de su única discreción.

c. En el caso de que el Inquilino, o los invitados del Inquilino, de alguna manera hayan causado o contribuido al daño de la Propiedad, el Arrendador tendrá el derecho de rescindir este Contrato en cualquier momento, y el Inquilino será responsable de todas las pérdidas, incluyendo, pero no limitado a daños y costos de reparación, así como a la pérdida de ingresos por alquiler.

d. El Arrendador no estará obligado a reparar o reemplazar cualquier propiedad traída a la Propiedad por el Inquilino.

Cláusula 15. Seguro para Inquilinos.

El Inquilino reconoce que la póliza de seguro de propiedad del Arrendador no cubrirá daños o pérdidas de la propiedad personal del Inquilino. El Inquilino obtendrá una póliza de seguro para inquilinos que:

- reembolsar al Arrendador por el costo del incendio o daños causados por el agua por el Inquilino o los invitados del Inquilino, y el vandalismo a la Propiedad

- indemnizar al Arrendador contra la responsabilidad ante terceros por cualquier negligencia por parte del Inquilino, los invitados del Inquilino o los invitados; y

- cubrir daños a las posesiones personales del Inquilino a un mínimo de $100,000.

El Inquilino proporcionará al Arrendador una prueba de dicha póliza al entregar al Arrendador un certificado de seguro emitido por la compañía de seguros dentro de los quince (15) días de _____. La póliza nombrará al Arrendador como un "asegurado adicional." El Inquilino proporcionará al Arrendador un certificado de seguro en cada renovación. El Inquilino no permitirá que dicha política caduque durante el período de alquiler. La falta de obtención y mantenimiento de una póliza de seguro para inquilinos será tratada como un incumplimiento material de este Contrato.

Cláusula 16. Mascotas.

Ningún animal puede ser mantenida en la Propiedad, sin previa autorización escrita del Arrendador, excepto los animales necesitados para los inquilinos que tienen una discapacidad, como ese término se entiende por la ley, y _____ , de acuerdo con las condiciones siguientes: _____ .

Cláusula 17. Derecho del Arrendador al Acceso a la Propiedad.

El Arrendador o agentes del Arrendador pueden entrar a la Propiedad, en caso de emergencia, para hacer reparaciones o mejoras, o para mostrar la Propiedad a potenciales nuevos inquilinos o compradores en perspectiva. También podrá entrar para la inspección anual para revisar la seguridad o chequear problemas de mantenimiento. Excepto en caso de emergencia, por el abandono de la Propiedad por parte del Inquilino, orden de la corte, o cuando no sea práctico, el Arrendador deberá notificarle al Inquilino de su intención de entrar a la Propiedad con _____ de anticipación.

Cláusula 18. Ausencias Prolongadas del Inquilino.

El Inquilino debe notificar al Arrendador con anticipación si el Inquilino estará ausente de la Propiedad durante _____ días consecutivos o más. Durante este tiempo, el Arrendador podrá entrar, cuando sea necesario, a la Propiedad para mantenimiento y inspeccionar en busca de daños y reparaciones necesarias.

Cláusula 19. Tomar Posesión de la Propiedad.

a. *Falla del Inquilino en tomar posesión de la Propiedad.*

Si después de haber firmado este Contrato, el Inquilino no toma posesión de la Propiedad, aún será responsable por pago de la renta y cumplimiento de todos los demás términos de este Contrato.

b. *Falla del Arrendador en entregar la Propiedad.*

Si el Arrendador no puede entregar la posesión de la Propiedad al Inquilino, por cualquier razón fuera de su control, incluyendo, pero no limitado a, falta de desocupación de los ocupantes anteriores, destrucción parcial o completa de la Propiedad, el Inquilino tendrá el derecho de terminar este Contrato, mediante aviso previo y apropiado como lo señala la ley. En tal situación, la responsabilidad del Arrendador al Inquilino, estará limitada a la devolución de todas las cantidades previamente pagadas por el Inquilino al Arrendador.

Cláusula 20. Normas y Regulaciones del Inquilino.

☐ El Inquilino reconoce lo recibido y que ha leído una copia de las Normas y Regulaciones del Inquilino; que están marcados con "Accesorio _____" y están adjuntas e incorporadas al presente Contrato. El Inquilino entiende que violaciones serias o repetidas de las reglas pueden ser motivo de terminacion de este Contrato.

Cláusula 21. Pago del Abogado y Costos de la Corte en Caso de un Juicio.

☐ En cualquier acción jurídico-legal para hacer cumplir total o parcialmente este Contrato, la persona que gana ☐ no deberá / ☐ deberá recuperar honorarios justos del abogado y costos de la corte.

Cláusula 22. Divulgaciones.

El Inquilino reconoce que el Arrendador le ha hecho las siguientes divulgaciones con respecto a la Propiedad:

☐ *Declaración de Información sobre Pintura a Base de Plomo y/o Peligros de la Pintura a Base de Plomo* y el folleto *Proteja a su Familia Contra el Plomo en el Hogar.*

☐ Otras divulgaciones: _____

_____

_____ .

Cláusula 23. Personal Autorizado para Recibir Documentos Legales.

El Arrendador, la persona que administre la Propiedad, y a quien haya designado el Arrendador, están autorizados para aceptar servicio de proceso, y recibir otras noticias y demandas, las cuales pueden ser entregadas a:

☐ El Arrendador, a la siguiente dirección: _____

☐ El Administrador, a la siguiente dirección: _____

☐ A la persona designada que se llama: _____ ,

a la siguiente dirección: _____

Cláusula 24. Disposiciones Adicionales.

Disposiciones adicionales son las siguientes: _____

_____

_____

_____

_____

Cláusula 25. Validez de las Cláusulas de este Contrato.

Si un tribunal considera que una parte de este Contrato no es válida, su invalidez no afectará la validez o aplicabilidad de ninguna otra disposición de este Contrato.

Cláusula 26. Razones para Cancelar el Contrato de Arrendamiento.

El incumplimiento de cualesquiera de los términos de este Contrato por parte del Inquilino o sus invitados, o la relación falsa de un hecho esencial en la Solicitud de Alquiler del Inquilino, es motivo de rescisión del Contrato de arrendamiento, seguido con la debida notificación al Inquilino de acuerdo con lo requerido por la ley.

Cláusula 27. Contrato Completo.

Este documento constituye el Contrato completo entre el Inquilino y el Arrendador, y el Arrendador y el Inquilino no han hecho otro compromiso, además que los contenidos en este Contrato o los señalados por la ley. Cualquier modificación a este Contrato, tiene que ser por escrito y firmado por el Arrendador y el Inquilino.

Fecha   Arrendador o su representante   Título

Número y Nombre de la Calle

Ciudad   Estado   Código Postal   Teléfono

Email

Fecha   Inquilino   email   Teléfono

Fecha   Inquilino   email   Teléfono

Fecha   Inquilino   email   Teléfono

Fixed-Term Residential Lease

Clause 1. Identification of Landlord and Tenant

This Agreement is between _____

_____ ("Tenant") and

_____ ("Landlord").

Each Tenant is jointly and severally liable for the payment of rent and performance of all other terms of this Agreement.

Clause 2. Identification of Premises

Subject to the terms and conditions in this Agreement, Landlord rents to Tenant, and Tenant rents from Landlord, for residential purposes only, the premises located at _____

_____ (the Premises). Rental of the Premises also

includes: _____

_____

_____ .

Rental of the Premises excludes: _____

_____

_____ .

Clause 3. Limits on Use and Occupancy

The Premises are to be used only as a private residence for Tenant(s) listed in Clause 1 of this Agreement,

and their minor children: _____. Occupancy by guests for more than

_____ , is prohibited without Landlord's written consent and will be considered

a breach of this Agreement.

Clause 4. Term of the Tenancy

The term of the rental will begin on _____ , and end on _____

_____ .

Clause 5. Payment of Rent

Regular monthly rent

Tenant will pay to Landlord a monthly rent of $_____ , payable in advance on the first day of each month, except when that day falls on a weekend or legal holiday, in which case rent is due on the next business day. Rent will be paid as follows, or in another manner as Landlord designates from time to time:

Delivery of payment

Rent will be paid:

☐ by mail, to _____

☐ in person, at _____

☐ electronically, to _____

Form of payment

Landlord will accept payment in these forms:

☐ cash

☐ personal check made payable to _____

☐ certified funds or money order made made payable to _____

☐ credit or debit card

☐ other electronic funds transfer: _____

Prorated first month's rent

☐ On signing this Agreement, Tenant will pay to Landlord for the period of _____ through

_____ the sum of $ _____ as rent, payable in advance of the start of the tenancy.

☐ Upon move-in, Tenant will owe as rent the prorated rent specified above, plus one full month's rent in the

amount designated above, for a total of $ _____.

Clause 6. Late Charges

Because Landlord and Tenant agree that actual damages for late rent payments are very difficult or impossible

to determine, Landlord and Tenant agree to the following:

- Tenant will pay Landlord a late charge if Tenant fails to pay the rent in full within _____ days

    after the date it is due.

- The late charge will be $ _____, plus $ _____ for each individual day that the rent

    continues to be unpaid. The total late charge for any one month will not exceed $ _____.

Landlord does not waive the right to insist on payment of the rent in full on the date it is due.

Clause 7. Returned Check and Other Bank Charges

If any check offered by Tenant to Landlord in payment of rent or any other amount due under this Agreement

is returned for lack of sufficient funds, a "stop payment," or any other reason, Landlord will make a demand for

payment and otherwise pursue remedies as allowed by law.

Clause 8. Security Deposit

On signing this Agreement, Tenant will pay to Landlord the sum of $ _____ as a security deposit. Tenant may not, without Landlord's prior written consent, apply this security deposit to the last month's rent or to any other sum due under this Agreement. Within _____ after Tenant has vacated the Premises, returned keys, and provided Landlord with a forwarding address, Landlord will return the deposit in full or give Tenant an itemized written statement of the reasons for, and the dollar amount of, any of the security deposit retained by the Landlord, along with a check for any deposit balance.

[optional clauses, if any]

Clause 9. Utilities

Tenant will pay all utility charges, except for the following, which will be paid by Landlord:

_____

_____ .

Clause 10. Prohibition of Assignment and Subletting

Tenant will not sublet any part of the Premises or assign this Agreement without the prior written consent of Landlord. Violating this clause is grounds for terminating the tenancy.

☐ a. Tenant shall not sublet or rent any part of the Premises for short-term stays of any duration, including, but not limited to, vacation rentals.

☐ b. Short-stay rentals are prohibited except as authorized by law. Any short-stay rental is expressly conditioned upon the Tenant's following all regulations, laws, and other requirements as a condition to offering a short-stay rental. Failure to follow all laws, ordinances, regulations, and other requirements, including any registration requirement, will be deemed a material, noncurable breach of this Agreement and will furnish cause for termination.

Clause 11. Tenant's Maintenance Responsibilities

Tenant will: (1) keep the Premises clean, sanitary, and in good condition and, upon termination of the tenancy, return the Premises to Landlord in a condition identical to that which existed when Tenant took occupancy, except for ordinary wear and tear; (2) immediately notify Landlord of any defects or dangerous conditions in and about the Premises of which Tenant becomes aware; and (3) reimburse Landlord, on demand by Landlord, for the cost of any repairs to the Premises, including Landlord's personal property therein, damaged by Tenant or Tenant's guests or business invitees through misuse or neglect.

Tenant has examined the Premises, including appliances, fixtures, carpets, drapes, and paint, and has found them to be in good, safe, and clean condition and repair, except as noted in the Landlord-Tenant Checklist.

Clause 12. Repairs and Alterations by Tenant

a. Except as provided by law, or as authorized by the prior written consent of Landlord, Tenant will not make any repairs or alterations to the Premises, including nailing holes in the walls or painting the rental unit.

b. Tenant will not, without Landlord's prior written consent, alter, rekey, or install any locks to the Premises or install or alter any security alarm system. Tenant will provide Landlord with a key or keys capable of unlocking all such rekeyed or new locks as well as instructions on how to disarm any altered or new security alarm system.

Clause 13. Violating Laws and Causing Disturbances

Tenant is entitled to quiet enjoyment of the Premises. Tenant and guests or invitees will not use the Premises or adjacent areas in such a way as to: (1) violate any law or ordinance, including laws prohibiting the use, possession, or sale of illegal drugs; (2) commit waste (severe property damage); or (3) annoy, disturb, inconvenience, or interfere with the quiet enjoyment and peace and quiet of any other tenant or nearby resident.

Clause 14. Damage to the Premises

In the event the Premises are partially or totally damaged or destroyed by fire or other cause, the following will apply:

a. Premises totally damaged and destroyed. Landlord will have the option to: (1) repair such damage and restore the Premises, with this Agreement continuing in full force and effect, except that Tenant's rent will be abated while repairs are being made; or (2) give written notice to Tenant terminating this Agreement at any time within thirty (30) days after such damage, and specifying the termination date; in the event that Landlord gives such notice, this Agreement will expire and all of Tenant's rights pursuant to this Agreement will cease.

b. Premises partially damaged by fire or other cause. Landlord will attempt to repair such damage and restore the Premises within thirty (30) days after such damage. If only part of the Premises cannot be used, Tenant must pay rent only for the usable part, to be determined by Landlord. If Landlord is unable to complete repairs within thirty (30) days, this Agreement will expire and all of Tenant's rights pursuant to this Agreement will terminate at the option of either party. Whether the Premises are totally or partially destroyed will be decided by Landlord, in the exercise of its sole discretion.

c. In the event that Tenant, or Tenant's guests or invitees, in any way caused or contributed to the damage of the Premises, Landlord will have the right to terminate this Agreement at any time, and Tenant will be responsible for all losses, including, but not limited to, damage and repair costs as well as loss of rental income.

d. Landlord will not be required to repair or replace any property brought onto the Premises by Tenant.

Clause 15. Renters' Insurance

Tenant acknowledges that Landlord's property insurance policy will not cover damage to or loss of Tenant's personal property. Tenant will obtain a renters' insurance policy that will:

- reimburse Landlord for cost of fire or water damage caused by Tenant or Tenant's guests, and vandalism to the Premises
- indemnify Landlord against liability to third parties for any negligence on the part of Tenant, Tenant's guests, or invitees; and
- cover damage to Tenant's personal possessions to a minimum of $100,000.

Tenant will provide Landlord with proof of such policy by giving Landlord a certificate of insurance issued by the insurance company within fifteen (15) days of _____. The policy will include Landlord as an "additional insured." Tenant will provide Landlord with a certificate of insurance upon every renewal. Tenant will not allow such policy to expire during the rental term. Failure to obtain and maintain a renters' insurance policy will be treated as a material breach of this Agreement.

Clause 16. Pets

No animal may be kept on the Premises without Landlord's prior written consent, except animals needed by tenants who have a disability, as that term is understood by law, and _____ ,

_____

under the following conditions: _____

_____ .

Clause 17. Landlord's Right to Access

Landlord or Landlord's agents may enter the Premises in the event of an emergency, to make repairs or improvements, or to show the Premises to prospective buyers or tenants. Landlord may also enter the Premises to conduct an annual inspection to check for safety or maintenance problems. Except in cases of emergency, Tenant's abandonment of the Premises, court order, or where it is impractical to do so, Landlord will give Tenant _____ notice before entering.

Clause 18. Extended Absences by Tenant

Tenant will notify Landlord in advance if Tenant will be away from the Premises for _____ or more consecutive days. During such absence, Landlord may enter the Premises at times reasonably necessary to maintain the property and inspect for damage and needed repairs.

Clause 19. Possession of the Premises

a. *Tenant's failure to take possession.*

If, after signing this Agreement, Tenant fails to take possession of the Premises, Tenant will still be responsible for paying rent and complying with all other terms of this Agreement.

b. *Landlord's failure to deliver possession.*

If Landlord is unable to deliver possession of the Premises to Tenant for any reason not within Landlord's control, including, but not limited to, failure of prior occupants to vacate or partial or complete destruction of the Premises, Tenant will have the right to terminate this Agreement upon proper notice as required by law. In such event, Landlord's liability to Tenant will be limited to the return of all sums previously paid by Tenant to Landlord.

Clause 20. Tenant Rules and Regulations

☐ Tenant acknowledges receipt of, and has read a copy of, the Tenant Rules and Regulations, which are labeled Attachment _____ and attached to and incorporated into this Agreement by this reference. Tenant understands that serious or repeated violations of the rules may be grounds for termination.

Clause 21. Payment of Court Costs and Attorneys' Fees in a Lawsuit

In any action or legal proceeding to enforce any part of this Agreement, the prevailing party

(choose one: will not/will*)* recover reasonable attorneys' fees and court costs.

Clause 22. Disclosures

Tenant acknowledges that Landlord has made the following disclosures regarding the Premises:

☐ *Disclosure of Information on Lead-Based Paint and/or Lead-Based Paint Hazards,* and the booklet, *Protect Your Family From Lead in Your Home.*

☐ Other disclosures: _____

_____

_____

_____

Clause 23. Authority to Receive Legal Papers

The Landlord, any person managing the Premises, and anyone designated by the Landlord are authorized to accept service of process and receive other notices and demands, which may be delivered to:

☐ The Landlord, at the following address: _____

_____

☐ The manager, at the following address: _____

_____

☐ The following person, at the following address: _____

_____

Clause 24. Additional Provisions

Additional provisions are as follows: _____

_____

_____

_____

_____

Clause 25. Validity of Each Part

If a court holds any portion of this Agreement to be invalid, its invalidity will not affect the validity or enforceability of any other provision of this Agreement.

Clause 26. Grounds for Termination of Tenancy

The failure of Tenant or Tenant's guests or invitees to comply with any term of this Agreement, or the misrepresentation of any material fact on Tenant's rental application, is grounds for termination of the tenancy, with appropriate notice to Tenant and procedures as required by law.

Clause 27. Entire Agreement

This document constitutes the entire Agreement between the parties, and no promises or representations, other than those contained here and those implied by law, have been made by Landlord or Tenant. Any modifications to this Agreement must be in writing, signed by Landlord and Tenant.

_____ _____ _____
Date   Landlord or Landlord's Agent   Title

_____
Street Address

_____ _____ _____ _____
City   State   Zip   Phone

_____
Email

_____ _____ _____ _____
Date   Tenant   email   Phone

_____ _____ _____ _____
Date   Tenant   email   Phone

_____ _____ _____ _____
Date   Tenant   email   Phone

Contrato de Arrendamiento Residencial a Plazo Fijo

Cláusula 1. Identificación del Arrendador y del Inquilino

Este Contrato es entre _____ ("Inquilino") y
_____ ("Arrendador").

Cada Inquilino es responsable del pago de renta y del cumplimiento de todos los demás términos de este Contrato.

Cláusula 2. Identificación de la Propiedad

De acuerdo con los términos y condiciones establecidos en este Contrato, el Arrendador alquila al Inquilino, y el Inquilino alquila al la Propiedad del Arrendador sólamente para residir, la propiedad ubicada en, _____ ("la Propiedad"). Alquiler de la Propiedad tambien incluye: _____ .

Alquiler de la Propiedad excluye: _____ .

Cláusula 3. Límitaciones en el Uso y Ocupación

La Propiedad se utilizará sólo como residencia privada por el Inquilino designado en la Cláusula 1 de este Contrato y sus hijos menores: _____ .

Está prohibido que invitados habiten la Propiedad por más de _____

excepto con previo consentimiento por escrito del Arrendador. De lo contrario, será considerado como una violación a este Contrato.

Cláusula 4. Período de Arrendamiento

El alquiler comenzará el día _____ de _____ de _____ ,

y terminará el día _____ de _____ de _____ .

Cláusula 5. Renta y Fechas de Pago

Renta Regular Mensual.

El Inquilino pagará por adelantado, una renta mensual de $ _____ , el primer día del mes; excepto cuando éste día sea en un fin de semana o en un día feriado oficial, en cuyo caso debe ser pagada el próximo día laboral. La renta se pagará de la siguiente manera, o de otra manera como el Arrendador designe de vez en cuando:

Entrega de Pago.

La renta será pagado:

☐ Por correo, dirigido a _____

☐ Personalmente, en _____

☐ electrónicamente, a _____

Forma de Pago.

El Arrendador recibirá los pagos en:

☐ efectivo

☐ cheque personal escrito en favor de _____

☐ fondos certificados o giro postal escrito en favor de _____

☐ tarjeta de crédito o de débito

☐ otra transferencia electrónica de fondos: _____

Prorrateo del primer mes de renta.

☐ Al firmar este Contrato, el Inquilino pagará al Arrendador por el período de _____

a través de _____ la suma de $ _____ como renta, pagadero

antes del inicio del arrendamiento.

☐ Al mudarse, el Inquilino debe como alquiler la renta prorrateado especificado anteriormente, más un

mes completo de alquiler en la cantidad designada anteriormente, para un total de $ _____ .

Cláusula 6. Cobros por Mora.

Como Arrendador y Inquilino están de acuerdo que los daños actuales para pagos de renta tarde son muy

difíciles o imposibles de determinar, Arrendador y Inquilino están de acuerdo con lo siguiente:

- El Inquilino pagará al Arrendador un cargo por retraso si el Inquilino no paga el alquiler en su totalidad

  dentro de _____ días después de la fecha en que se debe.

- El cargo por retraso será $ _____ más $ _____ por cada día individual que el

  alquiler continúa sin pagar. El cargo total por retraso para cualquier mes no excederá $ _____ .

El Arrendador no descartará el derecho de insistir en el pago total de la renta en la fecha debida.

Cláusula 7. Pagos por Cheques Sin Fondo y Recargos Bancarios.

En el caso de cualquier cheque, ofrecido por el Inquilino al Arrendador como pago de renta o cualquier otra

suma debida bajo este Contrato, sea regresado por insuficiencia de fondos, un "paro de pago," o cualquier otra

razón, el Arrendador hará una demanda de pago y buscar otro tipo de recursos como permitido por la ley.

Cláusula 8. Depósito de Garantía.

Al firmar el presente Contrato, el Inquilino pagará al Arrendador, la cantidad de $ _____ como

depósito de seguridad. Este depósito no puede aplicarse al último mes de renta o a cualquier cantidad

debida bajo este Contrato; excepto con previo consentimiento por escrito del Arrendador. Dentro de

_____ después de que el Inquilino haya desocupado la Propiedad, haya

entregado las llaves y proveído la dirección donde contactarse, el Arrendador le entregará el depósito en su

totalidad o le detallará de manera escrita las razones y la cantidad que es retenido por él Arrendador, junto con

un cheque por la cantidad de su diferencia.

[Si quiere incluir alguna cláusula opcional, escríbalo aquí]

Cláusula 9. Servicios Públicos.

El Inquilino pagará todos los servicios públicos, exceptuando los siguientes, los cuales serán pagados por el Arrendador: _____

_____ .

Cláusula 10. Prohibición de Traspaso o Subarrendamiento.

El Inquilino no puede subarrendar cualquier parte de la Propiedad o traspasar este Contrato, sin previo consentimiento por escrito del Arrendador. Violación de esta cláusula es un violación material y incurable de este Contrato y puede ser motivo de su terminación.

☐ a. El Inquilino no debería subarrendar o alquilar de cualquier parte de la Propiedad para estancias cortas de cualquier duración, incluyendo pero no limitado a alquileres de vacaciones.

☐ b. Alquileres a corto plazo son prohibidos, excepto los que son autorizado por ley. El Inquilino debe seguir todas las regulaciones, leyes, y otros requisitos como condición para poder ofrecer un alquiler a corto plazo. El incumplimiento de las leyes, ordenanzas, regulaciones, y otros requerimientos, incluso cualquier requisito de registro, se considerará un violación material y incurable de este Contrato y puede ser motivo de su terminación.

Cláusula 11. Responsabilidad del Inquilino de Mantenimiento de la Propiedad.

El Inquilino acepta: (1) mantener la Propiedad limpia e higiénica, en buena condición, y cuando el arrendamiento termine, regresar la Propiedad al Arrendador en idéntica condición a la que existía cuando la habitaron, exceptuando el deterioro causado por el uso; (2) notificar de inmediato al Arrendador, sobre cualquier defecto o condición peligrosa que note en o alrededor de la Propiedad; y (3) reembolsar al Arrendador, bajo demanda de Arrendador, los costos de cualquier reparación de daños a la Propiedad, ocasionados por uso indebido o negligencia del Inquilino o sus invitados.

El Inquilino ha revisado la Propiedad, incluyendo los aparatos electrodomésticos, accesorios, alfombras, cortinas, y pintura, y los ha encontrado en buenas condiciones, seguras, y limpias, exceptuando las que están en la Lista Arrendador-Inquilino.

Cláusula 12. Reparaciones y Modificaciones Hechas por el Inquilino.

a. Exceptuando lo provisto por la ley o con la autorización previa y por escrito del Arrendador, el Inquilino no debe hacer modificaciones o reparaciones en la Propiedad, incluído el hacer hoyos en las paredes o pintar el unidad de alquiler.

b. El Inquilino no debe alterar las cerraduras, ni cambiarlas, ni instalar o modificar el sistema de alarma; excepto que haya recibido del Arrendador, una autorización previa y por escrito. El Inquilino deberá proveer al Arrendador una copia de llave o llaves para abrir cada cerradura modificada o nueva, y instrucciones de cómo desarmar un sistema de alarma de seguridad modificado o nuevo.

Cláusula 13. Disturbios y Violar Leyes.

El Inquilino tiene derecho a un disfrute tranquilo de la Propiedad. El Inquilino y sus invitados no deben usar la Propiedad o áreas aledañas, de manera que: (1) viole cualquier ley o reglamento, incluyendo leyes que prohiben el uso, posesión o venta ilegal de drogas; (2) permite el uso abusivo de la Propiedad (daño serio a la Propiedad) o crear o tolerar una molestia; o (3) provocar disturbios, provocar inconvenientes, o interferir en el disfrute de paz y tranquilidad de otros inquilinos o vecinos.

Cláusula 14. Daños a la Propiedad.

En el caso de que la Propiedad esté parcial o totalmente dañada o destruida por un incendio u otra causa, se aplicará lo siguiente:

a. La Propiedad totalmente dañada o destruida. El Arrendador tendrá la opción de: (1) reparar dichos daños y restaurar la Propiedad, con este Contrato continuando en pleno vigor y efecto, excepto que la renta del Inquilino será reducida o disminuida mientras se realizan las reparaciones; o (2) dar aviso por escrito al Inquilino terminando este Contrato en cualquier momento dentro de los treinta (30) días después de dicho daño, y especificando la fecha de terminación; en caso de que el Arrendador dé dicha notificación, este Contrato expirará y todos los derechos del Inquilino de conformidad con este Contrato cesarán.

b. La Propiedad parcialmente dañada por incendio u otra causa. El Arrendador intentará reparar dichos daños y restaurar la Propiedad dentro de los treinta (30) días posteriores a dicho daño. Si sólo una parte de la Propiedad no se puede utilizar, el Inquilino debe pagar la renta sólo por la parte utilizable, que será determinado por el Arrendador. Si el Arrendador no puede completar las reparaciones en un plazo de treinta (30) días, este Contrato expirará y todos los derechos del Inquilino de conformidad con este Contrato terminarán a elección de cualquiera de las partes. Si la Propiedad son total o parcialmente destruidas será decidida por el Arrendador, en el ejercicio de su única discreción.

c. En el caso de que el Inquilino, o los invitados del Inquilino, de alguna manera hayan causado o contribuido al daño de la Propiedad, el Arrendador tendrá el derecho de rescindir este Contrato en cualquier momento, y el Inquilino será responsable de todas las pérdidas, incluyendo, pero no limitado a daños y costos de reparación, así como a la pérdida de ingresos por alquiler.

d. El Arrendador no estará obligado a reparar o reemplazar cualquier propiedad traída a la Propiedad por el Inquilino.

Cláusula 15. Seguro para Inquilinos.

El Inquilino reconoce que la póliza de seguro de propiedad del Arrendador no cubrirá daños o pérdidas de la propiedad personal del Inquilino. El inquilino obtendrá una póliza de seguro para inquilinos que:

- reembolsar al Arrendador por el costo del incendio o daños causados por el agua por el inquilino o los invitados del Inquilino, y el vandalismo a la Propiedad
- indemnizar al Arrendador contra la responsabilidad ante terceros por cualquier negligencia por parte del Inquilino, los invitados del Inquilino o los invitados; y
- cubrir daños a las posesiones personales del Inquilino a un mínimo de $100,000.

El Inquilino proporcionará al Arrendador una prueba de dicha póliza al entregar al Arrendador un certificado de seguro emitido por la compañía de seguros dentro de los quince (15) días de _____ .
La póliza nombrará al Arrendador como un "asegurado adicional". El Inquilino proporcionará al Arrendador un certificado de seguro en cada renovación. El Inquilino no permitirá que dicha política caduque durante el período de alquiler. La falta de obtención y mantenimiento de una póliza de seguro para inquilinos será tratada como un incumplimiento material de este Contrato.

Cláusula 16. Mascotas.

Ningún animal puede ser mantenida en la Propiedad, sin previa autorización escrita del Arrendador, excepto los animales necesitados para los inquilinos que tienen una discapacidad, como ese término se entiende por la ley, y _____ , de acuerdo con las condiciones siguientes:

_____ .

Cláusula 17. Derecho del Arrendador al Acceso a la Propiedad.

El Arrendador o agentes del Arrendador pueden entrar a la Propiedad, en caso de emergencia, para hacer reparaciones o mejoras, o para mostrar la Propiedad a potenciales nuevos inquilinos o compradores en perspectiva. También podrá entrar para la inspección anual para revisar la seguridad o chequear problemas de mantenimiento. Excepto en caso de emergencia, por el abandono de la Propiedad por parte del Inquilino, orden de la corte, o cuando no sea práctico, el Arrendador deberá notificarle al Inquilino de su intención de entrar a la Propiedad con _____ de anticipación.

Cláusula 18. Ausencias Prolongadas del Inquilino.

El Inquilino debe notificar al Arrendador con anticipación si el Inquilino estará ausente de la propiedad durante _____ días consecutivos o más. Durante este tiempo, el Arrendador podrá entrar, cuando sea necesario, a la Propiedad para mantenimiento y inspeccionar en busca de daños y reparaciones necesarias.

Cláusula 19. Tomar Posesión de la Propiedad.

a. *Falla del Inquilino en tomar posesión de la Propiedad.*

Si después de haber firmado este Contrato, el Inquilino no toma posesión de la Propiedad, aún será responsable por pago de la renta y cumplimiento de todos los demás términos de este Contrato.

b. *Falla del Arrendador en entregar la Propiedad.*

Si el Arrendador no puede entregar la posesión de la Propiedad al Inquilino, por cualquier razón fuera de su control, incluyendo, pero no limitado a, falta de desocupación de los ocupantes anteriores, destrucción parcial o completa de la Propiedad, el Inquilino tendrá el derecho de terminar este Contrato, mediante aviso previo y apropiado como lo señala la ley. En tal situación, la responsabilidad del Arrendador al Inquilino, estará limitada a la devolución de todas las cantidades previamente pagadas por el Inquilino al Arrendador.

Cláusula 20. Normas y Regulaciones del Inquilino.

☐ El Inquilino reconoce lo recibido y que ha leído una copia de las Normas y Regulaciones del Inquilino; que están marcados con "Accesorio _____" y están adjuntas e incorporadas al presente Contrato. El Inquilino entiende que violaciones serias o repetidas de las reglas pueden ser motivo de terminacion de este Contrato.

Cláusula 21. Pago del Abogado y Costos de la Corte en Caso de un Juicio.

☐ En cualquier acción jurídico-legal para hacer cumplir total o parcialmente este Contrato, la persona que gana ☐ No deberá / ☐ deberá recuperar honorarios justos del abogado y costos de la corte.

Cláusula 22. Divulgaciones.

El Inquilino reconoce que el Arrendador le ha hecho las siguientes divulgaciones con respecto a la Propiedad:

☐ *Declaración de Información sobre Pintura a Base de Plomo y/o Peligros de la Pintura a Base de Plomo* y el folleto *Proteja a su Familia Contra el Plomo en el Hogar.*

☐ Otras divulgaciones: _____

_____ .

Cláusula 23. Personal Autorizado para Recibir Documentos Legales.

El Arrendador, la persona que administre la Propiedad, y a quien haya designado el Arrendador, están autorizados para aceptar servicio de proceso, y recibir otras noticias y demandas, las cuales pueden ser entregadas a:

☐ El Arrendador, a la siguiente dirección: _____

_____

☐ El administrador, a la siguiente dirección: _____

_____

☐ A la persona designada que se llama: _____ ,

a la siguiente dirección: _____

Cláusula 24. Disposiciones Adicionales.

Disposiciones adicionales son las siguientes: _____

_____

_____

_____

_____ .

Cláusula 25. Validez de las Cláusulas de este Contrato.

Si un tribunal considera que una parte de este Contrato no es válida, su invalidez no afectará la validez o aplicabilidad de ninguna otra disposición de este Contrato.

Cláusula 26. Razones para Cancelar el Contrato de Arrendamiento.

El incumplimiento de cualesquiera de los términos de este Contrato por parte del Inquilino o sus invitados, o la relación falsa de un hecho esencial en la Solicitud de Alquiler del Inquilino, es motivo de rescisión del Contrato de arrendamiento, seguido con la debida notificación al Inquilino de acuerdo con lo requerido por la ley.

Cláusula 27. Contrato Completo.

Este documento constituye el Contrato completo entre el Inquilino y el Arrendador, y el Arrendador y el Inquilino no han hecho otro compromiso, además que los contenidos en este Contrato o los señalados por la ley. Cualquier modificación a este Contrato, tiene que ser por escrito y firmado por el Arrendador y el Inquilino.

Fecha	Arrendador o su representante	Título

Número y Nombre de la Calle

Ciudad	Estado	Código Postal	Teléfono

Email

Fecha	Nombre del Inquilino	email	Teléfono
Fecha	Nombre del Inquilino	email	Teléfono
Fecha	Nombre del Inquilino	email	Teléfono

Disclosure of Information on Lead-Based Paint and/or Lead-Based Paint Hazards

Lead Warning Statement

Housing built before 1978 may contain lead-based paint. Lead from paint, paint chips, and dust can pose health hazards if not managed properly. Lead exposure is especially harmful to young children and pregnant women. Before renting pre-1978 housing, lessors must disclose the presence of known lead-based paint and/or lead-based paint hazards in the dwelling. Lessees must also receive a federally approved pamphlet on lead poisoning prevention.

Lessor's Disclosure

(a) Presence of lead-based paint and/or lead-based paint hazards (check (i) or (ii) below):

   (i) _____ Known lead-based paint and/or lead-based paint hazards are present in the housing (explain).

   _____

   _____

   (ii) _____ Lessor has no knowledge of lead-based paint and/or lead-based paint hazards in the housing.

(b) Records and reports available to the lessor (check (i) or (ii) below):

   (i) _____ Lessor has provided the lessee with all available records and reports pertaining to lead-based paint and/or lead-based paint hazards in the housing (list documents below).

   _____

   _____

   (ii) _____ Lessor has no reports or records pertaining to lead-based paint and/or lead-based paint hazards in the housing.

Lessee's Acknowledgment (initial)

(c) _____ Lessee has received copies of all information listed above.

(d) _____ Lessee has received the pamphlet *Protect Your Family from Lead in Your Home.*

Agent's Acknowledgment (initial)

(e) _____ Agent has informed the lessor of the lessor's obligations under 42 U.S.C. 4852d and is aware of his/her responsibility to ensure compliance.

Certification of Accuracy

The following parties have reviewed the information above and certify, to the best of their knowledge, that the information they have provided is true and accurate.

Lessor	Date	Lessor	Date
Lessee	Date	Lessee	Date
Agent	Date	Agent	Date

Declaración de Información sobre Pintura a Base de Plomo y/o Peligros de la Pintura a Base de Plomo

Declaración sobre los Peligros del Plomo

Las viviendas construidas antes del año 1978 pueden contener pintura a base de plomo. El plomo de pintura, pedazos de pintura y polvo puede representar peligros para la salud si no se maneja apropiadamente. La exposición al plomo es especialmente dañino para los niños jóvenes y las mujeres embarazadas. Antes de alquilar (rentar) una vivienda construida antes del año 1978, los arrendadores tienen la obligación de informar sobre la presencia de pintura a base de plomo o peligros de pintura a base de plomo conocidos en la vivienda. Los arrendatarios (inquilinos) también deben recibir un folleto aprobado por el Gobierno Federal sobre la prevención del envenenamiento de plomo.

Declaración del Arrendador

(a) Presencia de pintura a base de plomo y/o peligros de pintura a base de plomo (marque (i) ó (ii) abajo):

(i) _____ Confirmado que hay pintura a base de plomo y/o peligro de pintura a base de plomo en la vivienda (explique).

_____

(ii) _____ El arrendador no tiene ningún conocimiento de que haya pintura a base de plomo y/o peligro de pintura a base de plomo en la vivienda.

(b) Archivos e informes disponibles para el vendedor (marque (i) ó (ii) abajo):

(i) _____ El arrendador le ha proporcionado al comprador todos los archivos e informes disponibles relacionados con pintura a base de plomo y/o peligro de pintura a base de plomo en la vivienda (anote los documentos abajo).

_____

(ii) _____ El arrendador no tiene archivos ni informes relacionados con pintura a base de plomo y/o peligro de pintura a base de plomo en la vivienda.

Acuse de Recibo del Arrendatario o Inquilino (inicial)

(c) _____ El arrendatario ha recibido copias de toda la información indicada arriba.

(d) _____ El arrendatario ha recibido el folleto titulado *Proteja a Su Familia del Plomo en Su Casa.*

Acuse de Recibo del Agente (inicial)

(e) _____ El agente le ha informado al arrendador de las obligaciones del arrendador de acuerdo con 42 U.S.C. 4852d y está consciente de su responsabilidad de asegurar su cumplimiento.

Certificación de Exactitud

Las partes siguientes han revisado la información que aparece arriba y certifican que, según su entender, toda la información que han proporcionado es verdadera y exacta.

_____ _____   _____ _____
Arrendador   Fecha   Arrendador   Fecha

_____ _____   _____ _____
Arrendatario   Fecha   Arrendatario   Fecha

_____ _____   _____ _____
Agente   Fecha   Agente   Fecha

Are You Planning to Buy or Rent a Home Built Before 1978?

Did you know that many homes built before 1978 have **lead-based paint?** Lead from paint, chips, and dust can pose serious health hazards.

Read this entire brochure to learn:

- How lead gets into the body
- How lead affects health
- What you can do to protect your family
- Where to go for more information

Before renting or buying a pre-1978 home or apartment, federal law requires:

- Sellers must disclose known information on lead-based paint or lead-based paint hazards before selling a house.
- Real estate sales contracts must include a specific warning statement about lead-based paint. Buyers have up to 10 days to check for lead.
- Landlords must disclose known information on lead-based paint and lead-based paint hazards before leases take effect. Leases must include a specific warning statement about lead-based paint.

If undertaking renovations, repairs, or painting (RRP) projects in your pre-1978 home or apartment:

- Read EPA's pamphlet, *The Lead-Safe Certified Guide to Renovate Right,* to learn about the lead-safe work practices that contractors are required to follow when working in your home (see page 12).

Protect
Your
Family
From
Lead in
Your
Home

United States
Environmental
Protection Agency

United States
Consumer Product
Safety Commission

United States
Department of Housing
and Urban Development

June 2017

Lead Gets into the Body in Many Ways

Adults and children can get lead into their bodies if they:

- Breathe in lead dust (especially during activities such as renovations, repairs, or painting that disturb painted surfaces).

- Swallow lead dust that has settled on food, food preparation surfaces, and other places.

- Eat paint chips or soil that contains lead.

Lead is especially dangerous to children under the age of 6.

- At this age, children's brains and nervous systems are more sensitive to the damaging effects of lead.

- Children's growing bodies absorb more lead.

- Babies and young children often put their hands and other objects in their mouths. These objects can have lead dust on them.

Women of childbearing age should know that lead is dangerous to a developing fetus.

- Women with a high lead level in their system before or during pregnancy risk exposing the fetus to lead through the placenta during fetal development.

Simple Steps to Protect Your Family from Lead Hazards

If you think your home has lead-based paint:

- Don't try to remove lead-based paint yourself.

- Always keep painted surfaces in good condition to minimize deterioration.

- Get your home checked for lead hazards. Find a certified inspector or risk assessor at epa.gov/lead.

- Talk to your landlord about fixing surfaces with peeling or chipping paint.

- Regularly clean floors, window sills, and other surfaces.

- Take precautions to avoid exposure to lead dust when remodeling.

- When renovating, repairing, or painting, hire only EPA- or state-approved Lead-Safe certified renovation firms.

- Before buying, renting, or renovating your home, have it checked for lead-based paint.

- Consult your health care provider about testing your children for lead. Your pediatrician can check for lead with a simple blood test.

- Wash children's hands, bottles, pacifiers, and toys often.

- Make sure children eat healthy, low-fat foods high in iron, calcium, and vitamin C.

- Remove shoes or wipe soil off shoes before entering your house.

Check Your Family for Lead

Get your children and home tested if you think your home has lead.

Children's blood lead levels tend to increase rapidly from 6 to 12 months of age, and tend to peak at 18 to 24 months of age.

Consult your doctor for advice on testing your children. A simple blood test can detect lead. Blood lead tests are usually recommended for:

- Children at ages 1 and 2
- Children or other family members who have been exposed to high levels of lead
- Children who should be tested under your state or local health screening plan

Your doctor can explain what the test results mean and if more testing will be needed.

Health Effects of Lead

Lead affects the body in many ways. It is important to know that even exposure to low levels of lead can severely harm children.

In children, exposure to lead can cause:

- Nervous system and kidney damage
- Learning disabilities, attention-deficit disorder, and decreased intelligence
- Speech, language, and behavior problems
- Poor muscle coordination
- Decreased muscle and bone growth
- Hearing damage

Brain Nerve Damage
Hearing Problems
Slowed Growth
Digestive Problems
Reproductive Problems (Adults)

While low-lead exposure is most common, exposure to high amounts of lead can have devastating effects on children, including seizures, unconsciousness, and in some cases, death.

Although children are especially susceptible to lead exposure, lead can be dangerous for adults, too.

In adults, exposure to lead can cause:

- Harm to a developing fetus
- Increased chance of high blood pressure during pregnancy
- Fertility problems (in men and women)
- High blood pressure
- Digestive problems
- Nerve disorders
- Memory and concentration problems
- Muscle and joint pain

Where Lead-Based Paint Is Found

In general, the older your home or childcare facility, the more likely it has lead-based paint.[1]

Many homes, including private, federally-assisted, federally-owned housing, and childcare facilities built before 1978 have lead-based paint. In 1978, the federal government banned consumer uses of lead-containing paint.[2]

Learn how to determine if paint is lead-based paint on page 7.

Lead can be found:

- In homes and childcare facilities in the city, country, or suburbs,
- In private and public single-family homes and apartments,
- On surfaces inside and outside of the house, and
- In soil around a home. (Soil can pick up lead from exterior paint or other sources, such as past use of leaded gas in cars.)

Learn more about where lead is found at epa.gov/lead.

---

[1] "Lead-based paint" is currently defined by the federal government as paint with lead levels greater than or equal to 1.0 milligram per square centimeter (mg/cm), or more than 0.5% by weight.

[2] "Lead-containing paint" is currently defined by the federal government as lead in new dried paint in excess of 90 parts per million (ppm) by weight.

Identifying Lead-Based Paint and Lead-Based Paint Hazards

Deteriorating lead-based paint (peeling, chipping, chalking, cracking, or damaged paint) is a hazard and needs immediate attention. **Lead-based paint** may also be a hazard when found on surfaces that children can chew or that get a lot of wear and tear, such as:

- On windows and window sills
- Doors and door frames
- Stairs, railings, banisters, and porches

Lead-based paint is usually not a hazard if it is in good condition and if it is not on an impact or friction surface like a window.

Lead dust can form when lead-based paint is scraped, sanded, or heated. Lead dust also forms when painted surfaces containing lead bump or rub together. Lead paint chips and dust can get on surfaces and objects that people touch. Settled lead dust can reenter the air when the home is vacuumed or swept, or when people walk through it. EPA currently defines the following levels of lead in dust as hazardous:

- 40 micrograms per square foot ($\mu g/ft^2$) and higher for floors, including carpeted floors
- 250 $\mu g/ft^2$ and higher for interior window sills

Lead in soil can be a hazard when children play in bare soil or when people bring soil into the house on their shoes. EPA currently defines the following levels of lead in soil as hazardous:

- 400 parts per million (ppm) and higher in play areas of bare soil
- 1,200 ppm (average) and higher in bare soil in the remainder of the yard

Remember, lead from paint chips—which you can see—and lead dust—which you may not be able to see—both can be hazards.

The only way to find out if paint, dust, or soil lead hazards exist is to test for them. The next page describes how to do this.

Checking Your Home for Lead

You can get your home tested for lead in several different ways:

- A lead-based paint **inspection** tells you if your home has lead-based paint and where it is located. It won't tell you whether your home currently has lead hazards. A trained and certified testing professional, called a lead-based paint inspector, will conduct a paint inspection using methods, such as:

  - Portable x-ray fluorescence (XRF) machine

  - Lab tests of paint samples

- A **risk assessment** tells you if your home currently has any lead hazards from lead in paint, dust, or soil. It also tells you what actions to take to address any hazards. A trained and certified testing professional, called a risk assessor, will:

  - Sample paint that is deteriorated on doors, windows, floors, stairs, and walls

  - Sample dust near painted surfaces and sample bare soil in the yard

  - Get lab tests of paint, dust, and soil samples

- A combination inspection and risk assessment tells you if your home has any lead-based paint and if your home has any lead hazards, and where both are located.

Be sure to read the report provided to you after your inspection or risk assessment is completed, and ask questions about anything you do not understand.

Checking Your Home for Lead, continued

In preparing for renovation, repair, or painting work in a pre-1978 home, Lead-Safe Certified renovators (see page 12) may:

- Take paint chip samples to determine if lead-based paint is present in the area planned for renovation and send them to an EPA-recognized lead lab for analysis. In housing receiving federal assistance, the person collecting these samples must be a certified lead-based paint inspector or risk assessor

- Use EPA-recognized tests kits to determine if lead-based paint is absent (but not in housing receiving federal assistance)

- Presume that lead-based paint is present and use lead-safe work practices

There are state and federal programs in place to ensure that testing is done safely, reliably, and effectively. Contact your state or local agency for more information, visit epa.gov/lead, or call **1-800-424-LEAD (5323)** for a list of contacts in your area.[3]

---

[3] Hearing- or speech-challenged individuals may access this number through TTY by calling the Federal Relay Service at 1-800-877-8339.

What You Can Do Now to Protect Your Family

If you suspect that your house has lead-based paint hazards, you can take some immediate steps to reduce your family's risk:

- If you rent, notify your landlord of peeling or chipping paint.

- Keep painted surfaces clean and free of dust. Clean floors, window frames, window sills, and other surfaces weekly. Use a mop or sponge with warm water and a general all-purpose cleaner. (Remember: never mix ammonia and bleach products together because they can form a dangerous gas.)

- Carefully clean up paint chips immediately without creating dust.

- Thoroughly rinse sponges and mop heads often during cleaning of dirty or dusty areas, and again afterward.

- Wash your hands and your children's hands often, especially before they eat and before nap time and bed time.

- Keep play areas clean. Wash bottles, pacifiers, toys, and stuffed animals regularly.

- Keep children from chewing window sills or other painted surfaces, or eating soil.

- When renovating, repairing, or painting, hire only EPA- or state-approved Lead-Safe Certified renovation firms (see page 12).

- Clean or remove shoes before entering your home to avoid tracking in lead from soil.

- Make sure children eat nutritious, low-fat meals high in iron, and calcium, such as spinach and dairy products. Children with good diets absorb less lead.

Reducing Lead Hazards

Disturbing lead-based paint or removing lead improperly can increase the hazard to your family by spreading even more lead dust around the house.

- In addition to day-to-day cleaning and good nutrition, you can **temporarily** reduce lead-based paint hazards by taking actions, such as repairing damaged painted surfaces and planting grass to cover lead-contaminated soil. These actions are not permanent solutions and will need ongoing attention.

- You can minimize exposure to lead when renovating, repairing, or painting by hiring an EPA- or state-certified renovator who is trained in the use of lead-safe work practices. If you are a do-it-yourselfer, learn how to use lead-safe work practices in your home.

- To remove lead hazards permanently, you should hire a certified lead abatement contractor. Abatement (or permanent hazard elimination) methods include removing, sealing, or enclosing lead-based paint with special materials. Just painting over the hazard with regular paint is not permanent control.

Always use a certified contractor who is trained to address lead hazards safely.

- Hire a Lead-Safe Certified firm (see page 12) to perform renovation, repair, or painting (RRP) projects that disturb painted surfaces.

- To correct lead hazards permanently, hire a certified lead abatement professional. This will ensure your contractor knows how to work safely and has the proper equipment to clean up thoroughly.

Certified contractors will employ qualified workers and follow strict safety rules as set by their state or by the federal government.

Reducing Lead Hazards, continued

If your home has had lead abatement work done or if the housing is receiving federal assistance, once the work is completed, dust cleanup activities must be conducted until clearance testing indicates that lead dust levels are below the following levels:

- 40 micrograms per square foot (μg/ft^2) for floors, including carpeted floors
- 250 μg/ft^2 for interior windows sills
- 400 μg/ft^2 for window troughs

For help in locating certified lead abatement professionals in your area, call your state or local agency (see pages 14 and 15), or visit epa.gov/lead, or call 1-800-424-LEAD.

Renovating, Repairing or Painting a Home with Lead-Based Paint

If you hire a contractor to conduct renovation, repair, or painting (RRP) projects in your pre-1978 home or childcare facility (such as pre-school and kindergarten), your contractor must:

- Be a Lead-Safe Certified firm approved by EPA or an EPA-authorized state program
- Use qualified trained individuals (Lead-Safe Certified renovators) who follow specific lead-safe work practices to prevent lead contamination
- Provide a copy of EPA's lead hazard information document, *The Lead-Safe Certified Guide to Renovate Right*

RRP contractors working in pre-1978 homes and childcare facilities must follow lead-safe work practices that:

- **Contain the work area.** The area must be contained so that dust and debris do not escape from the work area. Warning signs must be put up, and plastic or other impermeable material and tape must be used.

- **Avoid renovation methods that generate large amounts of lead-contaminated dust.** Some methods generate so much lead-contaminated dust that their use is prohibited. They are:
  - Open-flame burning or torching
  - Sanding, grinding, planing, needle gunning, or blasting with power tools and equipment not equipped with a shroud and HEPA vacuum attachment
  - Using a heat gun at temperatures greater than 1100°F

- **Clean up thoroughly.** The work area should be cleaned up daily. When all the work is done, the area must be cleaned up using special cleaning methods.

- **Dispose of waste properly.** Collect and seal waste in a heavy duty bag or sheeting. When transported, ensure that waste is contained to prevent release of dust and debris.

To learn more about EPA's requirements for RRP projects, visit epa.gov/getleadsafe, or read *The Lead-Safe Certified Guide to Renovate Right*.

Other Sources of Lead

Lead in Drinking Water

The most common sources of lead in drinking water are lead pipes, faucets, and fixtures.

Lead pipes are more likely to be found in older cities and homes built before 1986.

You can't smell or taste lead in drinking water.

To find out for certain if you have lead in drinking water, have your water tested.

Remember older homes with a private well can also have plumbing materials that contain lead.

Important Steps You Can Take to Reduce Lead in Drinking Water

- Use only cold water for drinking, cooking and making baby formula. Remember, boiling water does not remove lead from water.

- Before drinking, flush your home's pipes by running the tap, taking a shower, doing laundry, or doing a load of dishes.

- Regularly clean your faucet's screen (also known as an aerator).

- If you use a filter certified to remove lead, don't forget to read the directions to learn when to change the cartridge. Using a filter after it has expired can make it less effective at removing lead.

Contact your water company to determine if the pipe that connects your home to the water main (called a service line) is made from lead. Your area's water company can also provide information about the lead levels in your system's drinking water.

For more information about lead in drinking water, please contact EPA's Safe Drinking Water Hotline at 1-800-426-4791. If you have other questions about lead poisoning prevention, call 1-800 424-LEAD.*

Call your local health department or water company to find out about testing your water, or visit epa.gov/safewater for EPA's lead in drinking water information. Some states or utilities offer programs to pay for water testing for residents. Contact your state or local water company to learn more.

* Hearing- or speech-challenged individuals may access this number through TTY by calling the Federal Relay Service at 1-800-877-8339.

Other Sources of Lead, continued

- **Lead smelters** or other industries that release lead into the air.

- **Your job.** If you work with lead, you could bring it home on your body or clothes. Shower and change clothes before coming home. Launder your work clothes separately from the rest of your family's clothes.

- **Hobbies** that use lead, such as making pottery or stained glass, or refinishing furniture. Call your local health department for information about hobbies that may use lead.

- Old **toys** and **furniture** may have been painted with lead-containing paint. Older toys and other children's products may have parts that contain lead.[4]

- Food and liquids cooked or stored in **lead crystal** or **lead-glazed pottery or porcelain** may contain lead.

- Folk remedies, such as **"greta"** and **"azarcon,"** used to treat an upset stomach.

[4] In 1978, the federal government banned toys, other children's products, and furniture with lead-containing paint. In 2008, the federal government banned lead in most children's products. The federal government currently bans lead in excess of 100 ppm by weight in most children's products.

For More Information

The National Lead Information Center

Learn how to protect children from lead poisoning and get other information about lead hazards on the Web at epa.gov/lead, hud.gov/lead, or call **1-800-424-LEAD (5323)**.

EPA's Safe Drinking Water Hotline

For information about lead in drinking water, call **1-800-426-4791**, or visit epa.gov/lead for information about lead in drinking water.

Consumer Product Safety Commission (CPSC) Hotline

For information on lead in toys and other consumer products, or to report an unsafe consumer product or a product-related injury, call **1-800-638-2772**, or visit CPSC's website at cpsc.gov or saferproducts.gov.

State and Local Health and Environmental Agencies

Some states, tribes, and cities have their own rules related to lead-based paint. Check with your local agency to see which laws apply to you. Most agencies can also provide information on finding a lead abatement firm in your area, and on possible sources of financial aid for reducing lead hazards. Receive up-to-date address and phone information for your state or local contacts on the Web at epa.gov/safewater, or contact the National Lead Information Center at **1-800-424-LEAD**.

> Hearing- or speech-challenged individuals may access any of the phone numbers in this brochure through TTY by calling the toll-free Federal Relay Service at **1-800-877-8339**.

U. S. Environmental Protection Agency (EPA) Regional Offices

The mission of EPA is to protect human health and the environment. Your Regional EPA Office can provide further information regarding regulations and lead protection programs.

Region 1 (Connecticut, Massachusetts, Maine, New Hampshire, Rhode Island, Vermont)

Regional Lead Contact
U.S. EPA Region 1
5 Post Office Square, Suite 100, OES 05-4
Boston, MA 02109-3912
(888) 372-7341

Region 2 (New Jersey, New York, Puerto Rico, Virgin Islands)

Regional Lead Contact
U.S. EPA Region 2
2890 Woodbridge Avenue
Building 205, Mail Stop 225
Edison, NJ 08837-3679
(732) 321-6671

Region 3 (Delaware, Maryland, Pennsylvania, Virginia, DC, West Virginia)

Regional Lead Contact
U.S. EPA Region 3
1650 Arch Street
Philadelphia, PA 19103
(215) 814-2088

Region 4 (Alabama, Florida, Georgia, Kentucky, Mississippi, North Carolina, South Carolina, Tennessee)

Regional Lead Contact
U.S. EPA Region 4
AFC Tower, 12th Floor, Air, Pesticides & Toxics
61 Forsyth Street, SW
Atlanta, GA 30303
(404) 562-8998

Region 5 (Illinois, Indiana, Michigan, Minnesota, Ohio, Wisconsin)

Regional Lead Contact
U.S. EPA Region 5 (DT-8J)
77 West Jackson Boulevard
Chicago, IL 60604-3666
(312) 886-7836

Region 6 (Arkansas, Louisiana, New Mexico, Oklahoma, Texas, and 66 Tribes)

Regional Lead Contact
U.S. EPA Region 6
1445 Ross Avenue, 12th Floor
Dallas, TX 75202-2733
(214) 665-2704

Region 7 (Iowa, Kansas, Missouri, Nebraska)

Regional Lead Contact
U.S. EPA Region 7
11201 Renner Blvd.
WWPD/TOPE
Lenexa, KS 66219
(800) 223-0425

Region 8 (Colorado, Montana, North Dakota, South Dakota, Utah, Wyoming)

Regional Lead Contact
U.S. EPA Region 8
1595 Wynkoop St.
Denver, CO 80202
(303) 312-6966

Region 9 (Arizona, California, Hawaii, Nevada)

Regional Lead Contact
U.S. EPA Region 9 (CMD-4-2)
75 Hawthorne Street
San Francisco, CA 94105
(415) 947-4280

Region 10 (Alaska, Idaho, Oregon, Washington)

Regional Lead Contact
U.S. EPA Region 10
Solid Waste & Toxics Unit (WCM-128)
1200 Sixth Avenue, Suite 900
Seattle, WA 98101
(206) 553-1200

IMPORTANT!

Lead From Paint, Dust, and Soil in and Around Your Home Can Be Dangerous if Not Managed Properly

- Children under 6 years old are most at risk for lead poisoning in your home.

- Lead exposure can harm young children and babies even before they are born.

- Homes, schools, and child care facilities built before 1978 are likely to contain lead-based paint.

- Even children who seem healthy may have dangerous levels of lead in their bodies.

- Disturbing surfaces with lead-based paint or removing lead-based paint improperly can increase the danger to your family.

- People can get lead into their bodies by breathing or swallowing lead dust, or by eating soil or paint chips containing lead.

- People have many options for reducing lead hazards. Generally, lead-based paint that is in good condition is not a hazard (see page 10).

Consumer Product Safety Commission (CPSC)

The CPSC protects the public against unreasonable risk of injury from consumer products through education, safety standards activities, and enforcement. Contact CPSC for further information regarding consumer product safety and regulations.

CPSC
4330 East West Highway
Bethesda, MD 20814-4421
1-800-638-2772
cpsc.gov or saferproducts.gov

U. S. Department of Housing and Urban Development (HUD)

HUD's mission is to create strong, sustainable, inclusive communities and quality affordable homes for all. Contact HUD's Office of Healthy Homes and Lead Hazard Control for further information regarding the Lead Safe Housing Rule, which protects families in pre-1978 assisted housing, and for the lead hazard control and research grant programs.

HUD
451 Seventh Street, SW, Room 8236
Washington, DC 20410-3000
(202) 402-7698
hud.gov/offices/lead/

U. S. EPA Washington DC 20460
U. S. CPSC Bethesda MD 20814
U. S. HUD Washington DC 20410

EPA-747-K-12-001
June 2017

¿Está planeando comprar o alquilar una casa construida antes de 1978?

¿Sabía que muchas casas construidas antes de 1978 tienen **pintura con base de plomo**? El plomo en la pintura, las partículas y el polvo puede ser un peligro grave para la salud.

Lea todo este folleto para saber:

- Cómo entra el plomo en el cuerpo.
- Cómo el plomo afecta a la salud.
- Qué puede hacer para proteger a su familia.
- Adónde recurrir para obtener más información.

Antes de alquilar o comprar una casa o un apartamento construidos antes de 1978, la ley federal requiere lo siguiente:

- Los vendedores tienen que dar la información que posean acerca de la pintura con base de plomo o los peligros relacionados con dicha pintura antes de vender una casa.
- Los contratos de venta de inmuebles deben incluir una declaración de advertencia específica sobre la pintura con base de plomo. Los compradores tienen hasta 10 días para verificar la existencia de plomo.
- Los propietarios tienen que dar la información que posean acerca de la pintura con base de plomo y los peligros relacionados con dicha pintura antes de que el alquiler entre en vigencia. Los contratos de alquiler deben incluir una declaración de advertencia específica sobre la pintura con base de plomo.

Si emprenderá algún proyecto de renovación, reparación o pintura (RRP, por sus siglas en inglés) en su casa o apartamento construido antes de 1978:

- Lea el folleto de la EPA *Guía de prácticas acreditas seguras para trabajar con el plomo para remodeler correctamente.*

Proteja a su familia contra el plomo en el hogar

 EPA Agencia de Protección Ambiental de los Estados Unidos (EPA)

 Comisión de Seguridad de Productos del Consumidor de Estados Unidos (CPSC)

 Departamento de la Vivienda y de Desarrollo Urbano de los Estados Unidos (HUD)

Junio de 2017

Medidas sencillas para proteger a su familia contra los peligros relacionados con el plomo

Si cree que su casa tiene pintura con base de plomo:

- No trate de remover usted mismo la pintura con base de plomo.

- Mantenga siempre las superficies pintadas en buenas condiciones para minimizar el deterioro.

- Haga que examinen su casa para identificar peligros relacionados con el plomo. Encuentre un inspector certificado o un asesor de riesgos en epa.gov/lead.

- Hable con el propietario para que arregle las superficies con pintura descascarada o picada.

- Limpie con regularidad los pisos, los antepechos de las ventanas y las demás superficies.

- Tome precauciones para evitar la exposición al polvo de plomo al remodelar.

- Al realizar renovaciones, reparaciones o pintura, contrate solamente a empresas de renovación certificadas en prácticas seguras con el plomo aprobadas por el estado o la EPA.

- Antes de comprar, alquilar o renovar su casa, hágala examinar para ver si tiene pintura con base de plomo.

- Consulte con su profesional de la salud sobre pruebas para detectar la presencia de plomo en sus hijos. El pediatra puede comprobar la presencia de plomo con un simple análisis de sangre.

- Lave con frecuencia las manos, los biberones, los chupones y los juguetes de los niños.

- Asegúrese de que los niños coman alimentos saludables, bajos en grasa, y altos en hierro, calcio y vitamina C.

- Quítese los zapatos o lave la tierra de los zapatos antes de entrar a su casa.

El plomo entra al cuerpo de muchas maneras

El plomo puede entrar en el cuerpo de adultos y niños si:

- Respiran el polvo de plomo (especialmente durante las actividades de renovación, reparación y pintura que alteran las superficies pintadas).

- Tragan polvo de plomo que se ha acumulado en alimentos, superficies donde se preparan alimentos y otros lugares.

- Comen partículas de pintura o tierra que contengan plomo.

El plomo es especialmente peligroso para los niños menores de 6 años.

- A esta edad, el cerebro y el sistema nervioso de los niños son más sensibles a los efectos dañinos del plomo.

- El cuerpo en crecimiento de los niños absorbe más plomo.

- Los bebés y los niños pequeños se llevan las manos y otros objetos a la boca con frecuencia. Dichos objetos pueden estar cubiertos de polvo de plomo.

Las mujeres en edad de concebir deben saber que el plomo es peligroso para el feto en desarrollo.

- Las mujeres que tienen un nivel alto de plomo en su cuerpo antes del embarazo o mientras están embarazadas podrían exponer al feto al plomo a través de la placenta durante su desarrollo.

Efectos del plomo en la salud

El plomo afecta el cuerpo de muchas maneras. Es importante saber que aun una exposición a niveles bajos de plomo puede afectar al niño gravemente.

En los niños, la exposición al plomo puede causar:

Daño nervioso en el cerebro

Problemas auditivos

Crecimiento más lento

Problemas digestivos

Problemas en la reproducción (adultos)

- Daño al sistema nervioso y los riñones.

- Problemas de aprendizaje, desorden de deficiencia de atención y disminución de la capacidad intelectual.

- Problemas del habla, del lenguaje y de comportamiento.

- Pobre coordinación muscular.

- Disminución en el crecimiento muscular y de los huesos.

- Daño en la audición.

Mientras que la exposición a niveles bajos de plomo es más común, la exposición a niveles altos de plomo puede causar efectos devastadores en los niños, incluso convulsiones, pérdida del conocimiento y, en algunos casos, la muerte.

Aunque los niños son especialmente susceptibles a la exposición al plomo, también puede ser peligroso para los adultos.

En los adultos, la exposición al plomo puede causar:

- Daño a un feto en desarrollo.

- Mayor probabilidad de tener tensión arterial alta durante el embarazo.

- Problemas de fertilidad (en hombres y mujeres).

- Tensión arterial alta.

- Problemas digestivos.

- Trastornos nerviosos.

- Problemas de memoria y concentración.

- Dolores musculares y articulares.

3

Verifique el nivel de plomo en su familia

Haga que examinen a sus niños y a su casa si cree que esta tiene plomo.

El nivel de plomo en la sangre de los niños tiende a aumentar con rapidez entre los 6 y 12 meses de edad, y tiende a llegar al nivel más alto entre los 18 y 24 meses de edad.

Consulte a su médico en cuanto a la necesidad de examinar a sus niños. Un sencillo análisis de sangre puede detectar la presencia de plomo. Los análisis de sangre para detectar plomo se recomiendan generalmente para:

- Niños de 1 a 2 años de edad.

- Niños u otros miembros de la familia que hayan estado expuestos a niveles altos de plomo.

- Niños que deben examinarse en virtud del plan local o estatal de exámenes médicos.

Su médico puede explicarle los resultados de las pruebas y decirle si es necesario realizar más análisis.

4

Dónde se encuentra la pintura con base de plomo

Generalmente, cuanto más vieja sea su casa o centro de cuidado infantil, mayor será la posibilidad de que tenga pintura con base de plomo.[1]

Muchas viviendas —incluidas las viviendas privadas, las de propiedad federal y las que reciben ayuda federal— y centros de cuidado infantil construidos antes de 1978 tienen pintura con base de plomo. En 1978, el gobierno federal prohibió el uso por parte del consumidor de pintura que contenga plomo.[2]

En la página 7, encontrará cómo establecer si la pintura tiene plomo.

El plomo puede encontrarse en:

- Casas y centros de cuidado infantil en la ciudad, el campo o los suburbios;

- Casas y apartamentos unifamiliares privados y públicos;

- Superficies dentro y fuera de la casa; y

- La tierra alrededor de la casa (la tierra puede acumular plomo de la pintura exterior u otras fuentes, tales como la gasolina con plomo que se usaba en el pasado en los automóviles).

Obtenga más información sobre dónde se encuentra plomo en epa.gov/lead.

---

[1] En la actualidad, el gobierno federal define la "pintura con base de plomo" como pintura con niveles de plomo superiores o iguales a 1.0 miligramo por centímetro cuadrado (mg/cm) o con más de 0.5 % por peso.

[2] En la actualidad, el gobierno federal define la "pintura que contiene plomo" como plomo en pintura nueva seca que supere las 90 partes por millón (ppm) por peso.

Identificando la pintura con base de plomo y los peligros de la pintura con base de plomo

La pintura con base de plomo deteriorada (descascarada, picada, pulverizada, agrietada o dañada) es un peligro y requiere atención inmediata. La **pintura con base de plomo** también puede ser un peligro si se encuentra en superficies que los niños puedan morder o que se desgasten mucho, tales como:

- Ventanas y antepechos de ventanas.

- Puertas y marcos de puertas.

- Escaleras, pasamanos, barandas y porches.

La pintura con base de plomo generalmente no es peligrosa si está en buenas condiciones y no está en una superficie de impacto o de fricción, como en una ventana.

El polvo de plomo puede formarse al raspar, lijar o calentar la pintura con base de plomo. También se forma cuando las superficies pintadas que contienen polvo se golpean o frotan entre sí. Las partículas y el polvo de la pintura que contiene plomo pueden acumularse en superficies y objetos que las personas tocan. El polvo de plomo que se ha acumulado puede volver a mezclarse con el aire cuando se aspira o barre la casa, o cuando las personas caminan sobre el mismo. Actualmente, la EPA define como peligrosos los siguientes niveles de plomo en el polvo:

- 40 microgramos por pie cuadrado (µg/pie²) o más en pisos, incluidos pisos alfombrados.

- 250 µg/pie² o más en los antepechos de ventanas interiores.

El plomo en la tierra puede ser peligroso cuando los niños juegan en tierra descubierta o cuando las personas meten tierra en la casa con los zapatos. Actualmente, la EPA define como peligrosos los siguientes niveles de plomo en la tierra:

- 400 partes por millón (ppm) o más en áreas de juego de tierra descubierta.

- 1,200 ppm (promedio) o más en la tierra descubierta del resto del jardín.

Recuerde que el plomo de las partículas de pintura —que puede ver— y el polvo de plomo —que tal vez no pueda ver— pueden ser peligrosos.

La única forma de saber si existe peligro debido a la presencia de plomo en pintura, polvo o tierra es realizando pruebas. En la página siguiente se describe cómo hacer esto.

Verificando si su casa tiene plomo

Puede evaluar su casa de diferentes maneras para determinar si tiene plomo:

- Una **inspección** de la pintura con base de plomo le dirá si su casa tiene pintura con base de plomo y dónde se localiza. Sin embargo, esta inspección no le dirá si en su casa existen actualmente peligros relacionados con el plomo. Un profesional experto en pruebas capacitado y certificado, que se llama inspector de pintura con base de plomo, realizará la inspección de la pintura utilizando métodos como:

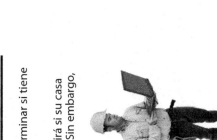

  - Máquina portátil de fluorescencia por rayos X (XRF, por sus siglas en inglés).
  - Pruebas de laboratorio de muestras de pintura.

- Una **evaluación de riesgo** le dirá si en su casa existe actualmente algún peligro relacionado con el plomo debido a la presencia de plomo en la pintura, el polvo o la tierra. También le dirá qué acciones debe llevar a cabo para eliminar estos peligros. Un profesional experto en pruebas capacitado y certificado, que se llama asesor de riesgo, hará lo siguiente:

  - Tomará muestras de la pintura deteriorada de puertas, ventanas, pisos, escaleras y paredes.
  - Tomará muestras del polvo cerca de las superficies pintadas y muestras de tierra descubierta del patio.
  - Hará pruebas de laboratorio con las muestras de pintura, polvo y tierra.
  - Una combinación de evaluación de riesgo e inspección le dirá si en su casa hay pintura con base de plomo, si existe algún peligro relacionado con el plomo y dónde se localizan ambos.

Asegúrese de leer el informe que le entreguen una vez finalizada la inspección o la evaluación de riesgo, y pregunte todo lo que no entienda.

Verificando si su casa tiene plomo (continuación)

Al preparar un trabajo de renovación, reparación o pintura en una casa construida antes de 1978, los renovadores certificados para prácticas seguras con el plomo (vea la página 12) pueden:

- Tomar muestras de partículas de pintura para determinar si hay pintura con base de plomo en el área que se prevé renovar y enviarlas para analizar a un laboratorio especializado en plomo reconocido por la EPA. En viviendas que reciben ayuda federal, la persona que recolecte estas muestras debe ser un evaluador de riesgo o inspector certificado de pintura con base de plomo.

- Utilizar juegos de pruebas reconocidos por la EPA para determinar si no hay pintura con base de plomo (no se deben usar en viviendas que reciban ayuda federal).

- Suponer que hay pintura con base de plomo y utilizar prácticas de trabajo seguras con el plomo.

Existen programas estatales y federales para garantizar que las pruebas se realicen de modo seguro, confiable y con eficacia. Comuníquese con la agencia estatal o local para obtener más información, visite epa.gov/lead o llame al **1-800-424-LEAD (5323)** para obtener una lista de contactos en su área.[3]

---

[3] Las personas con impedimentos auditivos o del habla pueden acceder a este número a través del sistema TTY llamando al Federal Relay Service (Servicio Federal de Retransmisión) al 1-800-877-8399.

Lo que usted puede hacer en estos momentos para proteger a su familia

Si sospecha que su casa tiene algún peligro relacionado con pintura con base de plomo, puede tomar algunas medidas inmediatas para reducir el riesgo de su familia:

- Si alquila, infórmele al propietario si hay pintura descascarándose o picándose.

- Mantenga las superficies pintadas limpias y sin polvo. Limpie semanalmente los pisos, los marcos y antepechos de las ventanas y las demás superficies. Use un trapeador o una esponja con agua tibia y un limpiador para usos múltiples. (Recuerde: nunca mezcle productos de amoníaco con blanqueadores, ya que pueden formar gases peligrosos.)

- Limpie inmediatamente y con cuidado las partículas de pintura sin generar polvo.

- Enjuague bien y con frecuencia las esponjas y las cabezas de los trapeadores mientras limpia las áreas sucias o con polvo, y vuelva a hacerlo cuando termine de limpiar.

- Lávese con frecuencia las manos y también las de sus hijos, especialmente antes de comer, antes de la siesta y antes de irse a dormir.

- Mantenga limpias las áreas de juego. Lave con regularidad los biberones, los chupones, los juguetes y los animales de peluche.

- No permita que los niños muerdan los antepechos de las ventanas ni las demás superficies pintadas, ni tampoco que coman tierra.

- Al realizar renovaciones, reparaciones o pintura, contrate a empresas de renovación certificadas en prácticas seguras con el plomo aprobadas por el estado o la EPA (vea la página 12).

- Límpiese o quítese los zapatos antes de entrar a la casa para evitar meter el plomo de la tierra.

- Asegúrese de que los niños coman alimentos nutritivos, bajos en grasa y altos en hierro y calcio, tales como las espinacas y los productos lácteos. Los niños con una dieta adecuada absorben menos plomo.

Reduciendo los peligros del plomo

Alterar la pintura con base de plomo o remover incorrectamente el plomo puede aumentar el peligro para su familia, ya que esparce aún más el polvo de plomo en la casa.

- Además de la limpieza diaria y la buena nutrición, usted puede reducir **temporariamente** los riesgos relacionados con la pintura con base de plomo tomando medidas, como la reparación de las superficies pintadas que estén dañadas y plantar césped para cubrir la tierra contaminada con plomo. Estas medidas no son soluciones permanentes y necesitarán atención continua.

- Para minimizar la exposición al plomo cuando renueve, repare o pinte su casa, contrate a un renovador certificado por el estado o la EPA que esté capacitado en el uso de prácticas de trabajo seguras con el plomo. Si es una persona que suele hacer los trabajos por su cuenta, aprenda a utilizar prácticas de trabajo seguras con el plomo en su casa.

- Para remover permanentemente los peligros relacionados con el plomo, debe contratar a un contratista certificado para que "remueva" el plomo. Los métodos para remover (o eliminar permanentemente el peligro) incluyen la eliminación, el sellado o el revestimiento de la pintura con base de plomo con materiales especiales. Simplemente pintar sobre la pintura que presenta riesgos con una pintura común no es un control permanente.

Siempre recurra a un contratista certificado que esté capacitado para corregir los peligros relacionados con el plomo de manera segura.

- Contrate a una empresa certificada en prácticas seguras con el plomo (vea la página 12) para realizar proyectos de renovación, reparación o pintura (RRP) a fin de no alterar las superficies pintadas.

- Para corregir permanentemente los peligros relacionados con el plomo, contrate a un profesional certificado para que "remueva" el plomo. Esto asegurará que el contratista sepa cómo trabajar en forma segura y tenga el equipo apropiado para limpiar minuciosamente.

Los contratistas certificados contratarán a trabajadores cualificados y seguirán reglas estrictas de seguridad según lo dicta el estado o el gobierno federal.

Reduciendo los peligros del plomo (continuación)

Si en su casa se realizó un trabajo para remover el plomo o si se trata de una vivienda que recibe ayuda federal, una vez que se termine el trabajo, deben realizarse las actividades de limpieza del polvo hasta que las pruebas de aprobación indiquen que los niveles de polvo de plomo están por debajo de los siguientes niveles:

- 40 microgramos por pie cuadrado (μg/pie^2) en pisos, incluidos pisos alfombrados.

- 250 μg/pie^2 en los antepechos de ventanas interiores.

- 400 μg/pie^2 en los canales de ventanas.

Para obtener ayuda para localizar en su área profesionales certificados que remuevan el plomo, llame a la agencia estatal o local (vea las páginas 14 y 15), visite epa.gov/lead o llame al **1-800-424-LEAD.**

Renovación, reparación o pintura

Si contrata a un contratista para que realice proyectos de renovación, reparación o pintura (RRP) en una casa o centro de cuidado infantil construidos antes de 1978 (como centros preescolares y jardines de infancia), el contratista debe:

- Ser una empresa certificada en prácticas seguras con el plomo, aprobada por la EPA o por un programa estatal autorizado por la EPA.

- Utilizar personas cualificadas y capacitadas (renovadores certificados en prácticas seguras con el plomo) que empleen prácticas de trabajo seguras con el plomo específicas, a fin de evitar la contaminación con plomo.

- Darle una copia del documento informativo de la EPA sobre peligros relacionados con el plomo que se titula *Guía de prácticas acreditas seguras para trabajar con el plomo para remodeler correctamente.*

Los contratistas de RRP que trabajen en casas o centros de cuidado infantil construidos antes de 1978 deben seguir prácticas de trabajo seguras con el plomo que:

- **Contengan el área de trabajo.** Debe contenerse el área para que el polvo y los escombros no se escapen del área de trabajo. Deben colocarse letreros de advertencia, y debe usarse cinta y material plástico u otro tipo de material impermeable.

- **Eviten los métodos de renovación que generan grandes cantidades de polvo contaminado con plomo.** Algunos métodos producen tanto polvo contaminado con plomo que su uso está prohibido. Entre estos métodos se incluyen:

  - Quema o flameado a llama abierta.

  - Lijado, esmerilado, cepillado, uso de pistolas de aguja o limpieza a chorro con herramientas eléctricas y equipos sin cubierta y accesorio de aspiradora HEPA.

  - Pistola de aire caliente a temperaturas superiores a 1100 °F.

- **Limpien minuciosamente.** El área de trabajo debe limpiarse diariamente. Una vez terminado todo el trabajo, debe limpiarse el área con métodos de limpieza especiales.

- **Eliminen los desechos adecuadamente.** Recoja los residuos en una bolsa o lámina de alta resistencia y séllela. Cuando transporte los residuos, asegúrese de que la bolsa o lámina esté bien cerrada para que el polvo y los escombros no se escapen.

Para obtener más información sobre los requisitos de la EPA para los proyectos de RRP, visite epa.gov/getleadsafe o lea la *Guía de prácticas acreditas seguras para trabajar con el plomo para remodeler correctamente.*

Otras fuentes de plomo

Plomo en el agua potable

Las fuentes más comunes de plomo en el agua potable son las tuberías, grifos y accesorios de plomo.

Las tuberías de plomo son más factibles de encontrar en las ciudades más antiguas y en las casas construidas antes de 1986.

El plomo en el agua potable no presenta ningún olor ni sabor.

Para saber con seguridad si tiene plomo en el agua potable, debe hacerla analizar.

Recuerde que las casas más viejas con un pozo privado también pueden tener materiales de plomería que contengan plomo.

Medidas que puede tomar para reducir el plomo en el agua potable

- Use solo agua fría para beber, cocinar y preparar la leche del bebé. Recuerde que hervir el agua no elimina el plomo de esta.

- Antes de beber el agua, deje corriendo el grifo para purgar las tuberías del hogar, tomando una ducha, lave la ropa sucia o lave los trastes.

- Limpie regularmente el filtro del grifo (también llamado aireador).

- Si usa un filtro certificado para eliminar el plomo, no olvide leer las instrucciones para aprender cuándo cambiar el cartucho. El uso de un filtro después de su vencimiento puede hacerlo menos eficaz en la eliminación del plomo.

Comuníquese con su empresa de suministro de agua para determinar si la tubería que conecta su casa a la cañería de agua principal (llamada línea de servicio) es de plomo. Su empresa de agua local también puede brindarle información sobre los niveles de plomo en el agua potable de su sistema.

Para obtener más información sobre el plomo en el agua potable, comuníquese con Línea directa de la EPA sobre el agua potable (en inglés) al **1-800-426-4791**. Si tiene otras preguntas sobre la prevención del envenenamiento por plomo, llame al **1-800 424-LEAD**.*

Llame a su departamento de salud local o a su empresa de agua para averiguar cómo obtener un análisis del agua de su casa, o visite epa.gov/safewater para ver información de la EPA sobre el plomo en el agua potable. Algunos estados o empresas de servicios públicos ofrecen programas para pagar el análisis del agua de los residentes. Comuníquese con el servicio público de agua local o estatal para obtener más información.

* Las personas con dificultades del habla o la audición pueden acceder a este número a través de TTY llamando al Servicio Federal de Transmisión de Información al 1-800-877-8339.

Otras fuentes de plomo (continuación)

- **Los hornos de fundición de plomo** u otras industrias que emiten plomo al aire.

- **Su trabajo.** Si trabaja con plomo, podría traerlo a su casa en el cuerpo o la ropa. Báñese y cámbiese la ropa antes de volver a su casa. Lave la ropa de trabajo por separado del resto de la ropa de la familia.

- **Los pasatiempos** que usan plomo, tales como hacer trabajos en cerámica, pintar en vidrio o restaurar muebles. Llame al departamento de salud local para obtener información sobre los pasatiempos en los que puede usarse plomo.

- Los **juguetes** y **muebles** viejos que pueden haberse pintado con pintura que contenga plomo. Los juguetes viejos y otros productos para niños pueden contener partes con plomo.[4]

- Los alimentos y líquidos cocinados o almacenados en **cristal de plomo**, o en **cerámica o porcelana con esmalte de plomo** pueden contener plomo.

- Los remedios caseros, tales como **"greta"** y **"azarcón"**, que se usan para tratar padecimientos estomacales.

[4] En 1978, el gobierno federal prohibió los juguetes, otros productos para niños y los muebles con pintura que contenga plomo. En 2008, el gobierno federal también prohibió el plomo en la mayoría de los productos para niños, y actualmente prohíbe el plomo en cantidades superiores a 100 ppm por peso en la mayoría de los productos para niños.

Para obtener más información

The National Lead Information Center (Centro Nacional de Información sobre el Plomo)

Averigüe cómo proteger a los niños del envenenamiento por plomo y obtenga otra información sobre los peligros relacionados con el plomo por Internet en epa.gov/lead y hud.gov/lead, o llame al **1-800-424-LEAD (5323)**.

Línea directa de agua potable segura de la EPA

Para obtener información sobre el plomo en el agua potable, llame al **1-800-426-4791** o visite epa.gov/lead para obtener información sobre el plomo en el agua potable.

Línea directa de la Comisión de Seguridad de Productos del Consumidor de Estados Unidos (CPSC)

Para pedir información relacionada con el plomo en los juguetes y en otros productos del consumidor, o para denunciar un producto del consumidor inseguro o una lesión relacionada con un producto, llame al **1-800-638-2772**, o visite el sitio web de la CPSC en cpsc.gov o saferproducts.gov.

Agencias del medio ambiente y de salud estatales y locales

Algunos estados, tribus y ciudades tienen sus propias reglas relacionadas con la pintura con base de plomo. Consulte con su agencia local para ver cuáles leyes se le aplican. La mayoría de las agencias también pueden proporcionarle información para encontrar en su área una empresa para remover el plomo, y para conseguir posibles fuentes de ayuda económica para la reducción de los peligros relacionados con el plomo. Obtenga direcciones e información telefónica actualizadas de contactos locales o estatales por Internet en epa.gov/lead, o comuníquese con el Centro Nacional de Información sobre el Plomo llamando al **1-800-424-LEAD**.

Las personas con impedimentos auditivos o del habla pueden acceder a cualquiera de los números de teléfono que se indican en este folleto a través del sistema TTY llamando en forma gratuita al Federal Relay Service (Servicio Federal de Retransmisión) al **1-800-877-8339.**

Oficinas regionales de la Agencia de Protección Ambiental de los Estados Unidos (EPA)

La misión de la EPA es proteger la salud de los seres humanos y el medio ambiente. La Oficina Regional de la EPA puede darle más información sobre la normativa y los programas de protección contra el plomo.

Región 1 (Connecticut, Massachusetts, Maine, New Hampshire, Rhode Island, Vermont)

Regional Lead Contact
(Contacto regional para el plomo)
U.S. EPA Region 1
Suite 1100 (CPT) One Congress Street
Boston, MA 02114-2023
(617) 918-1524

Región 2 (New Jersey, New York, Puerto Rico, Virgin Islands)

Regional Lead Contact
(Contacto regional para el plomo)
U.S. EPA Region 2
2890 Woodbridge Avenue
Building 205, Mail Stop 225
Edison, NJ 08837-3679
(732) 321-6671

Región 3 (Delaware, Maryland, Pennsylvania, Virginia, DC, West Virginia)

Regional Lead Contact
(Contacto regional para el plomo)
U.S. EPA Region 3
1650 Arch Street
Philadelphia, PA 19103
(215) 814-2088

Región 4 (Alabama, Florida, Georgia, Kentucky, Mississippi, North Carolina, South Carolina, Tennessee)

Regional Lead Contact
(Contacto regional para el plomo)
U.S. EPA Region 4
AFC Tower, 12th Floor, Air, Pesticides & Toxics
61 Forsyth Street, SW
Atlanta, GA 30303
(404) 562-8998

Región 5 (Illinois, Indiana, Michigan, Minnesota, Ohio, Wisconsin)

Regional Lead Contact
(Contacto regional para el plomo)
U.S. EPA Region 5 (DT-8J)
77 West Jackson Boulevard
Chicago, IL 60604-3666
(312) 886-7836

Región 6 (Arkansas, Louisiana, New Mexico, Oklahoma, Texas y 66 tribus)

Regional Lead Contact
(Contacto regional para el plomo)
U.S. EPA Region 6
1445 Ross Avenue, 12th Floor
Dallas, TX 75202-2733
(214) 665-2704

Región 7 (Iowa, Kansas, Missouri, Nebraska)

Regional Lead Contact
(Contacto regional para el plomo)
U.S. EPA Region 7
11201 Renner Blvd.
WWPD/TOPE
Lenexa, KS 66219
(800) 223-0425

Región 8 (Colorado, Montana, North Dakota, South Dakota, Utah, Wyoming)

Regional Lead Contact
(Contacto regional para el plomo)
U.S. EPA Region 8
1595 Wynkoop St.
Denver, CO 80202
(303) 312-6966

Región 9 (Arizona, California, Hawaii, Nevada)

Regional Lead Contact
(Contacto regional para el plomo)
U.S. EPA Region 9 (CMD-4-2)
75 Hawthorne Street
San Francisco, CA 94105
(415) 947-4280

Región 10 (Alaska, Idaho, Oregon, Washington)

Regional Lead Contact
(Contacto regional para el plomo)
U.S. EPA Region 10
Solid Waste & Toxics Unit (WCM-128)
1200 Sixth Avenue, Suite 900
Seattle, WA 98101
(206) 553-1200

Comisión de Seguridad de Productos del Consumidor de Estados Unidos (CPSC)

La CPSC protege al público contra el riesgo irrazonable de daños causados por productos del consumidor a través de educación, actividades relacionadas con normas de seguridad y aplicación de la ley. Comuníquese con la CPSC para obtener más información sobre los reglamentos y la seguridad de los productos del consumidor.

CPSC
4330 East West Highway
Bethesda, MD 20814-4421
1-800-638-2772
cpsc.gov o saferproducts.gov

Departamento de la Vivienda y de Desarrollo Urbano de los Estados Unidos (HUD)

La misión del HUD es crear comunidades fuertes, sustentables e inclusivas, así como hogares de calidad asequibles para todos. Comuníquese con la Oficina de Hogares Saludables y Control de Peligros Relacionados con el Plomo del HUD para obtener más información acerca de la Regla sobre Viviendas Seguras en relación con el Plomo, que protege a las familias que residen en viviendas construidas antes de 1978 que reciben ayuda económica, y acerca de los programas de control de los peligros relacionados con el plomo y de subvenciones para investigación.

HUD
451 Seventh Street, SW, Room 8236
Washington, DC 20410-3000
(202) 402-7698
hud.gov/offices/lead/

EPA-747-K-13-001
Junio de 2017

U. S. EPA Washington DC 20460
U. S. CPSC Bethesda MD 20814
U. S. HUD Washington DC 20410

¡IMPORTANTE!

El plomo de la pintura, del polvo y de la tierra en la casa y alrededor de esta puede ser peligroso si no se maneja adecuadamente

- Los niños menores de 6 años son los que corren mayor riesgo de envenenamiento por plomo en la casa.

- La exposición al plomo puede hacerle daño a los niños pequeños y aun a los bebés antes del nacimiento.

- Es probable que las casas, las escuelas y los centros de cuidado infantil construidos antes de 1978 contengan pintura con base de plomo.

- Aun los niños que aparentan estar saludables pueden tener niveles peligrosos de plomo en el cuerpo.

- Alterar las superficies con pintura con base de plomo o remover incorrectamente la pintura con base de plomo puede aumentar los peligros para su familia.

- El plomo puede entrar en el cuerpo de las personas al respirar o tragar polvo de plomo, o al comer tierra o partículas de pintura que contengan plomo.

- Las personas tienen muchas opciones para reducir los peligros relacionados con el plomo. Generalmente, la pintura con base de plomo que está en buenas condiciones no es peligrosa (vea la página 10).

Rental Application

A separate application is required from each applicant age 18 or older.

Date and time received by Landlord _____

THIS SECTION TO BE COMPLETED BY LANDLORD

Address of property to be rented: _____

Rental term: ☐ month-to-month   ☐ lease from _____ to _____

Amounts Due Prior to Occupancy

First month's rent: .... $_____

Security deposit: .... $_____

Credit check fee: .... $_____

Other (specify): _____ $_____

TOTAL $_____

Applicant

Full Name—include all names you use or have used in the past: _____

Home Phone: _____ Work Phone: _____

Cell Phone: _____ Email: _____

Social Security Number: _____ Driver's License Number/State: _____

Other Identifying Information: _____

Vehicle Make: _____ Model: _____ Color: _____ Year: _____

License Plate Number/State: _____

Additional Occupants

List everyone, including minor children, who will live with you:

Full Name	Relationship to Applicant
_____	_____
_____	_____
_____	_____
_____	_____
_____	_____

Rental History

FIRST-TIME RENTERS: INSTEAD ATTACH A DESCRIPTION OF YOUR HOUSING FOR THE PAST FIVE YEARS.

Current Address: _____

Dates Lived at Address: _____ Rent $ _____ Security Deposit $ _____

Landlord/Manager: _____ Landlord/Manager's Phone: _____

Reason for Leaving: _____

Previous Address: _____

Dates Lived at Address: _____ Rent $ _____ Security Deposit $ _____

Landlord/Manager: _____ Landlord/Manager's Phone: _____

Reason for Leaving: _____

Previous Address: _____

Dates Lived at Address: _____ Rent $ _____ Security Deposit $ _____

Landlord/Manager: _____ Landlord/Manager's Phone: _____

Reason for Leaving: _____

Employment History

EMPLOYEES: ATTACH TAX RETURNS FROM THE MOST RECENT TWO YEARS, PLUS PAY STUBS FROM THE PAST SIX MONTHS.
SELF-EMPLOYED APPLICANTS: INSTEAD ATTACH TAX RETURNS FOR THE PAST TWO YEARS.

Name and Address of Current Employer: _____

_____ Phone: (____) _____

Name of Supervisor: _____ Supervisor's Phone: (____) _____

Dates Employed at This Job: _____ Position or Title: _____

Name and Address of Previous Employer: _____

_____ Phone: (____) _____

Name of Supervisor: _____ Supervisor's Phone: (____) _____

Dates Employed at This Job: _____ Position or Title: _____

Income

1. Your gross monthly employment income (before deductions): $_____

2. Average monthly amounts of other income (specify sources): $_____

   _____ $_____

   _____ $_____

                                        TOTAL: $_____

Bank/Financial Accounts

	Account Number	Bank/Institution	Branch

Savings Account: _____

Checking Account: _____

Money Market or Similar Account: _____

_____

_____

_____

_____

Credit Card Accounts

Major Credit Card: ☐ VISA ☐ MC ☐ Discover Card ☐ Am Ex ☐ Other: _____

Issuer: _____ Account No. _____

Balance $_____ Average Monthly Payment $ _____

Major Credit Card: ☐ VISA ☐ MC ☐ Discover Card ☐ Am Ex ☐ Other: _____

Issuer: _____ Account No. _____

Balance $ _____ Average Monthly Payment $ _____

Loans

Type of Loan (mortgage, car, student loan, etc.)	Name of Creditor	Account Number	Amount Owed	Monthly Payment

Other Major Obligations (such as child support, alimony, tax liens, etc.)

Type	Payee	Amount Owed	Monthly Payment

Pets

Type	Breed	Sex	Age	Neutered/spayed?	Weight	Years owned

Miscellaneous

Describe water-filled furniture you want to have in the rental property: _____
_____ .

Do you smoke? ☐ yes ☐ no

Have you ever: Filed for bankruptcy? ☐ yes ☐ no How many times _____

Been sued? ☐ yes ☐ no How many times _____

Sued someone else? ☐ yes ☐ no How many times _____

Been evicted? ☐ yes ☐ no How many times _____

Explain (include dates) any "yes" listed above: _____
_____
_____

References and Emergency Contact

Personal Reference: _____ Relationship: _____

Address: _____

Email: _____ Phone: (___) _____

Personal Reference: _____ Relationship: _____

Address: _____

Email: _____ Phone: (___) _____

Contact in Emergency: _____ Relationship: _____

Address: _____

Email: _____ Phone: (___) _____

Source

Where did you learn of this vacancy? _____

_____

I certify that all the information given above is true and correct and understand that my lease or rental agreement may be terminated if I have made any material false or incomplete statements in this application. I authorize verification of the information provided in this application from my credit sources, credit bureaus, current and previous landlords and employers, and personal references. This permission will survive the expiration of my tenancy.

_____   _____

Applicant   Date

Notes (Landlord/Manager): _____

_____

_____

_____

_____

_____

_____

_____

_____

_____

Consent to Contact References and Perform Credit Check

I authorize _____

to obtain information about me from my credit sources, current and previous landlords, employers, and personal

references, to enable _____ to

evaluate my rental application.

I give permission for the landlord or its agent to obtain a consumer report about me for the purpose of this

application, to ensure that I continue to meet the terms of the tenancy, for the collection and recovery of any

financial obligations relating to my tenancy, or for any other permissible purpose.

_____

Applicant Signature

_____

Printed Name

_____

Address

_____

Phone Number

_____

Date

Tenant References

Name of Applicant: _____

Address of Rental Unit: _____

Previous Landlord or Manager

Contact (name, property owner or manager, address of rental unit): _____

_____

Date: _____

Questions

When did tenant rent from you (move-in and move-out dates)? _____

What was the monthly rent? _____   Did tenant pay rent on time?   ☐ Yes ☐ No

If rent was not paid on time, did you have to give tenant a legal notice demanding the rent?   ☐ Yes ☐ No

If rent was not paid on time, provide details _____

_____

Did you give tenant notice of any lease violation for other than nonpayment of rent?   ☐ Yes ☐ No

If you gave a lease violation notice, what was the outcome? _____

Was tenant considerate of neighbors—that is, no loud parties and fair, careful use of common areas?

_____

_____

Did tenant have any pets?   ☐ Yes   ☐ No   If so, were there any problems? _____

_____

Did tenant make any unreasonable demands or complaints?   ☐ Yes   ☐ No   If so, explain: _____

_____

Why did tenant leave? _____

_____

Did tenant give the proper amount of notice before leaving?   ☐ Yes   ☐ No

Did tenant leave the place in good condition? Did you need to use the security deposit to cover damage?

_____

Any particular problems you'd like to mention? _____

_____

Would you rent to this person again? _____

_____

Other comments: _____

_____

Previous Landlord or Manager

Contact (name, property owner or manager, address of rental unit): _____
_____

Date: _____

Questions

When did tenant rent from you (move-in and move-out dates)? _____

What was the monthly rent? _____ Did tenant pay rent on time? ☐ Yes ☐ No

If rent was not paid on time, did you have to give tenant a legal notice demanding the rent? ☐ Yes ☐ No

If rent was not paid on time, provide details _____
_____

Did you give tenant notice of any lease violation for other than nonpayment of rent? ☐ Yes ☐ No

If you gave a lease violation notice, what was the outcome? _____

Was tenant considerate of neighbors—that is, no loud parties and fair, careful use of common areas?
_____
_____

Did tenant have any pets? ☐ Yes ☐ No If so, were there any problems? _____
_____

Did tenant make any unreasonable demands or complaints? ☐ Yes ☐ No If so, explain: _____
_____

Why did tenant leave? _____
_____

Did tenant give the proper amount of notice before leaving? ☐ Yes ☐ No

Did tenant leave the place in good condition? Did you need to use the security deposit to cover damage?
_____

Any particular problems you'd like to mention? _____
_____

Would you rent to this person again? _____
_____

Other comments: _____
_____
_____
_____
_____
_____
_____

Employment Verification

Contact (name, company, position): _____

Date: _____ Salary $_____

Dates of Employment: _____

Comments: _____

_____

_____

_____

_____

_____

_____

_____

Personal Reference

Contact (name and relationship to applicant): _____

Date: _____ How long have you known the applicant?_____

Would you recommend this person as a prospective tenant? _____

Comments: _____

_____

_____

_____

_____

_____

_____

Credit and Financial Information

_____

_____

_____

_____

_____

Notes, Including Reasons for Rejecting Applicant

_____

_____

_____

_____

_____

Notice of Denial Based on Credit Report or Other Information

To: _____

    Applicant

_____

    Street Address

_____

    City, State, and Zip Code

Your rights under the Fair Credit Reporting Act and Fair and Accurate Credit Transactions (FACT) Act of 2003. (15 U.S.C. §§ 1681 and following.)

THIS NOTICE is to inform you that your application to rent the property at _____

_____ [rental property address] been denied because of [*check all that apply*]:

☐ Insufficient information in the credit report provided by:

    Credit reporting agency: _____

    Address, phone number, URL: _____

    _____

☐ Negative information in the credit report provided by:

    Credit reporting agency: _____

    Address, phone number, URL: _____

    _____

☐ The credit score supplied on the credit report, _____, was used in whole or in part when making the selection.

☐ The consumer credit reporting agency noted above did not make the decision not to offer you this rental. It only provided information about your credit history. You have the right to obtain a free copy of your credit report from the consumer credit reporting agency named above, if your request is made within 60 days of this notice or if you have not requested a free copy within the past year. You also have the right to dispute the accuracy or completeness of your credit report. The agency must reinvestigate within a reasonable time, free of charge, and remove or modify inaccurate information. If the reinvestigation does not resolve the dispute to your satisfaction, you may add your own "consumer statement" (up to 100 words) to the report, which must be included (or a clear summary) in future reports.

☐ Information supplied by a third party other than a credit reporting agency or you and gathered by someone other than myself or any employee. You have the right to learn of the nature of the information if you ask me in writing within 60 days of the date of this notice.

_____   _____

Landlord/Manager   Date

Notice of Conditional Acceptance Based on Credit Report or Other Information

To: _____
Applicant

_____
Street Address

_____
City, State, and Zip Code

Your application to rent the property at _____

_____ [rental property address] has been accepted, conditioned on your

willingness and ability to: _____

_____

Your rights under the Fair Credit Reporting Act and Fair and Accurate Credit Transactions (FACT) Act of 2003. (15 U.S.C. §§ 1681 and following.)

Source of information prompting conditional acceptance

My decision to conditionally accept your application was prompted in whole or in part by:

☐ Insufficient information in the credit report provided by

Credit reporting agency: _____

Address, phone number, URL: _____

_____

☐ Negative information in the credit report provided by:

Credit reporting agency: _____

Address, phone number, URL: _____

_____

☐ The consumer credit reporting agency noted above did not make the decision to offer you this conditional acceptance. It only provided information about your credit history. You have the right to obtain a free copy of your credit report from the consumer credit reporting agency named above, if your request is made within 60 days of this notice or if you have not requested a free copy within the past year. You also have the right to dispute the accuracy or completeness of your credit report. The agency must reinvestigate within a reasonable time, free of charge, and remove or modify inaccurate information. If the reinvestigation does not resolve the dispute to your satisfaction, you may add your own "consumer statement" (up to 100 words) to the report, which must be included (or a clear summary) in future reports.

☐ Information supplied by a third party other than a credit reporting agency or you and gathered by someone other than myself or any employee. You have the right to learn of the nature of the information if you ask me in writing within 60 days of the date of this notice.

_____   _____
Landlord/Manager   Date

Landlord-Tenant Checklist

Property Address: _____

General Condition of Rental Unit and Premises

	Move-In Condition Date of Walk-Through:	Move-Out Condition Date of Walk-Through:
Living Room		
Flooring		
Walls & ceiling		
Light fixtures		
Window treatments		
Windows & screens		
Doors & handles/locks		
Fireplace		
Smoke detector & CO detector		
Other		
Kitchen		
Flooring		
Walls & ceiling		
Light fixtures		
Window treatments		
Windows & screens		
Doors & handles/locks		
Cabinets		
Counters		
Stove/oven/range		
Refrigerator		
Dishwasher		
Garbage disposal		
Microwave		
Stove hood		
Sink & plumbing		
Other appliances		
Smoke detector & CO detector		
Other		

	Move-In Condition Date of Walk-Through:	Move-Out Condition Date of Walk-Through:
Dining Room		
Flooring		
Walls & ceiling		
Light fixtures		
Window treatments		
Windows & screens		
Doors & handles/locks		
Smoke detector & CO detector		
Other		
Bathroom		
Flooring		
Walls & ceiling		
Light fixtures		
Window treatments		
Windows & screens		
Doors & handles/locks		
Bathtub/shower (incl. attached door)		
Sink, counters, & plumbing		
Cabinets & storage		
Mirror(s)		
Toilet		
Ceiling fan/ventilation		
Other		
Bedroom #1		
Flooring		
Walls & ceiling		
Lighting fixtures		
Window treatments		
Windows & screens		
Doors & handles/locks		
Closet		
Smoke detector & CO detector		
Other		

	Move-In Condition Date of Walk-Through:	Move-Out Condition Date of Walk-Through:
Bedroom #2		
Flooring		
Walls & ceiling		
Lighting fixtures		
Window treatments		
Windows & screens		
Doors & handles/locks		
Closet		
Smoke detector & CO detector		
Other		
Other Areas		
Heating, A/C (mechanical room)		
Lawn/garden		
Stairs and landings		
Patio, terrace, deck, etc.		
Basement		
Garage		
Attic		
Entryway		
Laundry room		
Other		

☐ Tenants acknowledge that all smoke detectors were tested in their presence and found to be in working order, and that the testing procedure was explained to them. Tenants agree to promptly notify Landlord in writing should any smoke detector appear to be malfunctioning or inoperable. Tenants will not refuse Landlord access for the purpose of inspecting, maintaining, repairing, or installing legally required smoke detectors.

☐ Tenants acknowledge that all carbon monoxide detectors were tested in their presence and found to be in working order, and that the testing procedure was explained to them. Tenants agree to promptly notify Landlord in writing should any carbon monoxide detector appear to be malfunctioning or inoperable. Tenants will not refuse Landlord access for the purpose of inspecting, maintaining, repairing, or installing legally required carbon monoxide detectors.

Checklist for Furnished Property

	Move-In Condition Date of Walk-Through:	Move-Out Condition Date of Walk-Through:
Living Room		
Coffee table		
End tables		
Lamps		
Chairs		
Sofa		
Decorative items (unattached mirrors, rugs, pictures, vases, etc.)		
Electronics		
Other		
Kitchen		
Countertop appliances		
Dishes, silverware, & cookware		
Linens		
Chairs & stools		
Table		
Decorative items (unattached mirrors, rugs, pictures, vases, etc.)		
Other		
Dining Room		
Chairs		
Stools		
Table		
Lamps		
Decorative items (unattached mirrors, rugs, pictures, vases, etc.)		
Electronics		
Other		
Bathroom		
Shelves & storage (unattached)		
Shower curtain & rod		
Hamper		
Linens		
Decorative items (unattached mirrors, rugs, pictures, vases, etc.)		
Other		

	Move-In Condition Date of Walk-Through:	Move-Out Condition Date of Walk-Through:
Bedroom #1		
Bed(s)		
Chairs		
Bureau		
Chests		
Dressing table		
Bedside tables		
Lamps		
Linens		
Decorative items (unattached mirrors, rugs, pictures, vases, etc.)		
Electronics		
Other		
Bedroom #2		
Bedroom #2 has no furnishings		
Other Areas		
Desks		
Shelves		
Books, games, media		
Decorative items (unattached mirrors, rugs, pictures, vases, etc.)		
Electronics		
Tools (yard and workshop)		
Trash & recycling bins		
Outdoor furniture		
Recreational equipment		
Other		

Use this space to provide any additional explanation:

_____

_____

_____

_____

_____

_____

Landlord-Tenant Checklist completed on moving in on _____
and approved by:

_____ and _____
Landlord/Manager   Tenant

                                                _____
                                                Tenant

                                                _____
                                                Tenant

Landlord-Tenant Checklist completed on moving out on _____
and approved by:

_____ and _____
Landlord/Manager   Tenant

                                                _____
                                                Tenant

                                                _____
                                                Tenant

Move-In Letter

Date _____

Tenant _____

Street Address _____

City and State _____

Dear _____ ,
                          Tenant

Welcome to _____
_____ [address of rental unit]. We hope you will enjoy living here.
This letter is to explain what you can expect from the management and what we'll be looking for from you.

1. Rent: _____
_____
_____ .

2. New Roommates: _____
_____
_____
_____
_____ .

3. Notice to End Tenancy: _____
_____
_____
_____ .

4. Deposits: _____
_____
_____ .

5. Manager: _____
_____
_____
_____ .

6. Landlord-Tenant Checklist: _____
_____
_____
_____
_____
_____ .

7. Maintenance/Repair Problems: _____

_____

_____

_____

_____

_____

8. Semiannual Safety and Maintenance Update: _____

_____

_____

_____

_____

_____

9. Annual Safety Inspection: _____

_____

_____

_____

_____

10. Insurance: _____

_____

_____

_____

_____

11. Moving Out: _____

_____

_____

_____

12. Changes to Your Contact Information: _____

_____

_____

Please let us know if you have any questions.

Sincerely,

_____   _____
Landlord/Manager   Date

I have read and received a copy of this statement.

_____   _____
Tenant   Date

Tenant's Notice of Intent to Move Out

Date _____

Landlord _____

Street Address _____

City and State_____

Dear _____ ,
　　　　　　　　　　Landlord

This is to notify you that the undersigned Tenant(s), _____

_____ , will be moving from

_____ ,

on _____ , _____ from today. This

provides at least _____ written notice as required in the rental

agreement.

Sincerely,

_____
Tenant

_____
Tenant

_____
Tenant

Move-Out Letter

Date _____

Tenant _____

Street Address _____

City and State _____

Dear _____ ,
Tenant

We hope you have enjoyed living here. In order that we can mutually end our relationship on a positive note, this move-out letter describes how we expect your unit to be left and what our procedures are for returning your security deposit.

Basically, we expect you to leave your rental unit in the same condition it was when you moved in, except for normal wear and tear. To refresh your memory on the condition of the unit when you moved in, I've attached a copy of the Landlord-Tenant Checklist you signed at the beginning of your tenancy. I'll be using this same form to inspect your unit when you leave.

Specifically, here's a list of items you should thoroughly clean before vacating:

- ☐ Floors
    - ☐ sweep wood floors
    - ☐ vacuum carpets and rugs (shampoo if necessary)
    - ☐ mop kitchen and bathroom floors
- ☐ Walls, baseboards, ceilings, and built-in shelves
- ☐ Kitchen cabinets, countertops and sink, stove and oven—inside and out
- ☐ Refrigerator—clean inside and out, empty it of food, and turn it off, with the door left open
- ☐ Bathtubs, showers, toilets, and plumbing fixtures
- ☐ Doors, windows, and window coverings
- ☐ Other _____

_____

_____

_____

_____

_____

If you have any questions as to the type of cleaning we expect, please let me know.

Please don't leave anything behind—that includes bags of garbage, clothes, food, newspapers, furniture, appliances, dishes, plants, cleaning supplies, or other items that belong to you.

Please be sure you have disconnected phone and utility services, changed your address for regular deliveries and subscriptions, and sent the post office a change of address form.

Once you have cleaned your unit and removed all your belongings, please call me at _____ to arrange for a walk-through inspection and to return all keys. Please be prepared to give me your forwarding address where we may mail your security deposit.

It's our policy to return all deposits either in person or at an address you provide within _____ _____ after you move out. If any deductions are made—for past-due rent or because the unit is damaged or not sufficiently clean—they will be explained in writing.

If you have any questions, please contact me at _____ .

Sincerely,

_____
Landlord/Manager

Index

Save 15% *off your next order*

Register your Nolo purchase, and we'll send you a **coupon for 15% off** your next Nolo.com order!

Nolo.com/customer-support/productregistration

On Nolo.com you'll also find:

Books & Software

Nolo publishes hundreds of great books and software programs for consumers and business owners. Order a copy, or download an ebook version instantly, at Nolo.com.

Online Forms

You can quickly and easily make a will or living trust, form an LLC or corporation, apply for a provisional patent, or make hundreds of other forms—online.

Free Legal Information

Thousands of articles answer common questions about everyday legal issues, including wills, bankruptcy, small business formation, divorce, patents, employment, and much more.

Plain-English Legal Dictionary

Stumped by jargon? Look it up in America's most up-to-date source for definitions of legal terms, free at Nolo.com.

Lawyer Directory

Nolo's consumer-friendly lawyer directory provides in-depth profiles of lawyers all over America. You'll find information you need to choose the right lawyer.

LEAR14